Growing Up Psychic

What Every Parent & Child Should Know
About Psychic Sensitivity

By

Rev. Lowell K. Smith

Growing Up Psychic

What Every Parent and Child Should Know About Psychic Sensitivity

ISBN: 978-0-615-33517-7

Disclaimer

All statements of fact, opinion, or analysis expressed are those of the author and do not reflect the official positions or views of the CIA or any other U.S. Government agency. Nothing in the contents should be construed as asserting or implying U.S. Government authentication of information or Agency endorsement of the author's views. This material has been reviewed by the CIA to prevent the disclosure of classified information.

Cover design by Ernesto De La Torre; intens80@hotmail.com

Dedication

This book is dedicated to

My Mom

Hattie Ford Allen-Milne

Acknowledgements

My deepest gratitude to all those people who have acknowledged and supported my psychic sensitivities over the years and helped me develop, expand, understand, and use them in service to others.

Although there are too many names to list here, I must mention my soul sister Angie Maggliozzi who has been and remains a rock of spiritual and emotional support for me over the many years. I also acknowledge my dear friend and wonderful student Mary-Siobhan McGibbon and her husband Gerry Rice who is my Web master. You are dear friends and great students and have helped me create this book by reading, making editing suggestions, and being totally supportive of my process. I thank you both from the bottom of my heart.

Thanks to my dear friend Sandra Strauss for your enthusiastic support of this book, when it was still just a thought. You helped make it possible. Your unstoppable energy is truly appreciated. To my friend and student Justina Munday, you have not only supported me greatly in establishing the *Indigos & Sensitives Support Group* but have served as facilitator in my absence. For that I am deeply grateful. As in many lifetimes you have been both a diligent student and valuable teacher.

I want to thank all of my clients and students for allowing me the opportunity to bring forth information that you have found of value. I am humbled beyond words and deeply moved by the many profound stories you sent me for inclusion in this book. I hope and trust that you know that it was not I, but the Father within that speaks through me. I simply remain an open channel.

And lastly, my heartfelt gratitude to Dotti McKee for your countless hours, valuable comments and occasional criticisims to help me make this book one that will captivate readers of every faith and belief. Thank you for working through the challenging process of preparing, reviewing, and editing the several versions of this manuscript.

With much love and appreciation,
Rev. Lowell K. Smith

Table of Contents

Why does that man not have any lights?

When the old man came into my grandfather's barbershop to get a haircut my grandpa greeted him with a friendly, "Hello Charlie, have a seat." I had seen him before when my grandpa Howard babysat me, but on this particular day there was something really different about that old man. He didn't have any *lights!* – the Aura that I always saw around people. That frightened me and I ran up to my grandpa who was cutting another man's hair and pulled frantically on his pant leg. "Grandpa, Grandpa, that man doesn't have any *lights!*" My grandpa stopped cutting the man's hair, swatted me on my behind and told me to go sit in the corner, be quiet and play with my toys. I did as I was told and kept quiet, but I kept looking at that old man, wondering why he looked so different; why didn't he have any *lights*?

When we went home for dinner, Grandpa told Grandma Hazel that I had been a bad boy and had embarrassed him. He explained what I had done. As we sat at the dining room table, I tried to explain that the old man did not have any *lights* and asked them what it meant. They told me to eat my supper and be quiet about it. When I asked them about it again after supper, they simply sent me to bed without my usual desert. I was a very confused little boy.

The next morning our next-door neighbor, the town sheriff, came to our house and told my grandpa that the old man Charlie had died. When the sheriff left, Grandpa began talking very angrily to Grandma Hazel about me being possessed by the devil and that he was going to have to "once and for all" make sure that I understood what I had done. Grandpa got his razor strap off the back of their bedroom door and called my name. I knew I was in BIG trouble. As I approached him, he grabbed me by the arm and yelled; *"You killed him, you killed him! You are wicked and I'm going to beat the devil out of you."* He hit me over and over yelling, "You are evil, you are an evil little boy." I don't remember what made him stop but I think I convinced him that I would never ever say anything about *lights* again.

As I crawled up the stairs and rolled into my bed that afternoon, I asked God and my "Angel Lady in White" to forgive me for causing that old man to die and said I didn't want to see *lights* around people, or ghosts, or *little people* any more.

Prologue

This book reflects my experiences growing up as a *psychically sensitive* child. It includes stories of my early childhood psychic experiences: seeing Auras, Ghosts, Nature Spirits, and Angels. I share how I was forced to turn off my "gift" at the tender age of about 6½, and how my sensitivities returned almost ten years later when I was reunited with my psychically sensitive mom.

The stories I include are based on my memories and experiences as best I can recall them and as such may be different from what others remember of the same incidents. I remain solely responsible for any errors or omissions.

Purpose

I wrote this book in the hopes of helping other *psychically sensitive* children as well as their parents, teachers, counselors and therapists understand and accept their psychic sensitivities. I believe this book will be especially helpful to the *New Age Kids* – the *Indigos, Crystals*, and *Star* children, most of whom have a great deal of natural psychic sensitivity. However, it is also my intent to help adults who grew up with psychic sensitivities and may have turned those sensitivities off, or may continue to have psychic experiences and be frightened by them or not know what to do with them.

I share my psychic experiences in an effort to help the reader validate similar experiences you may have had in your lives. My hope is to provide an understandable explanation of *Psychic phenomena* and *Metaphysical* information that will help you understand and put your own experiences into a useful perspective. I also hope to show that *psychic sensitivities* are a gift from, and an expression of, the Divine Source of one's being – what I refer to as God. They are not of the devil!!

Another purpose is to shift the reader's concept of who you are from a belief that, *"We are human beings with a Spirit,"* which is what most Christian religions teach, to an understanding that, *"We are Spiritual beings expressing through a physical body,"* which is what I, as a Spiritual Metaphysician, teach. When one makes that fundamental paradigm shift in thinking, it is natural to understand that everyone is *psychic* because the word psychic comes from the Greek word *psychikos* meaning "of the soul, mental." Psychic refers to the ability to perceive things hidden from the five physical senses (sight, smell, hearing, taste, and touch) via some form of extra-sensory perception (ESP).

Format

I have chosen to convey this information as an autobiography with explanatory comments and instructions about the underlying Metaphysics of Psychic phenomena: What it is. How it manifests. What I believe it means. How to control the experiences and not be frightened by them. How to use your sensitivities and experiences to increase your own and others Spiritual understanding. As well as how an increased awareness of psychic phenomena can help you create a better and closer relationship with the Divine Source of your being.

As you read about my psychic adventures while growing up, I believe many of you will be able to relate to these experiences and recognize that you have also had intuitive and *psychic* moments throughout your life, which you may have ignored or discounted as your imagination. Hopefully my "story" will help you reevaluate and validate your own previous and/or ongoing experiences so you can come to a better understanding of their meaning. I also include stories about learning Metaphysics and Spirituality, and how I was "guided" to become a Metaphysical teacher, a Minister and a Professional Psychic.

I include a chapter on the *New Age Kids* – the *Indigos*, *Crystals*, and *Star* children, and talk about my beginning to see them come into the earth plane in the early 1970's. I talk about their purpose, and what I believe this "phenomena" means for humanity. I have also included a checklist of characteristics to help those who don't see Auras determine whether you are, or someone you know is, a *New Age Kid* and how to deal or interact with those who are.

I wish you, the reader, increased health, happiness, abundance, greater love in your life and an expanded awareness of your own psychic sensitivities or intuitiveness, as well as a more loving and two-way communication with your Angels, your Spirit Guides, and the Divine Source of your being.

Rev. Lowell K. Smith
http://www.ReflectionsInLight.org

The Early Years

This lifetime, I was born at approximately 11:00 a.m. on December 29, 1939 in Detroit, Michigan as the middle child to my mother Hattie and my father Melvin. My older brother Robert Terry was about two and a half years old when I was born, and my younger sister Kathleen Diane came along about seventeen months later. I was born *psychically sensitive*, meaning that I have seen *lights* – what is commonly called an Aura – around people, animals and most plants all of my life. I have also *seen* or been *sensitive to* dead people (ghosts) and other "Spirits or Angelic beings" all my life and have been able to communicate with these ghosts, Angelic figures as well as Nature Spirits. Both my older brother and younger sister were also born "sensitive," although they have both handled their sensitivities differently.

My younger sister, Kathleen, although currently actively doing psychic readings in the Detroit area, recently told me that she turned her sensitivities off in her early 20's because when her stepdad Tom was diagnosed with cancer, she psychically knew he was going to die and she did not want to know that. My older brother, Terry, on the other hand, had similar sensitivities to mine as we were growing up together, but he almost always told me to ignore the ghosts, and Nature Spirits, (little people) when I asked him about them. So both of my natural siblings have psychic sensitivities even though they haven't always acknowledged or used them.

From my experience most children are born psychically "sensitive" to some degree, but turn it off by the age of about 6 or 7. Also, it is not uncommon for multiple children in a family to be "sensitive" when one or more of the parents are psychic, especially when the mother is psychic. However, even in those families with a psychically sensitive parent, not all of the parents are open with their own psychic sensitivity, and often discourage that sensitivity in their children believing that it is more important for them to "fit in" with their peers than be different. When a psychically sensitive child is born to a non-psychically sensitive family, they invariably feel different, isolated, and often are misunderstood.

As you will later learn, even though I was born to a psychically sensitive mother, I did not see or interact with her from the time I was about 2½ until I was 15 years old, so she was not around to help me with my sensitivities between those years. However, during those first 2½ years, I have some very good memories of her lights and other things I *saw*.

My Earliest Memories

One of my earliest memories is of the exceptionally beautiful and bright lights that were around my mother Hattie most of the time. She was very psychically sensitive herself, as was her mother, Vivian. Mom told me that when I was still in the crib, she was aware of my 'reading' and 'playing' with her *lights* or Aura. She said that she delighted in talking to me about my *lights* and other psychic things.

> *Initially all babies, toddlers and young children see or sense energies or lights around people, and will respond based on what they see or sense more than what that person is saying or doing. So do not discount your baby's or child's reaction to you or someone else and allow yourself (or even force yourself) to become curious and ask questions of your baby or child about what they see. Validate their sensitivities.*

As I grew and experienced interactions with my parents, other kids and other adults, I realized that nice or good people had bright vibrant yet soft 'feeling' lights, while bad, mean or angry people most often had *angry* or *"dirty lights,"* which often consisted of bright reds, oranges, sometimes greenish-yellow (deceitful), often brown, and black or dirty gray lights.

During the first two-and-a-half years of my life, my dad and mother fought a lot, and although I do not have clear memories of most of the fights, I do have specific bad memories of a couple really serious and violent fights. I mention this not because of the drama it tends to invoke, but because of the energies I remember *seeing* prior to and during these incidents.

Normally my mother's *lights* were a rather pleasant if somewhat diffused set of bright and shimmering blues, violets, greens, oranges, some reds, and some whites. However, right before the arguments or fights, my mother's *lights* would become very distorted with bright streaks of multiple shades of reds, yellows, browns and grays.

On the other hand, my dad's *lights* seemed to almost always have a lot of anger spewing everywhere. It was as if he was angry at the world, not just my mom, my brother, my sister, or me. During the serious arguments or fights, my dad's *lights* looked like an erupting volcano. As he became increasingly angry his *lights* would become "swirling clouds" of bright reds with lots of black, brown, gray and yellow streaks through them. They seemed to be "boiling clouds of danger," and it seemed to me like our very lives were being threatened. When my mother became particularly frightened, her *lights* would disappear as if she were leaving, which as a small child, really frightened me. Although I did not know it at the time, I now understand this to mean that my mother was completely withdrawing within herself. I suspect that we would follow suit, because usually after the fights, we were frightened, crying and otherwise making a lot of noise, which further angered my dad. I believe that during these times I would "go out of body" or otherwise close down and become as small as possible so as not to be noticed. As my psychotherapist told me many years later, I simply "disassociated" from what was going on because I feared for my life, an over-reaction perhaps, but as a small child it felt that way.

When my dad was not being angry or mean, his *lights* changed to softer shades of reds, pinks, some greens and paler blues. However, if we pouted or cried his *lights* would revert to angry clouds of reds. I am sure that my "sensitivities" to people's *lights* became heightened as a result. I realized that if I didn't pay very close attention, people could turn from being nice and friendly to being mean and violent with no apparent reason.

> *Babies, toddlers and young children 'see' or 'sense' powerful and scary energies or lights around people when those people are expressing anger, and will automatically begin to withdraw within themselves and shut down. This is a protective mechanism they naturally do when they become frightened, so do not discount your baby's or child's reaction to you or someone else's angry outbursts. You need to acknowledge to them that you got angry (or another person was angry) and let them know that they are still safe. Validate their sensitivities.*

I have a very vague memory of standing next to my baby sister's crib when I was a little over two thinking that I had to protect her from my dad's anger. In a recent conversation with Kathleen about this, she said that she too has memories of me being protective of her and feeling safe with me. She also reminded me that Mom repeatedly told us that I was always protective of her when I was very young.

Rover - My Guardian Dog

My mother's mother Vivian, whom we called Grandma Smith, had a Husky-Collie mixed breed dog named Rover that I loved and I still have warm memories of how "doggie" Rover smelled, and how gentle and sometimes "sparkly" his *lights* were. Whenever I was at Grandma Smith's house, and had been spanked or was frightened by the adults I would go and hide in Rover's doghouse and snuggle up next to him. When the adults came to find me, Rover would not let them near me, especially if I was sleeping. My mom used to tell a story about an incident when I was a little over two years old and we were visiting Grandma Smith's place. My dad had spanked me for some reason and I went out to the doghouse and snuggled up to Rover and told him that my dad had been mean to me. My mother said that when my dad, who actually liked Rover and often played with him, came to get me out of the doghouse, I would not leave. She said that when my dad went to grab me, Rover growled and nipped at him and would not let him near me. I knew that Rover was my protector and my friend.

> *Animals are very sensitive to energies. In fact it is that characteristic that allows them to be trained to be service animals where they can alert their owners to changes in their owner's physical health, such as stoke patients, and those who suffer from seizures, which the animals pick up from their owner's Auras. They have also proven to be very healing for autistic children and patients with Alzheimer's.*

> *Babies, toddlers or young children are very sensitive to animal energies and sometimes 'see' their lights and pretty much 'know' when it is safe. Most animals, especially dogs, are usually protective of young children. However, there are always exceptions so be alert. Again, allow yourself to become curious and ask questions of your baby or child about what they see – validate their sensitivities.*

Around that same time period my dad left my mother for good, following a particularly bad fight. My mother told me that over the next several months after my dad left, he would take us boys (my sister was too young) for a few hours to several days and then simply drop us off in the middle of the afternoon or night, often two or three blocks away from Grandma's house as a way of upsetting my mom. There was so much anger and animosity between them and as a young and sensitive child, I was very much aware of it, but clearly too young to understand what was going on.

The Divorce and Being Sent Away

Shortly after my dad quit coming to see us, a neighbor told my mom that he had joined the Army Air Corp *as a single person!* World War II was in progress and our young lives were about to change in ways I could not even imagine.

As my mom told the story, when she pressed for a divorce from my dad based on physical abuse and abandonment, the courts and the clerks were very unsympathetic. This was 1942 and WWII was in full swing and women asking for divorces from servicemen were looked down upon and treated badly – the facts were irrelevant.

During this time period, we lived with Grandma Smith, but for some reason, which was never explained, she kicked us out of her house. Although my mother would never talk about it, I suspect that my brother and I were too rambunctious for Grandpa Cam to handle. Mom later told me that she moved us into an old barbershop with no interior walls or heat, but the owner quickly put in partitions for privacy and a potbelly stove for warmth. My mom said that initially we slept on the floor until a dear friend of Grandma Smith gave Mom enough furniture to make it livable. When my sister and I recently discussed this time of our lives, she confirmed that she has vague memories of sleeping on the floor on blankets and pillows when she was still a baby.

My memories of my mother's *lights* during this time period are that they were very distorted and dim, which I have since come to understand is a sign of someone who is very depressed. On one occasion when we lived in the barbershop building, I followed my older brother to school and I remember the wonderfully bright and warm *lights* surrounding his teacher. When I asked my mom about this incident, years later, she told me that she remembered the teacher calling her at work and how delightful and understanding she was.

Shortly after we moved into the barbershop building, the Child Welfare Agency decided that my mother did not make enough money to support all three of us kids, and had a "caring" judge order that Terry and I be sent to a foster home. The Welfare Agency and the judge "thoughtfully" agreed that she could keep Kathleen. According to them, one child was all she could afford! Synchronistically my mother worked in a war factory in Detroit with a young lady, Lily Ann, whose mother ran a foster home for children in the Upper Peninsula. My mother painfully and reluctantly agreed to allow Terry and me to go there, praying that we would be well taken care of and provided for. She felt that she had no other choice.

Shortly after the court ordered that we be sent to a foster home, my mother arranged to have Lily Ann take us to her mothers' home near Manistique, Michigan. I have vague memories of Mom taking us to the train station dressed in grown-up suits, with our names and instructions pinned to our lapels. Mother drove us to the train station, hugged us and kissed us and told us to "be good little boys" then turned and left with tears steaming down her face. We then got on the train with her friend, destined for our new "home" 500 miles away. I was almost three and Terry was about five.

The Foster Home

As I began writing this book, I found that I still had some very specific memories of the foster home. For example, I remembered the name of the foster family; that we lived in a cabin or house on a lake near Manistique, Michigan; that there was an old icehouse and pit on the property; that we used to row our boat to an island; and that there was a floating dock that we would sometimes swim to. I also remembered that there was a nun in the family and that we were near a Catholic Church. In early 2008 I called my brother and told him I was interested in re-discovering the foster home. He remembered that the lake was called "Crooked Lake" and then shared a few other memories he had of that place and that period of our lives. That summer, following my 50th High School Class reunion, I drove to Manistique in the Upper Peninsula of Michigan. With the few vague memories I had, and my brother's information, I found the location of the foster home that my brother and I were sent as small boys.

Much to my amazement, one of the older brothers in the foster family named Robert, who was in the war when my brother and I were at the foster home, was still living in a house on Crooked Lake. When I drove out to the Crooked Lake campsite, I saw the beautiful lake with the island (which is actually a peninsula), and the old cabin we lived in, although it had changed in appearance over the years. When I met with Robert, his *lights* told me that he was very skeptical and that he was a very religious man. However, they also told me that he was open to at least listening to me. When I told him about my mother working in a war factory with a young lady, and that I remembered that there was a nun in the family, and described the old icehouse and ice pit and an old floating dock that is no longer there, he was very surprised. He was especially surprised that I remembered the icehouse and ice pit and the floating dock, which were long since gone. He said that he helped his dad build that floating dock before he left for the war. Robert confirmed that he had a younger sister, Lily Ann, who worked in the war factory in Detroit during that time period and that his youngest sister, Sister Mary Robert was indeed a nun. He then stunned me by saying that although Sister Mary Robert had recently died, Lily Ann was alive and living near Milwaukee, Wisconsin.

Robert called Lily Ann, had me talk to her, and I arranged to visit her that weekend. As I drove to see her I was excited at the thought of being able to meet and talk to this lady who worked with my mother in the war factory those many years ago. I was looking forward to hearing what she could tell me about our stay at that foster home and the train ride up north that took my brother and me away from our mother.

Meeting Lily Ann

When I drove to Lily Ann's home she greeted me warmly, listened to my memories and filled in many more details. It was an absolute joy to be with this wonderful lady who was now about 84 or so. Her energy was light and lively and her *lights* had the colors and pattern that I associate with "good people." It was a delight and honor to be in her presence. Lily Ann talked about working with my mother in the war factory and about the struggles my mother had raising three small children in those times. She shared her memories of our train ride up to her mother's home near Manistique. She said the train was completely packed with servicemen and there were no seats available. She was forced to stand on the platform between the cars, along with many other servicemen, while Terry and I sat quietly on the suitcase the entire time. She lovingly commented that we "hardly made a peep" even though it was cold and "raining like crazy with rain coming in through the doors."

Lily Ann said that we took the ferryboat across the Straits of Mackinac, and then boarded another train in St. Ignace, where we finally got seats, and continued our train ride to Manistique. Her parents met us at the train station and took us to her older sister's place in Manistique. Although I did not remember Lily Ann's mom and dad meeting us at the train station, I did remember the house in Manistique, which is near the Catholic Church and where we lived during the winter. I also remembered the cabin at Crooked Lake where we lived in the summer. Lily Ann's description of the train ride and her stories about working with my mom were very confirming and filled in a lot of holes regarding that period of my life. However, since Lily Ann was not around most of the time we were there, she could not confirm any of my memories of our time at the foster home.

Scoping Out The Foster Home Campsite

Prior to driving to visit with Lily Ann, I spent some time exploring the Crooked Lake campsite. Robert pointed me to where the original cabin was and graciously allowed me to go inside and look around. When I went inside to explore what memories I might recall and what things I might "pick up on" using my current psychic sensitivities, it took me several minutes of walking around in each room to regain a familiarity with this place. About the only thing I can honestly say I remember is the kitchen where I saw a ghost when I was there as a small boy. I have included that story later in this chapter.

As I continued to explore the campsite, I recalled a special hiding place in a marshy area near the cabin, where I used to play. This "hide away" was the first place I remember seeing and communicating with Nature Spirits[1] or *little people*. I walked over to it and although the vegetation had changed it quite a bit over the years, it still *felt* familiar. I "tuned in" to see if the Nature Spirits were still there and although I could not *see* them, I was able to *sense* them and I *heard* them speak to me in my mind. I *sensed* that they had not changed or aged the way I had, which I found rather humorous. I could hear them laughing in my mind about my realization. I just smiled and said "Hi guys, it's good to see that you are still here and that I am still able to at least *sense* your presence and be aware of you." I just got a *sense* of an acknowledgement, but that was sufficient confirmation for me.

Thinking back to when I was there as a small child, I enjoyed the memories I had of the years at that foster home. As I "traveled down memory lane," I realized that those were the years when I was becoming more and more aware of and sensitive to the energies or *lights* around people (their Aura). As I thought back to those years, it became clear that those were the years when I began to discern what the various colors and patterns of people's *lights* actually meant. I also recognized that it was during this time period that I discovered I could pick up on the thoughts of adults and could tell when they were not telling the truth.

Picking up on thoughts is different than seeing Auras. For me I usually 'see' something different in the person's Aura that catches my attention and then hear their thoughts in my head, or sometimes 'see' images related to what they are thinking about. Some of my students report that they just hear the thoughts, but don't notice a change in the Aura. The New Age Kids – Indigos, Crystals, and Star children, which I talk about in Chapter 8, are very sensitive to picking up on people's thoughts. As I teach my students, it is important not to pry in on other people's thoughts, but sometimes that does happen, so those of us who are 'sensitive' just have to be vigilant and circumspect.

As I continued to look back at that time period of my life, I remembered that was about the time when my Guardian Angel or my *Angel Lady in White*[2] began to appear to me on a regular basis. Prior to being at the foster

---

[1] I talk more about Nature Spirits or *little people* later in this chapter.

[2] My Guardian Angel was and still is a "being of light" that sometimes takes on a female humanly form. She has periodically appeared to me throughout my life, which has always been when I am under severe difficulty. She does not seem to

home, she only appeared to me the night my dad put a gun to my head and threatened to shoot me. I was about two years old and it was part of a huge fight my dad had with my mom. That night my *Angel Lady in White* hugged me and simply told me not to be frightened, that I would be safe and that she would always be with me.

I believe that during the years at the foster home, I was also receiving guidance from my Spirit Guides and Angelic beings and I know that as my sensitivities increased, I became more and more aware of ghostly apparitions, and aware of the Nature Spirits or *little people* so such occurrences became quite common for me.

I remember my *Angel Lady in White* instructing me not to talk to the nuns or priests about *seeing* their *lights*, or reading their thoughts, or about *seeing* the dead people I would sometimes see around them trying to get their attention. She told me that the priests and nuns thought it was evil and bad and that it frightened them, but that it wasn't bad or evil. She also told me not to talk to the adults about the Nature Spirits or *little people* (fairies and elves that I would see and play with down by the lake or in the woods) except for one lady, and that I would know who she was. I liked my *Angel Lady in White* and always looked forward to seeing her and talking to her. She usually appeared at nighttime but occasionally she would appear to me in church, or when I was talking with my Nature Spirit friends.

Early Psychic Experiences at The Foster Home

The following stories reflect the general character of the kind and types of *psychic* experiences I had while living at the foster home. I am sharing them so that both adults and children reading this might relate to and find comfort in them.

The Church Picnic

Shortly after we arrived at the foster home, we went to a picnic at the Catholic Church in town. People were gathered and talking in the picnic area next to the church where food was being served, and I, along with other children were playing. After awhile I had to go to the bathroom and went into the church through a side entrance I normally did not use. As I went down the hall looking for the bathroom, a priest and a woman came out from the

---

have a name. I usually just refer to her as my *Angel Lady in White*, because that is how she appears to me most of the time.

priest's office just as I was passing by. They were very surprised to see me, and the priest grabbed me by the collar and accused me of "snooping." I told him that I simply needed to use the bathroom and he swatted me on the butt and told me to "Go ahead but be quick about it and be sure to wash your hands." I could tell that both the priest and the lady were very embarrassed because their *lights* became quite "distorted." Although as a three year old I really did not understand what was going on, I felt as if I were prying. I never said a word to anyone about that "indiscrete" moment. However, over the years, I have seen that same energy pattern several times and it has usually been associated with people either caught in a lie or being caught doing something they believed they should not be doing.

A Dead Relative In The Kitchen

One day while playing in the kitchen of the cabin at the lake, I saw a very old man who I knew was dead, and I knew that he was either the father or grandfather of the nun, Sister Mary Robert. He seemed quite bent over and had a rather harsh voice. He told me that I needed to be very careful because "the older lady of the house was angry about something and she was looking for someone to scold." When I began talking to him and asking him questions, he seemed surprised that I could *see* him, but he then told me his name – I think it was Oscar or something like that. A little girl, one of the other foster children, was standing in the living room nearby and asked me who I was talking to. I told her his name and I could tell she was frightened because her *lights* became quite disturbed and she ran through the house yelling "He's talking to ghosts, he's talking to ghosts."

When the lady of the house came in to see what the commotion was, the little girl ran to her and told her that I was talking to a ghost. I noticed that the older lady's *lights* became flaming red and she grabbed me by the ear and demanded to know who I was talking to. When I told her the name that the old man gave me and pointed to where I saw him, her *lights* became very intense and much more distorted and she seemed to be very frightened. She screamed and dragged me out of the house calling for the men who were nearby. When she told one of the men what I had said and that she *felt* the dead man too, he told her that it was just her imagination. From then on while I was at the foster home, I only spoke to ghosts in my head and never aloud for others to hear.

If your baby or young child appears to be 'zoned out' or staring into space and playing with or talking to 'someone' it could possibly be a dead relative who has come to interact with them. If they are frightened, it is important to tell them not to be afraid and to begin to say a Prayer of Protection similar to the 'Robe of Light Protection

Prayer[3] *below for them and 'demand' that all energies not of the Christ energy be gone. Always validate your baby's or child's experience and tell them that they need not be afraid. See if you can get them to describe what they see. It is most likely not their imagination.*

The Funeral and The Dead Person

At the funeral mass for a relative of the foster family, the man who was in the coffin appeared standing next to the head of the coffin as the priest was performing the mass. I *saw* him jumping up and clicking his heels together, and then put a hat on sideways and made faces at me. He was laughing and saying how great he felt, and that the joke was on the people who were there. He winked at me and then he disappeared. I tried to tell my brother, Terry, but he told me to ignore him and be quiet. When I tried to tell another kid he whispered something to his mother, Anne, and she looked at me and made the sign for me to be quiet, but in a nice gentle way. After the mass, Mrs. Anne took me aside and asked me what I had told her son. She seemed genuinely interested and not angry at all. Her *lights* were what I had come to understand as "curious" and rather than scold me for telling her what I saw she laughed and said something like "that was just like 'so and so.' He always liked being a clown." She told me not to tell others because they would not understand, and then she ruffled my hair and told me to go play. Her *lights* had a lot of soft pinks, violets, and purples in them, and the green lights coming from her hands felt very soothing. I liked her a lot and knew that she was the "friendly" adult that my *Angel Lady in White* had told me about. From that point forward, whenever Mrs. Anne came to the camp or I saw her at church, she gave me a hug and quietly asked if I had seen that dead man again.

Children often see or sense the dead person, as well as other dead relatives, at a funeral, even if they do not know who it is they are seeing. If they do, bring out an old family picture album and ask them if there is anyone they recognize. You (and they) might just be surprised at their answer.

---

[3] *Robe of Light Protection Prayer* for someone else – "I surround you in a robe of light, consisting of the Love and Power and Wisdom of God, not only for your protection but so that all who see it or come in contact with it, will be drawn back to God and healed."

When children (or adults) 'see' or 'sense' a dead person or ghost, it does not necessarily mean that entity (dead person) is 'trapped' or has not yet gone to the light, it may simply be that they are in that process, or they might want their story heard, or want to pass a message on to their loved ones. From my experience, unlike the ghosts typically depicted in 'The Ghost Whisperer,'[4] and 'Medium,'[5] which are excellent TV programs that depict a psychically sensitive person who can 'see' and communicate with ghosts, most ghosts are not trapped here until they can be 'led to the light.'

From my experience, many of the dead people I pick up on are simply 'remnant energies' or 'energies of time' meaning that there is an energy associated with an individual or event and I am simply able to tap into that energy, sometimes communicate with individuals involved, and many times 'see' the events around a particular situation.[6] I am seldom frightened by these energies, but they can at times become overwhelming. For example I refuse to visit the Gettysburg battlefield area because of the overpowering experience of death and slaughter that I picked up there many years ago. I had a similar experience when I visited Atlanta, Georgia several years earlier.

Nature Spirits - The Little People

My brother Terry and I really enjoyed the lake at the foster home campsite. It had a fairly large densely wooded peninsula and we liked to row our little boat there. As we got older, we would swim out to the floating dock out in the deeper water. The camp seemed to be quite large with several cabins around the property.

When my brother and I went out to play around the cabins or down by the lake I often *saw* Nature Spirits or *little people* who talked to me in my mind. When I talked to Terry about them he told me that although he *saw* them too, they were just in our imagination and that I should ignore them. He also told me not to talk to the adults about them because that would just get us into

---

[4] *The Ghost Whisperer* is a CBS TV series
[5] *Medium* is a CBS TV series
[6] I talk more about this in a later chapter where I talk about taking my "*Indigos & Sensitives*" group members to Weston House and other haunted places to see what we can pick up on and understand.

trouble. However, one day I drew up the courage to ask Sister Mary Robert about them. Sure enough she scolded me and told me that if I continued with these "tall stories," I would go straight to hell. After she told me this, I went down to the lake near an old tree where I *saw* several *little people* sitting on some lily pads. One of the *little people* said that I looked real sad and that I needed to understand they were not simply in my imagination but most people could not *see* them or interact with them the way I did. My *Angel Lady in White* appeared and said that these *little people* were not of the devil, but God's little "guardians of the land" – Nature Spirits who were my special little friends. Since even my brother was afraid to acknowledge them, I resolved to keep quiet about them but I continued to *see* and play with them.

Terminology

To help the reader understand what I am talking about when I refer to Nature Spirits (or *little people*), fairies, and elves, I offer the following:

The energies or entities that guard the plant kingdom include Devas or Elementals, Fairies, and Nature Spirits, or 'little people' and each of them have their role or purpose.

Deva's and Elementals *are different expressions of an energy form or 'being' associated with plants – flowers, bushes, and trees. They have never presented themselves in a physical form the way Nature Spirits have, only as an energetic presence that I am aware of and sometimes 'see.' When I have 'seen' them, they have presented themselves as a humanoid facial form on leaves or in the bark of a tree and I have been aware that what I was 'seeing' was a Deva. To me it is like 'seeing' or 'sensing' the Essence, or the life force energy of that plant.*

Fairies *on the other hand, which I have not 'seen' since I was a small child, but continue to be 'aware of' periodically, appear as small (about 3" – 4" in stature) humanoid forms with dragonfly like wings, very much like those depicted in movies but not quite as 'human' as they are depicted in the movies. My understanding of the purpose of Fairies is that they take care of the pollination process in the plant kingdom. As I was writing this at my Tucson, AZ home in May 2009, I became aware of several fairies 'flitting' around the beautiful orange flowers on our large Ocotillo plant in our back yard. When I 'saw' them out of the corner of my eye, I would 'look' to see them closer and they would be gone, but I could hear them talking to me in my mind, confirming that they were taking care of the pollination process.*

Nature Spirits or 'little people' appear to me as 'little humanoid beings' about 1 ft – 2 ft in stature that look very much like the leprechauns or elves depicted in movies. They seem to appear and disappear at will and 'flit' (instantly jump) from one place to another, and are protectors of the plant kingdom. When I was a small child I was able to communicate and interact with them on a regular basis. Now, I only 'see' them occasionally but am still able to communicate with them.

One day when I was outside by the icehouse with Mrs. Anne, I told her about the *little people* I *saw*, talked to and played with. As I did so, her *lights* became very bright and animated, but somehow cautious. She asked me very quietly if I had told anyone else and I told her only my brother, but that he told me to ignore them. She asked if I would show them to her and I took her to the tree by the lake. When my *little people* appeared to me, I pointed in their direction and said, "See?" She just looked and said, "Oh really?" As we sat down by the lake I noticed that her *lights* became very calm and focused – she was probably simply trying to "tune in." As we sat there, she asked if I had names for any of my little friends, and I said yes but they were not like normal peoples' names. She then wanted to know if she would be allowed to see them. When I asked "Turf" (the older little person) he said yes. Almost immediately she began to smile and giggle and said that this was the first time she had actually been able to see these *little people*. I remember her saying that she always believed they existed but had never actually seen them before. Her *lights* seemed to dance with joy – there was a lot of white, blue, orange, and violet in her Aura, and she seemed genuinely happy. She made me promise never to talk about these *little people* with others in the house because they would not understand and would probably punish me. That was one of my favorite and most delightful experiences and memories of my time at the foster home.

If your child talks about 'little people' in the forest, or fairies in a garden area, become curious and ask questions the way Mrs. Anne did. The important thing is to help them understand that they are not 'crazy,' but in fact their experience is real – these beings are real, it is just that most people cannot 'see' them. Ask your child to describe exactly what they are 'seeing' or 'sensing' and help them put it in perspective. You can make their experience memorable as well. Validate and ask questions.

Recently I became aware of several *little people* in the back yard of Pete and Maureen, friends from our Unity Church whom I enjoy hanging out with. They have a wonderful deck overlooking a waterfall that spills into a nice sized Coy fishpond, which is surrounded by a colorful flower garden. When I shared with them that I saw three *little people* and pointed to where I saw them, they took note but could not see them. A few months later when Maureen's amazing little granddaughter, Mae Rose, who was just two years old, was standing on the deck looking out at the flowers, Maureen asked her whether she saw any little fairies. Much to her amazement Mae said, "Yes." When Maureen said, "Oh, Wow. How many?" Mae very matter-of-factly stated "Three" pointing to each one saying "One, two, three. See?" She then turned around and pranced her little body back inside as if this was totally normal. Maureen was delighted to know that her little grandchild could *see* the *little people* the same way I do.

The Catholic Church – Hearing Jesus

While living at the foster home, we attended the Catholic Church in Manistique. Although I was too young to go to school and do not remember taking any "classes" from the nuns or priests, I have rather positive memories of the Church Mass and other services. I loved the "pomp and ceremony" associated with the Mass, and remember being very good about crossing myself and saying dinner grace when asked. My memories of the nuns are that, although they could be quite strict, they were very nice. However, I also have a memory of an older priest, whom I did not like because he was mean like my dad, and had dirty and somewhat deceitful *lights* much of the time. As I recall, there was a younger priest at the church as well who sometimes seemed lost or out of place when dealing with small children. His *lights* seemed to be OK but he did not seem to be comfortable around us little kids.

One Sunday I went to Mass with the foster family following a harsh spanking at the hands of a large and heavy man. As I recall, another foster child we called "Picklepuss" had "tattled" on me about my talking to ghosts, and this huge man had spanked me and told me that talking to ghosts was evil.

While the priest was saying the Mass and I was praying to God, "Please don't send me to hell for talking to ghosts," I heard a voice in my head that I "knew" or believed was *Jesus*. He told me that I was not a bad boy and that I was not going to hell. He said that the man who spanked me was simply a very angry man who was afraid of ghosts and that I needed to pray for him. I then "felt" this figure kneel down and hug me. As he stood up he put his hand on my head and sent me some kind of blessing; then he simply disappeared. The pain from the spanking left me and I felt like I had been "touched by an Angel" – it felt really good.

Leaving The Foster Home

The three or so years that my brother and I spent at the foster home were an adventure. It is not clear to me why we lost touch with our mother, but in my conversation with Lily Ann, she said that when her mother tried to find our grandfather, Terry could only tell them that his name was Grandpa Howard and that he had a barbershop. Somehow they got in touch with our grandfather and he came to get us.

Grandpa Howard used to tell the story that he came to get us in a horse drawn sleigh in the winter just before Christmas. My brother recently told me that he remembers that we took a Greyhound Bus from St. Ignace back to Grandpa Howard's place. I don't remember my grandpa coming to get us, or that trip to his house. However, it must have been a very exciting trip for a little six-year-old boy because it was during the winter. Back then it required a ferry ride across the frozen straits between the Upper and Lower Peninsula because the Mackinac Bridge was not built until 1957. I do however remember thinking that at least we would now be with our own family. Little did I realize how much our young lives were about to change – again.

Living With Grandpa Howard

Going from the foster home in the Northern Peninsula to my grandpa Howard's home should have been a good thing because we were going to live with our family. However, it turned out not to be because my grandpa was a Hell Fire and Brimstone Baptist who had been taught to hate Catholics. My first exposure to what this meant occurred one evening shortly after my brother and I arrived. Grandpa asked me to say "grace" at the dinner table and everyone bowed their heads. However, as I crossed myself and began to say the Catholic table blessing as I had been taught in the foster home, Grandpa stopped me in mid-sentence, grabbed me off my chair, spanked me and yelled, "You are going to hell if you ever do that again." I was very confused because I knew I had done the crossing correctly and was saying the table blessing accurately. I did not understand why he was so angry. Later that evening grandpa took me aside and apologized saying that what I did was "idol worship," which was very wrong, and that I should never do it again. Only later did I learn that the Baptist minister in grandpa's church taught that Catholics were "idol worshipers" because they worship the Virgin Mary and Saint's statues.

Later that night as I lay in bed, I remembered that when we first sat down to the table to eat, grandpa's *lights* were rather soft with warm colors and patterns, but when he grabbed me and spanked me, his *lights* immediately changed to a violent display of bright, foaming reds and dirty grays. As I lay in bed wondering what I had done wrong, my *Angel Lady in White* appeared to me and told me that crossing myself was perfectly fine as long as I didn't do it in front of grandpa. I quickly learned to watch grandpa's *lights* and to avoid him when I saw his *lights* change to deep reds and dirty grays. As sad as this may sound, I realized at the tender age of about six, that my grandpa Howard was not someone I could trust to be loving and caring. I learned that he, like my dad, could change very quickly from someone who seemed to be nice to someone who could quickly become violent.

Being Different

I do not know when I fully recognized that I was truly different from other children but I had begun to notice that I was while we were living at the foster home. As I began making more friends in Brooklyn where my grandpa lived, it became apparent that my friends did not see *lights* around people although several kids did talk about *seeing* and being frightened by ghosts. I also recognized that I was different from most adults, except of course for my mom and Mrs. Anne in the Upper Peninsula.

As I indicated previously, when a psychically sensitive child is born to a non-psychically sensitive family, they invariably feel different, isolated, and often are misunderstood. However for me, although I recognized that I was different, it did not seem to bother me as much as most other people I have met, or most children I have talked to. I suspect it is partially because although my brother told me what I was 'seeing' was my imagination, I somehow recognized that he 'saw' the same things I did – he just chose to ignore them.

As I learned while I was at the foster home, the *lights* I saw around people told me whether that person was happy, angry, or smiling while covering up something. It also told me whether they were healthy or ill. One day while playing at a neighbor's house I told the mother of one of my friends that I was sorry about her daughter's stomach problem but that I thought she would be OK although it would take awhile. The mother was shocked that I was aware of an illness with her daughter but a few days later she learned there was in fact a problem with her daughter's pancreas. It took several months, but she eventually did get well.

Physical abnormalities or sicknesses show up as a distortion in the Aura pattern. Most of the time, I also 'hear' words in my head telling me how to interpret what I am 'seeing.' Just prior to a person dying, a person's Aura often becomes very weak, and sometimes 'flickers' like a light that is about to go out. When I was a small child this frightened me because I did not know what it meant; I just knew that

it was not good. Over the years I have learned how to interpret this
'medical intuitive' information.

Grandma Hazel's Lights

Grandma Hazel was a rather depressed person who did not have children of her own and was not very happy that Grandpa Howard brought us two boys to live with them. Dealing with two very rambunctious little boys must have been an awful drain on her. Grandma Hazel's *lights* were normally not very bright anyway, and usually consisted of dark or "faded" colors. It was as if you took bright yellow, green, red and violet shirts, got them real dirty, then washed them and they faded. I called them *"dirty lights."* When Grandma Hazel would get upset at us her *lights* would get brighter but somehow still seemed to be "dirty" and sometimes I would tell her that she had *"dirty lights"* – not a very nice thing for a little boy to say, but that is what I did and that is how I still remember her.

One day, Grandma Hazel baked cookies and I took one from the counter before I had permission. When she saw what I had done, she became extremely upset and began to chase me around the house with a rolling pin in her hand. She was quite overweight and she could not catch me, so at one point she screamed my name to stop, and I noticed that her *lights* had become very red and broiling. They were very frightening to me because I knew that there was something seriously wrong with her physically. As she began to approach me, she fell down and I thought she was dead, but her *lights* told me that she was still alive but having problems with her heart. I ran to the next-door neighbor who called the ambulance and they rushed her to the hospital – Grandma Hazel had a slight heart attack. When my grandpa got home from the hospital, I was told that I was a bad boy because I had caused Grandma Hazel to have a heart attack. I really felt the pain and burden of that but when I went to bed that night my *Angel Lady in White* appeared and assured me that Grandma Hazel would be OK and that it was not my fault. She remained at my bedside until I went to sleep.

The next day I learned that Grandma Hazel would be fine but when she returned from the hospital she seemed more insecure and unsure of herself. She would often cling to my grandpa, who was not a very affectionate person anyway, and after that incident he seemed even more uncomfortable around her. His *lights* would become weaker when he was around her – not softer, just weaker – and he would usually just sit and listen to the radio (we did not have TVs back then) or read the local newspaper or sometimes the Detroit Free Press, deeply ensconced in the news of the War.

As Grandma Hazel began to recover, it became very easy for Terry and me to upset her. Whether it was going to the neighbor's house without telling her, or going fishing down at the Mill Pond, she would get upset. She also got upset when we went tramping through the woods or through the wheat, oat and corn fields that were all around the area. Grandpa allowed us those freedoms but grandma became overly worried about us when we did those things. Whenever she became upset, I would "check out" her *lights* to make sure she was physically all right and then pretty much ignore her.

Seeing My Dead Relatives

Shortly after I arrived at my grandpa's house, I became aware of several ghosts whom I recognized as dead relatives because there were pictures of them on the living room mantel, the dining room buffet, and on my grandparents' bedroom dressers. These "ghosts" included Grandpa's mother, his grandmother, and some aunts and uncles. They generally did not frighten me but some of them would periodically play tricks on me. They were delighted when they discovered that I could *see* them and sometimes talk to them, and one particularly nice lady who identified herself as Aunt Lucille, would often tuck me in at night. She was a very gentle, kind old lady and always said something to me in my mind prior to her showing herself so as not to frighten me. One of the ghosts that I particularly liked introduced himself as "Uncle Henry." He told me that he was a brother of my grandpa's dad, and I later learned he had been a favorite uncle of my grandpa. Uncle Henry had a gruff manner and talked rather fast, but generally he was a gentle Spirit.

Uncle Henry and the other ghosts would periodically tell me stories about my grandpa and sometimes about my grandma Hazel. When they first began to appear, I would tell my grandpa or grandma what they said – usually stories I could not have known about. This almost always got me into trouble. My brother told me to ignore them (the ghosts) but I was too fascinated with them not to talk to them and began to talk to them openly, rather than just in my mind. One time my grandma overheard me and asked me who I was talking to. When I told her, she told me that was evil and told my grandpa when he came home. I received a spanking and a stern talking to and from then on, I only spoke to them in my mind, unless nobody else was around.

I recognize that when children (or adults) 'see' or 'sense' a dead person or ghost, it can be very frightening. However, from my experience, most ghosts are not interested in scaring people; they simply want their 'story' to be heard. And those of us who are psychically sensitive are like a light bulb – that is our Auras indicate that we are sensitive to them. So like a moth is drawn to a light, they are drawn to our 'light.'

Although Uncle Henry was a rather benign ghost, he constantly played tricks like taking cards out of a deck and putting them in the sofa or under my grandparents' bed, for which my brother and I would often get blamed. He would say he was sorry after I got spanked for lying when I said I didn't do it. One day I *saw* Uncle Henry move my grandmother's favorite perfume bottle on her dresser just as she came into the room. Since I was near the dresser, she accused me of moving it and when I firmly said I hadn't touched it, she accused me of lying. I tried to tell her that it was Uncle Henry who moved the bottle not me, but she didn't believe me and accused me of making up stories.

Uncle Henry constantly tried to get my grandpa's attention and I tried to explain to him that Grandpa could not *see* nor *hear* him. He liked to tell me stories about my grandpa and the things he did when he was young. One day I made the mistake of telling my grandpa one of Uncle Henry's stories about my grandpa trying to put a stick up a horse's behind and the horse blowing manure on him in retaliation, which for a young seven-year old was particularly funny. However, as I repeated that story, Grandpa's *lights* got real dark red and gray and he grabbed my arm. "Who told you that story?" he screamed. "Uncle Henry did!" I said. "So who is Uncle Henry?" he asked. I pointed to the picture of his Uncle Henry on the living room mantel. My grandpa yelled, "That's not Uncle Henry, that's Walter. He died before you were born so you could not have talked to him." He told me to never talk about *seeing* and talking to ghosts again because that was evil. Although I continued to see Uncle Henry and other dead relatives, I stopped telling my grandparents about the stories they would tell me. I would occasionally talk to my brother about them but he always told me they were just my imagination and I should ignore them.

Several weeks after this incident, my grandpa's older sister, Aunt Bertha came to visit us and noticed the picture of Uncle Henry on the mantel. She picked up the picture and fondly talked about Uncle Henry, stating that he was a very good man and that although he was my grandpa's most beloved uncle, he did not like Grandpa very much because of his "tall tales" and exaggerations. Grandpa became very angry saying, "That's not Uncle Henry. His name was Walter!" Without missing a beat, Aunt Bertha said very emphatically, "Yes his name was Walter but we all called him Uncle Henry." I felt vindicated and pleased to know that I was correct about Uncle Henry. My grandpa continued to insist that his name was Walter, and later I overheard him tell Aunt Bertha that I had claimed to have seen and talked to

Walter. She seemed to get very upset that I might be talking to ghosts, but continued to insist that his name was Uncle Henry.

Real People vs. Dead People

One afternoon my grandpa's mother, grandmother and Uncle Henry were *telling* me stories about my grandpa. Grandma Hazel was in the back yard hanging clothes and I *saw* Uncle Henry and Grandpa's mother walk through the staircase wall and into my grandparents' bedroom and then back out again. All of a sudden I had the realization that real people could not do that and I understood that the main difference between real people and dead people (for me) was that dead people could walk through walls and real people could not. This remembrance was triggered many years later while watching the movie *The Beautiful Mind*. There is a scene in that movie where Professor John Nash, the main character, played by Russell Crowe, was walking around in circles on the Princeton campus saying to his *ghost*, "You're not real. You're not real." And his ghost saying, "You see me soldier." At that point, as I watched the movie, I had a flashback to the scene of Uncle Henry and Grandpa's mother walking through the wall. I remembered how wonderful that "discovery" was for me.

My dead relatives did not actually appear as physically real in body form as real people. However, they were normal human sized grayish semi-opaque figures that communicated with me in my mind. Also, they interacted with me in much the same way my living relatives did. So to me they were as 'real' as physical beings. The hugs that my dead Aunt Lucille gave me when she tucked me in for my afternoon naps were just as real and felt just as good as the hugs I received from my living relatives. That's how 'real' my dead relatives were for me.

Young children often 'see' or 'sense' dead people and will often interact with them. Like myself, they may not be sure if the person they are talking to or interacting with is dead or not. So do not discount your child's reaction to someone they say they 'see' or 'sense' and do not be frightened yourself. Become curious and ask questions of your child about what they 'see' or 'sense' – validate their sensitivities.

Seeing Jesus In The Baptist Church

Grandpa Howard and Grandma Hazel went to a "born again, hell-fire and brimstone Baptist church" that believed all people who were not Baptists were sinners and were going straight to hell. One Sunday shortly after we went to live with my grandpa, I was listening to the Baptist minister preach that Jesus said we were all sinners. Just then a figure that I recognized as Jesus appeared in the aisle next to me and said, "I didn't say those things." He then told me that we are not sinners, and that God loves all of us. Then he smiled at me, said I was a good little boy, and simply disappeared. As the minister continued to preach about how "each of us were sinners and that we did not deserve to look upon the face of the Lord," I heard Jesus voice (in my head) again say, "You are not sinners," which made me smiled.

At the end of the service as I was leaving with my grandpa, I stopped to shake the minister's hand and boldly told him "Jesus told me that he didn't say the things you said he said. He told me that we are not sinners, and that God loves all of us." The minister seemed very taken aback and my grandpa was very embarrassed and tried to quickly scoot me away, but the minister bent down and said to me, "Don't you know that it is a sin to make up stories and tell lies?" I told him that I was not lying, that I did see Jesus, and that he did tell me those things. The minister just shook his head and said something to my grandpa that I did not hear. However, when we got home, my grandpa became very upset and told Grandma Hazel that he had to do something about me and my stories. Later that afternoon Grandpa took me aside and told me that I shouldn't make up stories like that because that was bad. I tried to convince him that I really did see Jesus and that He really did tell me that we were not sinners, but there was just no way to make him understand or believe me.

Later that night as I lay in bed wondering why Jesus would tell me those things if they were not true, I heard His voice say to me that what he told me was true, but that the Minister and my grandpa were blind to the truth and I needed to pray for them.

> *Many young children experience 'visitations' by or communications with Spiritual Beings or Biblical characters. These are not simply imaginary beings, but most likely Angels or the energy of the character they experience. So do not discount your child's stories. Allow yourself, or force yourself, to become curious and ask questions about what they 'see' or experience – validate their sensitivities.*

The Little People At The Lake

Sunday afternoon picnics at one of the multiple lakes around Brooklyn were an important family get together. These always included several aunts and uncles, and sometimes neighbors. We all drove to a lake and the men went out in rowboats to fish while the women prepared the picnic meal and watched the kids. On one of our early trips to the lake, I was playing and I *saw* a *little person* or Nature Spirit by the dock. He looked like one of the *little people* I used to see at the lake in the Upper Peninsula. As I looked closer, I noticed several other *little people* as well and I ran to play with them and *talked* with them in my mind. I asked them about my Nature Spirit friend named "Turf" from Crooked Lake and they all seemed to know him. I was running on the dock and along the shore playing catch with them and just having a good time. One of the little guys named "Fleck" ran out onto the lily pads along the shoreline and several of his friends followed. They encouraged me to do the same, "You can't catch us, you can't catch us." I believed I could do the same thing so I ran and jumped onto a lily pad, only to discover that it would not hold me. Down I went into the water. I remember yelling at "Fleck" and the others that they had tricked me. They simply doubled up laughing at me. One of my aunts ran over to the dock and pulled me out of the water and asked me what I thought I was doing.

I told her I was playing tag with the *little people* and that they had told me to jump on the lily pad as they had done. Although my aunt laughed as she was drying me off, she scolded me loudly then quietly told me never to tell grandma or grandpa or any other adults about playing with *little people* because I would get into big trouble. She then told me to go play in the sun and dry off. When she went back to the other adults, she explained that I had thought the lily pads would hold me and so I had jumped on them. This brought great laughter from everyone. She did not tell them about the *little people* but looked over at me and winked. We went to that lake, and several others, many more times over the years and although I would *see* and play with the *little people*, I did not allow them to get me into trouble again.

The Old Man in The Barbershop

My grandpa had a barbershop in the town of Brooklyn, Michigan and I often played with my toys and watched as Grandpa cut hair. One day as I was playing with my toys, an older man from our hometown walked in. I recognized him because he was one of my grandpa's regular customers, and my grandpa greeted him with a friendly "Hello Charlie, have a seat." At first I just stared at him but soon I became very frightened because on this particular day he did not have any *lights*, which I had come to rely on to determine "good or nice" people from "angry or bad" people. I ran up to my grandpa and grabbed his trousers and in a very frightened voice said, "Grandpa, Grandpa, he doesn't have any lights." My grandpa stopped cutting the hair of the man in the barber's chair, made some apology to Charlie, and told me to go sit in the corner and be quiet until it was time to go home, which I obediently did. However, I continued to look at that old man and wondered why he didn't have any *lights*.

When we went home for dinner, Grandpa told Grandma Hazel about the incident and how I had embarrassed him. As we sat down to eat I tried to explain to them that Mr. Charlie did not have any *lights* and I asked them what that meant. They told me to eat my supper and be quiet about it. When I asked my grandpa again after supper why ole' man Charlie did not have any *lights*, he simply told me not to talk about *lights* again, swatted me on the butt, and sent me to bed without my usual desert. I was a very confused little boy. When my brother came to bed I tried to talk to him about what I *saw* but he was not interested. I eventually fell asleep wondering why that man did not have any *lights*.

The next morning our next-door neighbor, the town sheriff, came to our house and told my grandpa that ole' man Charlie had died. I remember thinking maybe that was why he did not have any *lights* and I became very frightened. The sheriff and my grandparents continued to talk for a short while, but when the sheriff left, my grandpa began talking very angrily to Grandma Hazel about me being possessed by the devil and that he was going to have to "once and for all" make sure that I understood what I had done. I remember being really scared because Grandpa's *lights* had become "boiling clouds of anger" like my dad's had the night of the big fight with my mom, and I knew it meant that he was very, very angry. I also noticed that Grandma Hazel's *lights* were somewhat boiling as well. At that point Grandpa got his razor strap off the back of their bedroom door and called my name for me to come to him. I was really scared but I knew I had to go to him, and I knew I was in BIG trouble. As I sheepishly approached him, he grabbed my arm and yanked me toward him and yelled, "You killed him, you killed him! I'm going to beat the devil out of you. You are wicked. Those heathen Catholics have corrupted you." He began spanking me with the razor strap more severely than I could ever remember being spanked before. I don't remember what made him stop but I think I convinced him that I would never ever say anything about *lights* again. I vaguely remember crawling up the stairs on my hands and knees because my butt and the back of my legs hurt too much to walk.

Asking That The Gift Be Taken Away

As I lay in bed that afternoon whimpering (I didn't dare cry out loud) I prayed to God and to my *Angel Lady in White* that I be forgiven for being evil and causing that man to die and that I did not want to go to hell. I also asked that my "gift" to *see lights* around people be taken away. My *Angel Lady in White* appeared beside my bed and told me that I had not caused that man to die and that he was fine. She even made him appear and he looked fine and even smiled at me and said he was sorry for getting me into trouble.

Even his *lights* were beautiful. I asked her again to please take "the gift" away, which she promised she would do. She then hugged me and made the pain go away, and stayed by my bed until I fell asleep.

When I awoke the next morning, not only was the spanking pain gone, but most of the spanking marks were gone as well, but so too was my *Angel Lady in White*. As I went downstairs for breakfast, I was aware that I felt very sad and somehow very different. That was a very somber day for me because I did not *see* or *hear* any dead relatives, and was aware that my grandma Hazel's distorted *lights* had all but disappeared. Although over the next few days and months I would periodically *hear* Uncle Henry or my grandpa's mother say something to me in my mind, like my brother Terry, I was able to simply ignore them. Thus, at the tender age of about 6½ I made a silent vow to stop listening to the voices in my head, ignore the *lights* I saw around people, no longer talk to dead Spirits, and quit running and jumping with my delightful *little people* friends.

The In Between Years

When my *Angel Lady in White* took my *gift* away as I had asked, my psychic world immediately turned black which made life much more depressing for me. I was no longer aware of the "dirty lights" around my grandma Hazel. However, neither was I aware of the *lights* around other people that had been such an important part of my ability to judge what people were thinking or how they were feeling. I was also no longer able to talk to and interact with Uncle Henry or other family ghosts, and my Spirit Guides and my *Angel Lady in White* stopped talking to me. Even the *little people* or Nature Spirits that I used to play with were gone. Although my childhood friendships and life continued, I became a very quiet, withdrawn and obedient little boy but was very sad most of the time. The most important aspect of *my world* was gone and having asked that my *gift* be taken away, I did not know how to get it back. Little did I realize how important that aspect of my world was until it was taken away. Now that it was gone I could no longer rely on my sensitivities to judge whether people were lying to me, or whether they would be nice or hurtful. And my Spirit Guides, my *Angel Lady in White,* and my *little people* friends whom I could always rely on to be loving and caring were no longer around.

> *When a child either voluntarily or is forced to turn off their psychic sensitivities it is a very dramatic experience for them because a part of their world – their reality – has been taken away from them. As with me, they could easily become depressed, withdrawn and sad, so pay attention to these symptoms.*

> *Similarly, if a child's sensitivities are ridiculed, told that they are evil or bad or otherwise not validated, it can cause the child to become depressed or act out with anger or rebelliousness, so again pay attention to what your child is saying and how they are reacting. The clues are there if you look for them.*

Dad Returns from WWII

Following the war, my dad returned with a new wife, Henrietta, and a three-year old stepchild and began working in my grandpa's barbershop. Over the next several years two more sisters were born and then sometime in 1948 my dad went back into the Air Force and was promptly shipped overseas to Guam. A few months later my stepmom packed up the five of us kids and drove to San Francisco where we caught a troop ship and sailed to Guam. We spent about a year in Guam and were then shipped to the

Philippines where we lived until the Korean War broke out in June 1950. I remember when my dad was called out in the middle of the night to go flying. His squadron flew to Japan and dropped the first troops in Korea. When he returned, he was immediately transferred to Japan and several weeks later we again followed. We spent about two years in Japan during which time my *psychic* world remained black and I remained a very withdrawn, sad and lonely kid.

As a "GI Brat" you learn not to make friends, or at least not close friendships because you are constantly moving. You also learn that in the military rank means everything! If your dad is an enlisted man, you cannot make friends (fraternize) with officer's kids. As an enlisted man's son I always felt less than and my friendship options were limited. During these years I lost contact with my friends and playmates from Brooklyn and I learned to pretty much keep to myself. I believe this was partially a result of my grandfather Howard's and my dad's temperament. Both my brother and I learned to be loners, and for whatever reason, we were not close. It wasn't that we didn't like each other, we just didn't exactly get along with each other, and so I have no real memories of us playing or doing fun things together during those years.

Near the end of the Korean War the whole family (my dad, stepmother and us five kids) took a troop ship back to the United States and took a sleeper train back to Michigan. My dad bought a farm near my grandpa's farm and the family settled there. We got back just in time for my older brother to start high school at Brooklyn, while I and my younger siblings went to a one-room school house about ½ mile up the gravel road from our farm house. For the next few years, while our stepmother and us kids lived on the farm, my dad was stationed at Selfridge AFB north of Detroit. It was about an hour or so drive from Brooklyn. He lived there during the week and came home on weekends.

Over the next several years three more children were born into our family, and my responsibilities on the farm as the second oldest became quite burdensome. Although I was able to go back to the Brooklyn High School for my freshman year, where all my childhood friends were, my dad moved the family up to Selfridge AFB for my sophomore year. We then moved back to the farm for my junior and senior years. That was a very socially disruptive thing for a sensitive, withdrawn and insecure teenager.

Meeting My Mom Again

Sometime after we returned from overseas, my brother discovered that our biological mother was still living in the Detroit area. He contacted her and learned that she had remarried and had two boys, and that she definitely wanted to see us. It was close to spring break and he arranged to have her come out to the farm where we lived. When our dad learned that Terry had found our mom and that she wanted to see us, he was very upset and refused to allow us to go see her and would not let her come see us unless he was present. Throughout those years he had remained a bitter enemy of our mom.

The first weekend Mom came to see us on the farm, I was NOT told she was coming. I later leaned that my dad had told Terry not to tell me, hoping that I would be away fishing or with my friends in Brooklyn, so that I would not be there when she came. However, when Mom, Tom and my sister Kathleen arrived, I was cleaning the barn doing my normal weekend chores, getting ready for my dad's critical inspection. I was surprised when my dad called me out of the barn and I saw him and this strange woman coming toward me. He came and stood beside me, put his arm around my shoulder, and said something like "Here he is." As I recall Mom responded with something like "I'm your mother. We haven't seen each other in a very long time." She went on about how cute and grown up I was, and then my dad tousled my hair (something he would sometimes do after beating me). I remember feeling very confused, nervous and strange about this whole situation. My dad then told my mom that I needed to complete my chores and motioned for her to leave. I told him that I had already done them but he pushed me toward the barn and commanded: "Well go do them again!" Then he turned and followed my mother up to the house. I never got to see my mom on that visit because my dad sent them away saying that I was too busy with chores to visit. When I later asked my dad why they had left, he lied and said something about my mom still not being interested in seeing me, which really felt bad. Only later did I learn the real story.

In spite of my dad's objections and attempts to make it difficult for my brother and me to visit Mom, that summer I began hitch hiking or taking the bus to go see her and would often spend several days on each visit. My mom was always very loving and caring and she seemed to think I was smart, which I had never heard before. She also told me I was good looking, which is another thing I hadn't heard before. My mom was a hugger, and although I wasn't familiar with hugs, I loved how good they felt, but I remember being very shy about hugging her back.

The more I learned from my visits with my mom, the more I liked her. She loved to talk about Astrology, Ghosts, UFO's and other "strange things" and I thoroughly enjoyed her stories. Although my stepdad Tom was not psychically sensitive and was not sure he believed everything Mom said, he loved and cared for her, Kathleen, and their two boys, Chris and Tim, and he knew how to express it. He also began showing more affection toward me the more we got to know one another. Getting to know and understand my mom's family was both wonderful and confusing at the same time, because while I was receiving lots of love, positive feedback, and a feeling of being included in this *new* family, life at home with my dad and stepmother was as harsh as ever.

Several months after Mom's first visit to our farm, she and I had a good talk about that initial meeting. She mentioned that as she approached the barn she sensed that something was very wrong. She saw me flinch when my dad came up beside me and said that she wanted to grab me and hold me but was still afraid of my dad's uncontrolled anger. She told me she could tell that I was confused about meeting her again and that I was obviously very frightened of my dad. She said they left because my dad told them to. He told her I was too busy with my chores to visit.

Turning The Gift Back On

After one of my early visits to Mom's home in Southgate, Michigan, my *Angel Lady in White* appeared to me in a dream and told me that it was time to turn my sensitivities back on. I was very surprised as this was not something I was asking for. When I shared my dream with my mom, she seemed very pleased and said she would help me. So with my mom's strong and loving encouragement and discussions of various experiences that she related to me, I began *seeing* and *sensing* lights around my neighbors, teachers, classmates, and ordinary people on the street again. I even began seeing my dad's *lights* again, and when he came home on the weekends I was now aware enough to avoid him when his *lights* were distorted. After awhile, I even began seeing Nature Spirits in the woods and by the lakes where I went fishing, and that was a delightful experience. I could always count on them to be loving and caring, although somewhat mischievous.

After meeting my mom and turning my sensitivities back on, I desperately longed to be with my Spirit Guides and Angels, not just be sensitive to them. Alas, I had much to learn and much yet to experience. Although I fully recognized that I could only be aware of them and their presence, not among them, that fact did not eliminate the desire. During the years out on the farm, I would often go outside on a clear dark night and just sob, asking to be "taken home to the stars" because I knew that was where I came from and where I again longed to be. How badly I wanted to return. At that time, a musical group named The Platters had a song entitled *"My Prayer"* whose lyrics were "My prayer is to linger with you," which for me meant the "star people" – my new found Angels and Spirit Guides. This longing was based on a false belief that the Angels and my Spirit Guides were somehow "out there" among the stars. Only years later did I realize or come to understand that they are in the Spirit domain, not "out there" somewhere and that it is my psychic sensitivity that allows me to communicate with them – in Spirit, through my mind. When I told Mom that I wanted to "go back to the stars" she just held me with tears in her eyes and said she understood. She told me that I had a lot of things to learn and do and that it was not my time to go. She always seemed to understand what I was referring to and would share with me her own experiences, her dreams of being among the stars, her meditations and other "out of body" experiences. Those stories always fascinated me and gave me a clear sense of hope. More and more I realized that she was my mom and I was her son – that was a new and marvelous feeling. I felt totally accepted.

*To help the reader understand what I mean when I refer to **Angelic Beings** and **Spirit Guides**, which I do throughout the remainder of this book, I offer the following explanation.*

***Angelic Beings** (Angels and Archangels) are Spiritual Beings that have never separated from the Divine source – never expressed in human form, and have never been caught up in the Karmic cycle. My 'Angel Lady in White' is an Angelic Being. They are available to anyone who calls upon the Divine essence for assistance or understanding as indicated in the Bible and other sacred teachings. From my experience, Angels rarely express themselves visually, but will or can express themselves in one's mind in a humanoid form, or simply create an awareness in ones mind of a high Spiritual presence that may or may not take on a humanoid expression – depending on what that person needs to identify with. When one does become aware of an Angelic Being, there is no mistake that you have met, seen or been in the presence of such 'energy.' For example, when I make contact with them, not just talk to them in my mind, but actually call upon them and experience their presence, I become aware of a powerfully loving presence, and I sometimes 'hear' a message in my 'inner ear.' Angelic Beings do not operate within the limitations of our physical realm and can readily cause 'miraculous' things to occur.*

***Spirit Guides** on the other hand are highly evolved Spiritual Beings that are separate from the Angelic realm. They may be entities that we have been with in a previous life but who have chosen to express in Spirit form and work from that domain during this lifetime. I often 'see' or am aware of Spirit Guides for clients or friends. These Spirit Guides are often Spiritual Teachers from a past life, and are always* *of a high vibrational energy. From my experience, everyone has one or more Spirit Guides available to them. However, they do not and cannot interfere with an individual's free will choices and actions. I believe they provide guidance through what we commonly call our conscience.*

In addition to *seeing* and talking to my Angelic beings and Spirit Guides, I began *seeing* dead people again, which at first was not a pleasant experience since I would often encounter them on my five-mile walk home from town along a dirt road with few farm houses and no street lights. As I began *seeing* and *sensing* things more completely, I was able to ask Mom about these things and she helped me understand how to distinguish my fears and imagination from my *psychic* sensitivities – my other "real world." One evening Mom, Tom, Kathleen and I were sitting in their living room listening to the radio. All of a sudden my mom, Kathleen and I *saw* this man walk through the front wall into the living room as if he were lost. Kathleen and I both just blurted out "Who is he?" and Mom laughed and said that he was a lost soul. She said that he was a neighbor who had died recently and we needed to "send him to the light." That was the first time I had ever heard a human say those words but I had remembered hearing it in my mind before. Tom was totally freaked out. He didn't see anything but he definitely knew that we all had seen something.

On another evening my mom, Kathleen, Tim and I were at Grandma Smith's house and Grandma Smith was reading "cards" – she used regular playing cards not Tarot cards – for my brother Tim. I was standing behind her looking over her shoulder and as she laid the cards out and began speaking, I could *see* what she was *seeing* and *knew* what she was going to say, and I very excitedly blurted out, "Grandma, I can see what you are reading," and began explaining what I was *seeing*, and she calmly said "You are right. See, the gift is coming back" and winked at my mom. Mom just smiled and later told me that that was how she got started many, many years ago. I was very excited as were Kathleen and Tim and we talked about it for several days.

About a year or so after I began my visits with Mom, my dad rented our farm and moved the family up to Selfridge AFB where he had been stationed since we came back from Japan. It was easier to visit Mom now because I was only about 30-40 minutes away, a much shorter hitchhike or bus ride, and I really thought that now my dad would not be as tired and angry all the time and perhaps things would be better at home. Unfortunately they were not.

The Master Appears

On one of my visits to my mom's house during that first year, my mother and I had an experience that profoundly affected both of us. One that she in fact talked about for many years. Although this story may sound exaggerated or fabricated, I can assure you it is true. Initially I was reluctant to include it, but my Spirit Guides told me that I needed to relate it so those who have had similar such experiences can take comfort in the fact that you are not alone.

We were sitting at the kitchen table and I was asking Mom what had I done so bad that my dad would continue to beat me. I could see that her heart was breaking for me and I suspected that she just wanted to go kill him. However, that evening, she simply sat beside me and held me with such love and understanding. All of a sudden a bright light figure began forming next to the table. It was the figure of Jesus. Although I had seen Jesus appear before, this "apparition" seemed more physically real to me than my other "encounters" with the Master. I remember hearing in my head a loving blessing upon both of us, and words to the effect that there was a great work that I needed to accomplish. Then the figure that had formed simply disappeared. We both just sat there in awe.

When I was able to speak, I asked Mom if she saw the figure of Jesus and she confirmed that she had. She then said that she heard him bless both of us and heard him tell her that I would not be taken from her again. I had not heard that part. We sat there for about half an hour and talked about what we actually saw and heard, what He looked like, and what He actually said. Then she got up and said, "With that, I think that we both need to go to bed and get a good night's sleep." She gave me a big hug and said, "Thank you for coming to me and finding me again. I thought I had lost you forever and now I know that I will have you around for as long as I live." She gave me a kiss on the cheek and we both went to bed.

Experiences like the one above are similar to Near Death Experiences. Many more people have them than most people think, and they usually profoundly affect one's life. So if your child or you have such an encounter with a High Spiritual presence, don't discount it and don't ignore the message that is conveyed – it is always a reaffirming message of hope and love and helps us realize that there is more to life than just our physical body.

When I awoke the next morning, Mom was in the kitchen with Tom telling him what we had experienced the night before. As I sat down at the table, he looked me in the eye and asked if what Mom said was true. When I said, "Yes," he just shook his head and said something like, "You guys must be something special" and Mom immediately replied, "That was not the point!" She said that the point for her was that she was assured that I would not be taken from her again and that there was something special that I was to do. Although I didn't say it at the time, the point for me was that I was assured that the Master would always be with me, which was very reassuring.

Years later, whenever we got together and happened to talk about that experience, Mom would tear up and say that she felt that I was a special child when I was born and that experience was validation for her. To me it was a reaffirmation of my connection to "the Master" and my source – God. Periodically over the years, Tom would ask me about that experience and each time he enjoyed listening to it all over again. I continued visiting with my mom, sister, half brothers and my stepdad, who was such a loving and warm individual. I also continued exploring my *psychic* sensitivities, the new things Mom was helping me become aware of, and I was learning how better to handle my dad's anger.

Unusual Encounters

Shortly after I began visiting my mom and learning all about my psychic sensitivities; what they included and how to control them, my mom introduced me to the concept of UFO's. I learned that she was well read about UFO's and I remember the fascinating pictures in a book she had by George Adamski.[7] At the time, I was not sure whether I believed in them or not. But, I knew that Mom did, and the stories she told about them were always fascinating. One of the things that made me seriously consider the very real possibility of their existence was that on several occasions Mom, my sister Kathleen and I would go out into the yard and mom would "call" them in her mind. Within a few minutes, multiple objects – sometimes two or three, sometimes many more – would appear as "lights in the sky." However, these lights did not move as airplanes, or even as shooting stars, but moved in a controlled fashion and often at very high rates of speed from one point in the sky to another. I began to believe that there might be something more to them than just my mom's imagination.

---

[7] http://en.wikipedia.org/wiki/George_Adamski. Mr. Adamski wrote several books on UFO's but I do not recall the title of the books that my mom had. See http://www.amazon.com and type in George Adamski for a listing of his books.

Although the reader might wonder what UFO's have to do with psychic phenomena or psychic experiences, I have to say that they do not, directly. However, if you remain open to the possibility of such things, and begin asking your Spirit Guides and Angels about them, you will most likely be surprised at the answers you become aware of or 'get.' For me the experiences I had regarding UFO's during this time in my life helped me believe in and relate to many other unusual experiences I was to have later in my life.

A Personal Encounter

The following story may seem far-fetched to some readers, but I assure you it is true. It is something that I have no scientific explanation for, but I know that it was not simply my imagination. I am simply reporting here what I saw at that time and what I believe it was.

Because my dad was in the Air Force, I was fascinated by and became very familiar with all military aircraft. I could easily recognize and identify them on sight and at the time of this incident could probably have told you their top speed, their armament, etc. One day my sister Kathleen and I were walking down Dix Highway towards the local recreation center when all of a sudden we saw a bright and shiny circular shaped object in the sky that I KNEW was NOT an aircraft. As we stood there watching, cars began stopping and people got out to see what it was. There was no sound associated with it but there did seem to be a "shimmering" energy field of some sort around it. It appeared to be about ½ mile away, about 1,000 feet up in the air, and about 30-40 feet in diameter with a dome-like shape on top and three dome-like structures underneath. It looked very similar to a picture that I had seen in one of mom's books on UFOs. It seemed to simply "hover" there for about ten minutes or more and then I heard two F-86 aircraft approach at high speed. They "buzzed" past it as it very slowly moved to our left. As the F-86s circled around and began to approach again, it slowly started going up. It went up at about a 60-70 degree angle and simply accelerated at an incredible speed. In a flash it was gone without a sound.

The people who had stopped and were looking began to excitedly talk about what they had just experienced. Kathleen and I just looked at each other and simultaneously blurted out, "Did you see that?" and then just laughed. We immediately turned around and headed back home. When we got home and excitedly told Mom about our experience she calmly just smiled and said, "I know." The next day, and several days later, there were reports in the local newspaper about F-86s being scrambled from the nearby Willow Run field and several quotes from people who had stopped to see it. However, no real explanation was ever provided. That was my first "real" encounter with a UFO. Clearly it was unidentified and clearly it flew – faster than anything I had ever seen fly before or since.

When I later talked to my mom about what I saw and asked what she thought it was, she began telling more stories about her experiences with UFOs. Although I had trouble believing they were all true, it was clear to me that *she* truly believed them.

Many years later, while working in the Air Force at Cape Canaveral, Florida I had another "credible" UFO experience. I was part of a team that was about to launch an Atlas missile when five objects were spotted on the radar at about 15,000 feet over the launch site. A group of us at the launch site went outside and saw them visually, as well. We could also see the two "chase planes" that were aloft waiting for the launch and could hear them over the radio reporting that they saw them too. The five objects remained stationary as the two planes approached. However, as the planes passed by them, the five objects all took off almost vertically and disappeared. In a flash they were gone. The launch was delayed "due to unforeseen technical difficulties" – at least that was the official reason given in the newspapers.

Over the years I have had several other "less sure" encounters with Unidentified Flying Objects. When I asked my Spirit Guides about these, I was told that many of those experiences were genuine and that there are many other entities from other star systems and dimensions. So my sense is that there is some sort of reality to UFOs. But I also understand that there are some reported encounters that have normal explanations. As with many things psychic, great discernment is required of all such experiences. I leave it to the reader to make up his or her own mind about what you believe.

My Best Friend Gerry

When we lived with my Grandpa Howard in Brooklyn before we went overseas my best friend Gerry, who had a twin sister, Janet, lived across the street. We were the same age and the very best of friends. Gerry had polio as a very young child and one leg was shorter than the other but he got around very well. Their mom and dad had been divorced for a long time and they lived with their mom who was very nice and from what I saw of their dad, he was a big and angry man. Gerry and Janet loved to hear about Uncle Henry and other ghosts and things that I *saw*, and about *seeing lights* around people. I told them their mom had nice *lights*. Neither of them was sensitive but they enjoyed the ghost stories. I also told them about the man without any *lights* in the barbershop who died and about my grandpa getting so angry and that I had asked my *Angel Lady in White* to take the *gift* away. They must have told their mom because one day a few days after the barbershop incident, she pulled me to her and said quietly that she knew that I did not kill ole' man Charlie, that I was a good boy, and that she was sorry about what my grandpa did. I remember how good that felt. I always liked Mrs. Patterson.

When we moved overseas, we lost track of each other but when we returned we picked up our friendship where we had left off, even though I lived on a farm five miles from town. I would ride my bike or hitch hike to town so we could spend time together. However, it wasn't until I went to high school that we were able to see each other every day and truly rekindle our friendship.

Gerry and I had a great time, especially after I got my first car, a really cool '49 Ford. Gerry bought his '55 Chevy the year before and we had lots of fun going to the drag races and driving around like teenagers do. Then, just a few weeks before graduation from high school, Gerry was driving with his girlfriend on one of the very winding back roads and his front tie rod broke, sending them head-on into a tree. Gerry was killed instantly and his girlfriend was badly injured. When I heard the news, I was devastated and in shock. In spite of my new *psychic* sensitivities I was not aware of Gerry's Spirit nor aware of any Angels around, which was quite depressing. Gerry's death filled me with great sadness and grief. I missed him terribly. When I talked to my mom about him, she very gently and simply told me that he was fine and was sending me "love and light" from the other side. Somehow I believed her and that was very reassuring

Only years later when I visited his grave site and was able to "tap into" Gerry's energy myself and communicate with his Spirit, was I able to come to peace with his passing. I remember telling him that I was very angry with him for leaving me and that I missed him terribly. I felt his energy and *heard* him say he was fine and that we would always be the "best of friends."

The Air Force Years

A couple of months after graduation from high school I joined the Air Force and was sent to Boot Camp in San Antonio, Texas. Following Boot Camp, I was sent to Aircraft and Missile Electrical Technician School in Rantoul, Illinois. Although school was difficult for me, I really enjoyed learning and graduated high enough in my class to be given the option of where I wanted to be stationed. I chose the 322nd Air Division in France. An alternative was Viet Nam and I know my Angels and Spirit Guides must have been watching out for me, because I never got caught up in that devastating conflict.

Following my Air Force Technical Training graduation, I returned to Brooklyn, said goodbye to Grandpa Howard and Grandma Hazel, my aunts and uncles, and my high school buddies. I also spent some time with my mom, Tom, Kathleen, Chris and Tim. We had a good and fun visit. I especially enjoyed my visit with Tom since I was now old enough to have a beer with him, an initiation rite that every young man savors. I then took the train to New York and spent a couple days with my dad and stepmom, which turned out to be the last time I would see them for 22 years.

My Experiences In Europe

When I left my dad's place, I caught a plane to Dreux AFB, France, where I spent the next 2½ years working on C-119 Flying Box Cars and C-130 Hercules aircraft. I was also assigned to a "traveling squad" – a team of selected specialists in the areas of hydraulics, engines, instruments, aircraft electrical systems, sheet metal specialists, etc. who got to fly all over Europe, the Near East, and Africa to fix "downed" aircraft. That part of my tour was very enjoyable – I learned a lot and I got to see a lot.

Shortly after arriving at the base I hit it off with a couple guys from the coal-mining region of Pennsylvania. John Henry, a hydraulics specialist who had a very gentle Spirit but was built like the man in the legendary song of the same name, had been there about four months. He and I became best of friends. The other guy was Pete, a new Aircraft Electrical Technician like myself, and an intellectual. Pete constantly quoted Keats, Chaucer, Whitman, Poe, and others. Both John and Pete had motorcycles – John a Triumph Bonneville and Pete a BSA 650 Golden Flash and we thoroughly enjoyed riding to Paris and being total tourists on the weekends. We also had a lot of fun and exciting experiences speeding through the back roads of France.

My Catholic Connections

When I discovered that my new Air Force buddies were Catholic, I decided to attend Mass with them one Sunday and much to their surprise and mine, I seemed to *know* the Latin Mass as if I had been attending Mass all my life. It felt so comfortable. Even though I had never taken Latin, the words and understanding automatically came to me. My buddies accused me of lying about my not having been to Mass before except when I was a small child. They did not understand my familiarity with the Mass ritual and verse, and neither did I. Even though I had spent about two years with my foster family who were Catholics, it did not seem reasonable to assume that I would have remembered it. Did I? Either that or could I have been exposed to it in a previous life? An intriguing possibility.

As my familiarity with the Mass increased, I began taking Catechism classes in preparation of converting to Catholicism. I also began having dreams and spontaneous recall (while awake) of having been a Priest in

France several hundred years previously. What really freaked me out were the strange experiences I began having while visiting various Catholic Cathedrals throughout Europe as part of my "traveling squad" trips. One Sunday after attending High Mass at the Sacré-Cœur cathedral on Montmartre, I was standing near the rear of the church looking at the altar and I found myself "transported in time" to about 250 years previously. I was a Priest wearing a black robe with a red rope sash or belt. I realized that I had indeed been a Catholic Priest. Unfortunately, as more information was revealed to me, I learned that in that lifetime I had used my position to seduce young women and I understood that I was going to have to somehow make up for those indiscretions. That was a very depressing recall, but it also confirmed for me why I had so readily picked up on the Mass. I thanked God for those insights and began lighting candles and beseeching forgiveness of my victims and for my transgressions at every Catholic Church I visited.

About a year later at a special Christmas High Midnight Mass with a choir of about fifty monks at the Notre Dame Cathedral, I had another past life recall experience. As the monks chanted the Mass and were singing the Alleluia Chorus, I found myself out of my body looking down upon myself and all of the other people present. I was surrounded by a "Choir of Angels" creating a harmonious melody in concert with the Monk Choir. They were creating an extremely loving and melodious vibration, which I experienced like sound. It seemed to cause my entire being, not just my body, to vibrate as if in absolute harmony with the vibrations. It was as if I were being enveloped in the most loving energy one can ever imagine. As the Choir ended, I found myself back in my body with the feeling that I had been touched by God himself. Words are inadequate to describe this most profound spiritual experience, but it affected me greatly for several months.

Following this experience, I was then shown another lifetime. I was again a priest and was performing Mass in a large Cathedral. As I saw this scene, I was aware that I had been a good and dedicated priest in that lifetime and was being thanked for the work that I had done and heard the words, "life is about balance." I was beginning to recognize that my spiritual development was progressing and my *psychic* awareness was expanding, not so much because I was studying, but because I was apparently being taught in my dreams and via my experiences.

My Bike Accident – The Last Rights

About six months after I arrived in France, my buddies and I purchased 50cc motorbikes, which although a lot slower than the motorcycles were a lot more fun to ride. One weekend, we rode through a small village called *Cruce Cruvé*, which had a nice little park with very nicely aligned trees. Racing in and out of those trees was something I simply had to do. I deliberately left the road only to find that there was a deep ditch between the trees and me. Well, my bike did not jump the ditch. I went flying through the air and struck a tree with my left shoulder. My head went forward and snapped violently to the left, and as a result when I came to rest, my head was turned off to the left even though I was looking forward. I also scraped a good portion of skin off my left cheek and fell to the ground bleeding and unconscious.

My buddies immediately called the Air Base for an ambulance. When the medics arrived and began to try to straighten my head, my buddy John Henry fortunately intervened and would not let them. His actions probably saved my life because my neck although not broken was hyper-extended and turned 90 degrees to the left. John rode with me in the ambulance and luckily one of my barracks' buddies was on duty at the hospital when the ambulance arrived. This proved to be synchronistic and most helpful because much of what I can now write about is because my buddies later shared this traumatic event with me.

When I arrived at the hospital I had slipped into a deep coma and was bleeding from my ears, eyes, nose and mouth. The doctors called for a neurosurgeon to be flown in from Bitburg, Germany because there were no neurosurgeons at Dreux. While waiting for his arrival, I was put in traction with a strap under my chin, attempting to stretch the neck back out to relieve pressure on my spine. The doctors felt that I would not survive the night and because my military records indicated I was Catholic, they called for a Catholic Chaplain. They also sent a telegram to both of my parents saying that I had been in a serious accident, had a broken neck, a severe brain concussion and was in critical condition. My mother later told me that she had awakened that morning very upset, yet not knowing why. My stepdad Tom said that she had been "on edge" all day, and that when an Air Force sergeant came up the steps with a telegram, she immediately started crying uncontrollably. Remember, a few years previously she had been told by "the Master" that I would not be taken away from her again. She later told me that when she saw the Air Force guy, she knew something was seriously wrong with me (not my brother who was also in the Air Force) and began questioning that "message." She said that she immediately went into her bedroom and began praying and went into an altered state.

I later learned that when the neurosurgeon arrived at the hospital, he determined that he could not operate due to my severe brain trauma. He decided to "tap" my brain to relieve the pressure, and hopefully prevent me from going into a deeper coma, and decided to manually manipulate my neck bones back into position then slowly relieve the hyperextension. Shortly after the neurosurgeon completed turning my head and neck back to its normal position and holding it in place with tension straps, he left and flew back to Germany.

When the Catholic Chaplain from the base chapel arrived, he began administering the Last Rights of the Church while a nurse was taking my pulse. The priest later told me that as he was giving me the Last Rights, an "Angel" suddenly appeared at the foot of my bed startling both him and the nurse. He said that when the "Angel" appeared, I came out of my deep coma, sat bolt upright in bed – in spite of the traction straps – and said "Mamma?" and then simply laid back down. He said that the "Angel" remained for several minutes and seemed to send some form of energy to me because my entire body relaxed and seemed to go to sleep rather than back into a coma. Then she simply disappeared. When I was released from the hospital and was able to talk to the nurse she said that she was profoundly affected by the experience. She said an Angelic figure appeared at the foot of my bed that completely freaked her out. She stated that she had never experienced anything like that before and hoped that she never did again. She was very shook up by the entire encounter.

When I went to see the priest about my Catechism classes, he said that I must be someone very special because he saw an Angel appear at the foot of my bed as he was giving me the Last Rights. He said that he had never seen anything like it before and felt that I had received a miracle healing because the doctors had told him that my injuries were extremely serious and that they did not believe I would survive. I learned from my medic buddy that the doctors chalked my miraculous recovery up to the fact that my coma must not have been as severe as they initially thought. He said that for several days they talked about the great readjustment my neurosurgeon had performed on my neck.

When I was finally able to contact my mother, she asked me who that person in the purple robe was beside my bed. She did not know I was taking Catholic Catechism classes. She then told me that she saw the nametag of the nurse who was standing there and even wrote her name down. My mom had deliberately Astral Projected[8] herself to the foot of my bed and *saw* me in

---

[8] Astral Projection is a process where one can project their consciousness to a distant location and be aware of what is going on at that distant location. Sometimes they can make others at that location aware of them, and can sometimes communicate with them.

traction, *saw* the nurse and the priest. She told me that my sister, Kathleen, had also seen the nurse and the priest in a dream that same night. I feel that I should have had a Near Death Experience from that incident, but as far as I can recall, I did not.

Although I could easily have become a paraplegic with the injuries I suffered, I did not. I believe that it was because of my mother's healing presence and energy, and a knowledgeable neurosurgeon that I recovered so completely. I have never had any after effects other than a few spots on my back that are either numb or overly sensitive, which I am told are probably due to spinal nerve damage as a result of the hyper-extension trauma to my neck. I continue to thank my mom, that neurosurgeon and God for that healing.

Chance Encounters

In addition to my interesting Catholic Priest past life recall experiences, and my bike accident experience, I had a number of other interesting, fun, and synchronistic encounters during my time in Europe. Sometime in the summer of 1959 I had a chance encounter with Elvis Presley while he was on military leave in Paris. Me and several other buddies ended up drinking beer with Elvis one Saturday afternoon. We simply sat around "trashing our TIs" (Technical Instructors) for about an hour in a pub. He was just one of the guys. That was the one and only time I ever saw him.

I also had a chance encounter with Willy Brandt[9] in Berlin on the day he gave his famous speech near the Brandenburg Gate shortly after the wall went up. I was in Berlin waiting to fly into Poland and was about a block away, but was close enough to hear his speech. Thirty years later, in 1991, a few years after the wall came down, I met Willy Brandt at an IBM Golden Circle event in Palm Springs, California. I told him that I felt it was synchronistic that I saw him in 1961 when the wall went up and then saw and talked with him 30 years later shortly after the wall came down.

In 1961 when French President Charles DeGaulle closed all of the American Air Bases, I was sent to England to complete my 3-year tour. While there I had a third chance encounter when a buddy took me to Liverpool, England to listen to a great band he had discovered. It turned out to be the Beatles. After that initial visit I used to go to "the Pool" (as we

---

[9] For younger readers, Willy Brandt was the mayor of Berlin when the Berlin Wall went up in 1961 and made an important speech near Brandenburg Gate.

called it) almost every weekend to hear them play in the Cavern Club. This was just before the Beatles made it big in America. Although I did not get to know them personally, I truly enjoyed listening to them and felt that they would one day become famous. So when the Beatles came to America and were on the Ed Sullivan show, it was "a rush" to be able to say that I saw them before they became famous. I have never seen them again so I cherish those times in the Cavern Club. Approximately nine months later I was sent to Patrick AFB near Cape Canaveral, Florida.

Back Home In America

When I arrived at Patrick AFB in February 1962 I was assigned to an Aircraft Electrical shop working on C-130s, which I loved. However, due to my past experience on the "traveling squad," my ability to work on multiple aircraft electrical systems, and my ability to quickly find problems, I was also assigned to work on the Astronauts F-106 aircraft. As an assigned crewmember I got to meet and interact with the original astronauts (Shepard, Grissom, Schirra, Cooper, White, etc.) on a regular basis and even got to fly with several of them.

Many years later I was at the Air and Space Museum in Washington, DC when then Admiral Alan Shepard came walking through the lobby with an entourage of people. When I saw him I spontaneously called out, "Commander Sheppard" – that was how I knew him when I worked on his aircraft. He stopped and came over to where I was standing and said, "Smitty?" – that is what he used to call me – and shook my hand and we spent a good five minutes or so exchanging memories and "pleasantries." Just another synchronistic chance encounter. When I learned that Alan Shepard died about a year later I was greatly saddened. He was a great pilot, a good man, and I loved working with him and flying with him.

Out on My Own as A Civilian

When I left the military in early 1962, I moved to Pennsylvania to take a job on the assembly line of the Boeing Vertol plant in Morton, which built CH-46 and CH-47 helicopters. A Boeing Industrial Engineer I had met at the Boeing Cape Canaveral facility got me the job. However, a few months later I was laid off. Thus began one of the most difficult periods of my life.

After losing my job at Boeing I soon ran out of money and moved into the YMCA in Chester, Pennsylvania. I sold my military uniforms, sold newspapers on the streets in Philadelphia, and took other odd jobs so I could eat and pay for my bed at the YMCA. However, I just wasn't that good at newspaper selling and could no longer pay the miniscule amount for my room. I took a chance, became homeless and began living in the 30th Street

Station Subway in Philadelphia, begging for meals out of the back doors of restaurants. My psychic sensitivities were not active at all as far as I can recall. Looking back, I don't know how I survived, but I did, and today I remind myself where I have been and thank God for helping me "make it through" that most difficult period of my life.

For readers who may question why I did not or could not use my psychic sensitivities to help me, I have to say that, at that time in my life I was not understanding or knowledgeable enough of my sensitivities to consciously use them to help myself. Although that may sound strange to some readers, it has been my experience that just because you have psychic sensitivities does not mean that you understand them or know how to control or use them. From my experience, this requires a dedicated effort. In my case, it took several years of studying Metaphysics, learning how to Meditate, and working with my psychic sensitivities to get to where I could consciously use them.

After about three months of living in the 30th Street Station Subway, I got a job as an Encyclopedia Salesperson. I answered an ad for a Sales Executive position and was naïve enough to think that I could be successful. I diligently learned the "spiel" and somehow God provided a miracle. I was able to make at least one to three sales a week, which gave me enough money for a room at my now very much appreciated home in the downtown Philadelphia YMCA. It was pretty liberating to no longer have to bum cigarettes or pick up butts off the street, or beg meals out of the back doors of restaurants. From my perspective things were looking up. Within a few months I was actually making money and was promoted to a manager position. However, it was hard to feel good about what I was doing. I felt badly for those people who bought encyclopedias when they could barely feed their children, but I convinced myself that they were giving their children an education.

Meeting Suzanne

As I have learned, there is a reason for everything and this job was no exception because I met my first wife, Suzanne Pratt, while trying to sell her a set of those darn encyclopedias. She was a graduate student at the University of Delaware working on her Masters Degree in American Studies. She was recently divorced and lived in a small apartment in New Castle, Delaware. Suzanne saw something in me that I did not see in myself. She thought I was smart and that I could be a lot more than I dreamed of. She soon convinced me to stop selling encyclopedias and move in with her. I followed her advice, quit my encyclopedia job, moved out of the YMCA and moved into her apartment. In no time I had a new job; this time I was selling carpet. It was still sales but now out of a store front rather than driving all over four states. As luck would have it, Suzanne's parents were building a new home in Smyrna, Delaware and desperately needed new carpet. My discount saved them a lot of money so my little job came in quite handy.

One night Suzanne asked me, "What would you really like to become?" Nobody had ever asked me that question before and as I thought about it, I responded, "If I could become an airline pilot or an engineer, I could actually feel proud of myself." She responded, "So why don't you see what it would take to do that?" For the first time in my life, I felt encouraged and empowered. I had met someone who believed in me.

In checking out the airlines, I learned that you needed to be no more than 26 years old, have two years of college education (or the equivalent), and have a pilot's license with an instrument rating. At the time I was 23 years old and did not believe I could meet those requirements before I was 26 so I began looking at the possibility of college. Suzanne was quite supportive and encouraging, even though I wasn't so sure I was smart enough to get into college, let alone get into an engineering program. With great trepidation, I met with the Dean of Admissions, filled out the application forms, and took the entrance exams. Much to my surprise, I passed them with very good scores and was admitted to the University of Delaware Electrical Engineering program. Little did I realize how much I was being guided. As a veteran I was eligible for the GI Bill and so all of my undergraduate and graduate schooling was supported by my GI Bill benefits. At the advice of the Admissions Office I took a summer course in Trigonometry and Analytic Geometry to get me up to speed so I could take Calculus in the fall. I studied constantly and was admitted in the fall of 1965.

The College Years and Discovering the A.R.E.

I felt like I was way over my head taking on the Electrical Engineering curriculum at Delaware and yet it was something I really wanted to do. The summer class in Trigonometry and Analytic Geometry was a real wake up call. It had been over five years since I graduated from high school and I needed to re-learn how to study, and that class helped a great deal.

My first year quickly taught me to ask for help from my Spirit Guides. I don't know where I learned how to do that, I think it just came naturally, but I found myself relying on prayer to get me through my schoolwork. Calling on my Spirit Guides to answer everyday problems was not something that I had done up to this point in my life. However, as I began studying and having difficulty with the Engineering material, I began asking for help and was pleasantly surprised that I got it. My first semester of Chemistry is a good example of how this worked. Although I studied very hard I just could not get the concepts of balancing Chemical Equations, and went into the final exam with 2 F's and 2 C's. The night before the exam, and then again as I sat down to take the three-hour final exam, I prayed for my Spirit Guides to be with me. As I looked over the test, I saw a lot of problems involving balancing chemical equations that I knew I could not answer. However, I also saw a number of "fill in the blank" and "multiple choice" questions and felt guided to just concentrate on those questions. I completed answering all of those questions, reviewed my answers and turned in my test. As I was leaving I *heard* in my head that I had done OK. Later my instructor told me that every question I answered was correct. I had passed the course with assistance from my Spirit Guides. However, I knew that I still needed to learn Chemistry. I waited until the following summer to re-take the 1st semester of Chemistry over again and finally "got it." I then took the 2nd semester of Chemistry and aced it, which allowed me to catch up with my classmates.

As I continued to rely on my Spirit Guides for assistance, my grasp of the engineering material increased and my understanding of how to tune in and listen deepened. They helped me focus my mind so I could study with clarity. After about a year and a half, my grades improved and I got on and remained on the Dean's List the remainder of my undergraduate and graduate years. I was also invited to join the Electrical Engineering Honor Society – Eta Kappa Nu – an achievement I would never have thought possible. I felt truly humbled and honored. I studied hard in college because I really loved what I was learning, while Suzanne taught Kindergarten and First grade in the local elementary school.

Expanding Our Spiritual and Metaphysical Circle

As Suzanne and I began to get to know each other better, I shared many of my psychic sensitivities and experiences with her. She was always supportive and was never jealous of my sensitivities. We enjoyed long conversations about *seeing* or *sensing* ghosts and Auras, and knowing things without having studied them. We tried to understand how things occurred, how to control them, and what the information I received meant. We questioned why it was being presented to me, and how she might open herself up to her own sensitivities, which she was eventually able to do.

Suzanne was a voracious reader, very interested in the occult and spirituality, and she introduced me to a lot of new information. Astrology was her main interest and she became very good at it. We discussed the books she was reading and many times I could tell her what information was on certain pages of the book. It seemed that I was being instructed while asleep or at other times throughout the day because she would ask me questions about books she was reading and somehow I knew the answers. She began to rely on my "insights."

Suzanne and I were both introverts and did not make friends easily. She was nine years older and as an only child, enjoyed being around people her parents' age rather than people my age or younger. As a result, we didn't create many friendships with my classmates. As my sensitivities became broader in perspective we recognized that we needed to seek out and meet with others who were also interested in the occult and spirituality. Since neither of us was interested in attending a church, we sought out friendships with people we met at various Spiritual and Psychic phenomena groups. At a local psychic fair, we met several people involved in a Mediumship (communicating with the dead) group, and a paranormal group studying Astrology, Numerology, etc. The Mediumship group was interested in ghosts and ghost stories, which I of course found fascinating since I had *seen* and talked with my family's dead relatives as a child.

The White Motorcycle

At one of our first Mediumship Group meetings, as I walked into the host's kitchen, I saw a picture of a young man about 18 years old on a "white" motorcycle on a bulletin board over the kitchen table. I immediately *knew* that he was dead and in fact that he had just died. I said something to Suzanne as we passed through the kitchen into the living room where the meeting was being held. Being that it was our first meeting, Suzanne and I

introduced ourselves, stated that we were interested in joining the gro
that I was "a medium" aware of "Spirits." The host thanked us for co
and I then curiously asked about the picture of the young man on the "white
motorcycle in the kitchen. The host explained that it was his son on his brand
new bike and stated that it was blue not white, which puzzled me because I
distinctly remember it being white.

About thirty minutes into the meeting, the phone rang and the hostess
answered it. She began crying uncontrollably as she told her husband that the
phone call was from the Delaware State Police. A drunk driver had just hit
their son's motorcycle and their son had died instantly. The man also broke
down and the meeting quickly came to an end. Before Suzanne and I could
leave, the father asked me why I had asked about the picture of his son on a
motorcycle when I came in, and why I had said it was white? I responded
that when I saw the picture as I entered their kitchen, I *knew* that young man
was dead and that he had just been killed. I told them that I struggled with
this *knowing* so I just kept quiet. I was half expecting the parents to lash out
at me, but instead they simply wanted to know if I was aware of their son's
Spirit and was he OK? You can't imagine how good it felt to be with people
who understood and were interested in me tuning into their son's Spirit. As I
tuned into his energy, I said he was going to be fine but that right now he was
very pissed. I told them that he was telling me that he had saved up for "that
bike" for over a year and he wanted to thank his dad for the last $200 he had
given him to buy it. His dad and mom both started laughing through their
tears and explained that their son had indeed scrimped and saved for over a
year to buy that bike and that just two weeks previously his dad had given
him the $200 to purchase it. This was one of my first experiences of
communicating information from a dead person without being chastised. To
see the comfort this brought to that family helped me realize the importance
of sharing my "gift."

My psychic sensitivities and my understanding of Metaphysics and
Spirituality continued to expand and Suzanne and I participated in many
other group gatherings on Auras and Energies, Haunted places and Ghosts,
Astrology and Numerology. I loved the Haunted house and Ghost meetings,
because invariably I would *see* discarnate entities and was usually able to
relay information the ghosts were trying to convey to people in the meetings.
I received much positive feedback and also learned that it was as important to
understand when I was wrong – and why, as it was to know when I was right.
Many times I learned more from being "wrong" because it forced me to
delve more deeply into what I was "tuning into" and examine why I
interpreted the information the way I did. I discovered that the information I

seldom "wrong" but my *interpretation* of that
...mes wrong or incomplete.

Blue Eyes

...an year in college Suzanne learned about a very
spiritua... ..., who was the subject of a book entitled *The Search for
the Girl with the Blue Eyes* by Jess Stearn. Mrs. G held a Spiritual Discussion
and Meditation Group in her apartment just a short distance from our
apartment. Suzanne began attending these meetings and would come home
with amazing stories about experiences that members in the group were
having. It was good practice for me to see if I could provide further
information. Sometimes my comments fit their experiences while other times
they seemed beyond what I was aware of or capable of understanding. After
a couple of months, the group suggested that Suzanne invite me to one of
their sessions. Little did Suzanne or I realize how great an impact this
meeting would have on my spiritual development and understanding.

As we sat on pillows on the floor in Mrs. G's apartment, she led a
discussion on Meditation, Astrology, and other Metaphysical topics and then
led us on a Guided Image Meditation, which she recorded. I had never
participated in a Guided Image Meditation before so I sat cross-legged and
simply listened to Mrs. G's voice and tried to follow her instructions. When
she told us to concentrate on our "third eye center," I suddenly felt a
"whoosh" sensation all over my body and found myself up in the clouds. I
began speaking about seeing four Master Guides and thousands of other
people in white who were saying, "Welcome back, welcome back." I
responded with "Welcome back? I haven't ever been here before." They
immediately responded with "Oh yes you have, many times." They then told
me about when I was last with them and showed me several visions.
Additionally, they showed me a partial key and a "book," which they called
the *Akashic Record*.[10] It wasn't really a book but it was like a book in that it
contained a lot of information. They told me that I had one-half of the key to
the book and that I needed to develop the other half of the key before I could

---

[10] The *Akashic Record*, also known as "The Book of Life," is a record in space and
time of an entity's [person's] existence throughout eternity. According to the
Edgar Cayce readings, the *Akashic Record* ". . . contains every deed, word, feeling,
thought, and intent that has ever occurred at any time in the history of the world."
See http://edgarcayce.org/about_edgarcayce/akashic_records/akashic_records.asp

open it. I had never heard the words *Akashic Record* before that night. I came out of that Guided Image Meditation experience quite confused but the leader and several members of the group were delighted and excitedly talking a mile a minute.

Mrs. G stated that for me to have such an experience on my first Guided Image Meditation indicated that I was a "very old and highly developed soul," another new phrase for me at that time. I then explained some of my psychic sensitivities and shared several stories about *seeing* dead people when I was a young child. I also described some experiences from our recent meetings with the Mediumship Group. Mrs. G and the other group members discussed how the group should further explore my newfound abilities and what we should do with the information received. I began attending the weekly meetings on a regular basis and learned from Mrs. G that my *Angel Lady in White* was my Guardian Angel and that she would always be near me as long as I was on the earth plane. I also learned that I had several other Spirit Guides and that I had spent an extended period of time on "the inner planes" (another new term for me) acting as a Guide for others. She explained that I was one of those souls who walked in both worlds (the inner planes and the real physical world), which explained why I was so sensitive and sometimes "in outer space." Suzanne just laughed in agreement when she said that. I attended those meetings for several years and continued to have out-of-body experiences and would often "channel" information for the group. I learned a great deal about myself, my abilities, and my past lives from those meetings and from the people attending them.

The summer following my freshman year of college, Suzanne and I decided to buy a house and get married. Since we both were very interested in Metaphysics, she was respectful and supportive of my psychic sensitivities, and she encouraged me to continue to go to school and get my degree, it seemed the logical thing to do. So we bought a house, moved in, and got married in front of the fireplace. That summer I worked as a design draftsman at a local Electrical Lighting and Power Design Company.

Discovering The A.R.E.

Through members of the Mediumship Group and Mrs. G's Spiritual Discussion Group, we learned about the Association for Research and Enlightenment (A.R.E.)[11] organization in Virginia Beach. Suzanne began

---

[11] See http://www.edgarcayce.org

devouring books about Edgar Cayce and was fascinated with the more than 15,000 psychic readings he gave before and during World War II. During our summer break, we drove to Virginia Beach, visited the old A.R.E. Headquarters building, which was the Edgar Cayce Hospital back in the late 1920's, and stayed at the old Marshals Hotel across the street from the A.R.E. Headquarters. We quickly developed several new long-time friendships with people who were just as excited about discovering the A.R.E. and the Edgar Cayce material as we were. We learned that the A.R.E. held several conferences at Virginia Beach throughout the year and that there were many Search For God (SFG) Study Groups, which are Spiritual Discussion Groups that study the Edgar Cayce readings, all around the world. Much to our delight, we discovered that there was one in Newark, Delaware. As soon as we returned home we contacted the leaders of that group, Ed and Barbara. Ed was coincidentally an Electrical Engineer working for the DuPont Corporation and he and Barbara and Suzanne and I hit it off well. We joined their group, which met in various people's homes and soon began having meetings in our own home as well.

As I studied and began to apply the SFG Material and other information revealed through the Edgar Cayce readings, much of what my Angels and Spirit Guides had been teaching me began to make sense and my sensitivities began to broaden into areas about which I had no previous knowledge. The Edgar Cayce readings validated many of my own Spiritual ideas. As we met more and more people associated with the A.R.E. and our SFG Study Group, Suzanne and I both agreed that this was the organization we wanted to be a part of, learn more about, and contribute to in any way we could. Our extended family became those friends from our weekly meetings and the conferences we attended in Virginia Beach – we had found a Spiritual home!

Ed and Barbara were interested in my psychic sensitivities and interested in developing their own as well. As we began participating in the group discussions, I was encouraged to speak up whenever I "picked up" something. One evening, while in a group meditation, I felt the presence of a deceased entity who seemed somewhat confused. As I tuned into his energy, I began to "channel" information from him. The entity seemed to be a drunk and I began speaking in a slurred voice. Ed recorded the channeled session so that we could listen to it later and try to learn what information might be available for the group. Channeling a "drunk" was a powerful example of how important it is to carefully discern the kind of energies or entities one allows to come through. When I came out of it, I felt drunk! As I continued to channel various entities, I soon realized that I needed to "discern" what kind of entities I was willing to channel. I also learned how to protect myself and only channel higher consciousness entities and beings. Those early sessions turned out to be valuable Spiritual growth and understanding lessons for myself as well as the other group members.

To protect myself so that I would only channel 'higher level' beings, prior to attempting to channel I pray and ask that only beings of the 'highest energy level' or 'highest nature' be allowed to channel information through me and that all other beings needing to communicate information to the group be filtered through the Angelic realm or my Spirit Guides. This process allows me to continue to channel information that will be helpful to the group I am channeling for, and assures that lower vibration entities do not come through directly. When information from a lower vibration entity needs to come through to convey some specific information to the group I am channeling for, that energy is raised by the Angelic realm or my Spirit Guides and conveyed as needed and I am not affected by any lower level vibration entities.

Over the next several years, in addition to our SFG Study Group meetings, Suzanne and I attended several A.R.E. Conferences in Virginia Beach and met many wonderful new friends from around the world, many whom I am still in contact with 40+ plus years later. At these early conferences, Suzanne and I met and became friends with many of the "old guard" at Virginia Beach, and were grateful for their insights and the wisdom they shared with us. This included such notables as Hugh Lynn Cayce, Edgar Evans Cayce, Gladys Davis Turner, Eula Allen, Harmon and June Bro, Bill and Elsie Sechrist, Dr. Harold Riley, Dr. Bill and Gladys McGarey, Mae St. Clair, Ruth Lenore, Everett Irion, and many more. Suzanne and I became "regulars" at the old Marshals Motel, as well as at the A.R.E. Headquarters.

The Creation Story Conference

One of our first conferences was *The Creation Story* Conference with Hugh Lynn Cayce, Eula Allen, Gladys Davis Turner, and others. At that conference I heard a story about creation that made total sense to me and I learned a great many other things that validated many of the Spiritual ideas that my Spirit Guides had told me over the years. I was "hooked for life!"

To help the reader understand why I was so "hooked" I offer the following synopsis story or explanation of what "The Creation Story" is according to the Edgar Cayce readings.[12]

The Creation Story basically describes the devolution [in consciousness] of mankind from being a Spirit that was one with God to a human being that separated him/her/it self from God.

In a nutshell, the Edgar Cayce readings state that we – Spiritual Beings – were created as "companions" when God expressed himself/herself. We were all created as "drops of water out of the ocean of God" and were given Free Will to co-create whatever we desired. The Edgar Cayce readings refer to that "experience" as the **1ˢᵗ Root Race**. We were simply an expression of God – a Spirit – yet with "consciousness" of our oneness with God.

At some point, these Free Will Spirits began recognizing themselves as individuated Spirits – that is, as separate drops or buckets separate from the ocean – and began co-creating out of their desire (and nature) to create, but they began doing so not in accord with "natural law." They were creating in Spirit – thought forms, not physical forms. These Spirits began losing their awareness of being one with God – God consciousness, and became more aware of their separateness – individuated consciousness. That "period" or expression is considered the **2ⁿᵈ Root Race**.

Eons went by and many more "individuated expressions of God" got "caught up in" creating, and in their creations, and began creating "beings" that could come and go from what came to be the physical plane. Many of the stories of mythological creatures are based upon this creation process. It was sort of like being able to create a quasi-physical form, experience that creation, and then simply uncreate or de-materialize it. These Spirits began losing more and more of their awareness of being one with God – God consciousness, and became

---

[12] The Creation Story was originally described in 3 booklets written by Eula Allen entitled *Before The Beginning, The River of Time*, and *You Are Forever*. A more recent book that includes anthropological evidence and is a much more comprehensive and understandable explanation was written by Kathy Callahan, Ph.D. entitled *Multisensory Human - The Evolution of the Soul*, A.R.E. Press, May 2005.

more and more aware of their separateness – their individuated expression or consciousness. Not Thy will but mine! Many of these beings got caught up in the creations they had created and lost consciousness of the fact that they had created the being or object and became "encased" in their own creations. This period was the **3rd Root Race**. The readings say that the "beings" that were present in Lemuria or Mu and in the early period of Atlantis were of this "nature."

Many more eons passed and the story goes that an expression that led the first "grouping" (the 1st Root Race) to begin to create not in accord with natural law, recognized that he [not a male energy form but an androgynous being] and others needed to find a way to help those beings who had "got caught up in this process" to find a way back to God Consciousness. The story continues that they chose a physical being in the earth plane and "evolved the DNA structure" [my words not Edgar Cayce's] and created a human form, which became what Cayce referred to as "the Adamic consciousness" body. A physical form with total loss of consciousness of its oneness with God – an individuated expression, yet with a spark of the Divine within. Basically "a physical body with a Spirit" which is what most Christian religions teach. That is the **4th Root Race,** which is where the Biblical Creation starts.

The readings state that this "physical expression" happened in five different regions, simultaneously in the five races;

- The Red in the Atlantis region,
- The Brown in the Andes,
- The Yellow in the Gobi,
- The Black in the Sudan, and
- The White in the Carpathian and Caucasus mountain region.

The readings go on to say that the evolution of mankind, from the Adamic consciousness to the Christ consciousness as expressed in Jesus represents the evolution [in consciousness] of believing *"We are human bodies with a Spirit"* to *"We are Spiritual beings expressing in a physical form,"* which is what The Master Jesus was able to express or manifest.

As I heard and thought about this Story of Creation that came through the Edgar Cayce readings, it really made sense to me. A lot more sense than the story I had been taught in both the Catholic Church and the Baptist Church. It also made a lot more sense than what I knew from my understanding of sciences' view of creation. That is why I was hooked.

Hugh Lynn's Admonishment and Eula Allen's Encouragement

At the Creation Story Conference, I felt that I had truly found a Spiritual home where I could explore and expand my spiritual understanding and share and develop my psychic sensitivities. However, when I privately shared my psychic experiences with Hugh Lynn Cayce, the son of Edgar Cayce, he strongly discouraged me from developing them further or from using them. He stated that I needed to concentrate on developing my spiritual understanding first and only after I was able to meditate on a daily basis and really understood the material in the Edgar Cayce readings should I venture into "Opening yourself up to those energies." He stated that whatever psychic abilities I had would become manifest naturally as a result of my Spiritual development.

Although I was somewhat discouraged by Hugh Lynn's admonition, a very kind and gentle "little old lady" named Eula Allen, who had overheard my conversation with Hugh Lynn took me aside to speak with me. She said that she had overheard what I had told Hugh Lynn and then asked me what I *saw* with her and what I *picked up* when she mentioned a friend's name. When I told her what I *saw* and *sensed* with her, and what I *sensed* when I tuned into her friend's name, she just smiled and said that I was right on. She winked at me and said that she had her own sensitivities and could recognize another "sensitive old soul." She then told me I should ignore Hugh Lynn's admonitions and encouraged me to explore and develop both my psychic sensitivities and my spiritual understanding. She also told me that I needed to recognize who I was within myself and to get started working on what I came here to do. I felt both honored and humbled by her comments. Over the years, whenever I returned to Virginia Beach I made an effort to meet with Eula. Our conversations invariably turned to how I was using my psychic abilities and the importance of using my *gift* to help others.

When Eula Allen died in 1978 I was greatly saddened, but about a month after her passing, I *heard* her talking to me saying that I needed to get on the ball and start teaching. That was all I *heard*. Years later while facilitating a discussion on Edgar Cayce's Creation Story using *The Creation Trilogy* that Eula Allen wrote many years previously, I *heard* her voice saying, "Well done" and I realized that I had become a teacher of Metaphysics as she so lovingly suggested so many years previously. I was doing what I was sent here to do.

A.R.E's Prison Program

After that Creation Story conference, I began to Meditate on a regular basis as Hugh Lynn had suggested and continued to develop and expand my awareness of my psychic sensitivities as Eula Allen had recommended. As I studied the Edgar Cayce readings and many other Metaphysical and Spiritual topics, I discovered that Meditation significantly increased my psychic sensitivities as well as my understanding of Metaphysical principles.

When I got back from the Creation Story conference, I learned that our SFG Study Group leader Ed had begun working with the A.R.E. Prison Program, helping prisoners take responsibility for their past actions and present behavior. At the end of one of our Study Group meetings, Ed asked me to see what I could *pick up* from letters he had received from several prisoners. He wanted me to learn what was being requested from each prisoner, and how to best work with them. We sat at our dining room table and he placed each envelope and letter under my hands as I sat with my eyes closed. I simply talked about what I *sensed* from each letter. I stated that one person was simply using the program to try to get more lenient treatment and suggested that Ed not respond to his letter for at least a month. On another letter, I *felt* exchanging letters with this person would be much better than a face-to-face visit. On yet another, I *sensed* this person was the younger of two people in prison. I stated that I felt that his dad was also in prison and that a written communication and then a face-to-face meeting would be helpful for this younger person. Ed took the letters, thanked me, and everyone left.

About two weeks later, Suzanne and I met Ed and Barbara in Rehoboth Beach, Delaware. As they walked toward us, Ed began excitedly shouting, "You're not going to believe this, you're not going to believe this." When they reached us, he excitedly repeated; "You're not going to believe this because I'm not sure I believe it myself." He then proceeded to tell me about the letters I had psychometrized.[13] Ed said that he had received several more letters and learned that, sure enough, the person I said was simply using the Prison Program to get leniency was in fact abusing the system. Ed said that the person I felt needed written communication rather than a face-to-face meeting was responding very well to his letters. But then Ed dropped the bombshell. He said he had received a letter from the person I said had a father in prison. As he opened it, he noticed the return address indicated Sr. so he checked the previous letter. Much to his surprise it said Jr. In his letter the father stated that he knew his son had written to Ed and he hoped that Ed would help his son because he didn't want him ending up like he did – a

---

[13] Psychometry is the art of "picking up" information by tuning into an object.

three-time convicted felon. It was a very strong validation of my accuracy but more importantly that my psychic *gift* could indeed be used to help Ed and others.

I continued to use my psychic sensitivities in our SFG Study Group meetings and over the years Hugh Lynn and I had many conversations about our differences of opinion regarding developing and using one's psychic sensitivities. Until his death in July 1982, Hugh Lynn adamantly opposed psychic development as part of the A.R.E. curriculum. Little did Hugh Lynn or I suspect that many years later I would become one of the Certified Psychics for the A.R.E.

Attending A Psychics' Conference

The summer between my sophomore and junior year, 1967, Suzanne and I attended a Psychic and Spiritual Development and Healing Conference at a small college near West Point, New York. This was our first conference featuring many well known and respected Psychics, Mediums, Channelers, Healers, Palmists, Astrologers, etc. and we were very excited to be there.

Rescue Mediumship

The first day we arrived we attended a presentation and discussion held by David and Rosalind McKnight on "Rescue Mediumship." This was a term that neither Suzanne nor I knew anything about, but since I had been doing some channeling of difficult entities within our SFG Study Group, we were very interested in what the McKnights had to say. Shortly after we got to the meeting, Suzanne wasn't feeling well and left to take a short nap in our room while I stayed and took notes.

The McKnights explained that Rescue Mediumship was used by mediums to speak with those Spirits who were trapped in the "in between," meaning between this life and the next – what Catholicism refers to as Purgatory. They explained that "trapped Spirits" are those who have died and are still in shock of dying or are unable to let go of their physical lifetime and their loved ones left behind. As Spirits, they are drawn to psychically sensitive people (like the McKnight's or myself) because they know we can *see* and *hear* them. A good example of this is the TV series, *"Ghost Whisperer"* by John Gray and James Van Prague, which I referenced previously. They then did a short meditation in preparation for Rosalind to open herself to channel. As the meditation began, I immediately found myself outside my body and began channeling an entity that needed rescuing. I was not prepared for this and neither were David and Rosalind. They had to help the entity I was channeling, and then had to bring me back to a normal state, which meant clearing me from the effects of the entity I had channeled.

At this point in time I had not yet discovered how to channel only 'higher level' entities as I discussed earlier.

In the meantime, Suzanne was sleeping and was awakened with the sound of my voice. She heard me "call her" from the open window in our room so she went to the window to see where I was. She again heard my voice saying that I was in trouble, and knew something was not right. She got dressed and immediately went to the McKnight meeting just as they were bringing me out. The McKnights commented that it was extremely rare for someone unfamiliar with their work to spontaneously go into an altered state and channel. They felt I was clearly quite sensitive, but cautioned that I needed to be more careful and protective of how I did it, and what energies or entities I drew to me. The meeting ended and Suzanne and I joined several people from the group for dinner. The people that had been in the McKnight session filled Suzanne in on what happened and then began asking questions about my psychic sensitivities. They recommended that I meet with the other Psychics and Mediums who were at the conference.

A Healing Blanket of Light

The next day we met with several of the Mediums and Psychics, and I felt like a huge sponge soaking up information. Suzanne was equally fascinated with the information and presenters and scheduled a Healing session later that afternoon with a black healer named Rev. Henry Rucker. We learned that Henry was quite famous for his healing work and Suzanne asked that I sit in on the session to see what I might pick up. At the scheduled time, we went to the room and noticed that Rev. Rucker had just arrived and was obviously very tired. His energy was very low, and afterwards Suzanne and I talked about thinking "boy this is going to be a waste of time and money." Rev. Rucker sat down opposite Suzanne and asked her how she felt and what she wanted. She stated that she felt tired much of the time and that her joints were swollen and sore and that she would like the pain and stiffness to go away. He talked about how healing works and how our thinking strongly influences the healing process. As he was talking, he put his hand up, spread his fingers and then very slowly brought his hand down in front of Suzanne. As he did this, I was totally captivated by what I *saw*. This "very tired and non-energetic man" began to create an extremely powerful and bright white and green light from his hand. As he slowly lowered his hand in front of Suzanne, a blanket of bright white and green light enveloped her body and her energy pattern began to soften. She literally began to relax in her chair and was very surprised that her pain was beginning to go away and that her body was feeling much more relaxed. Henry said the healing would continue over the next several hours and she should probably take a short nap; she would feel much more energized afterwards. We got up, thanked him and left, noting that his physical energy was still quite low. The whole process took no more than 30 minutes.

When Suzanne and I talked about the experience, she said that as he raised his hand and then brought it down slowly in front of her, she felt this very loving and soothing energy descend upon her body. She said that her pain and the swollenness in her joints immediately disappeared. She was so grateful and truly amazed. We went back to the room and she took a short nap. Meanwhile I went outside to try to understand what I had just seen and experienced. As I did a short meditation I heard a voice in my head say, "You can't always judge by appearances." I then saw Henry's face smiling back at me. He winked and instantly disappeared. When Suzanne awoke almost two hours later, she reported that the joint swelling and stiffness were gone as was the constant pain she had experienced. Although she wasn't ready for a marathon, her energy was much greater than it had been in a very long time and her Aura pattern indicated that her strength was much greater as well.

Watching Professionals Deliver Messages

The program that evening consisted of several Psychics and Mediums giving "messages" for people in the audience. This was my first experience of watching professionals give messages in this manner. As the Spirit entities talked to the Mediums, I could *see* and/or *hear* what they were going to say to the person before they said it. After about the third such experience, I got very excited and began whispering to Suzanne, jabbing her in the ribs with my elbow. I told her that I could *hear* and *see* what the Psychics and Mediums on stage were *hearing* and *seeing*. For me this was a major affirmation of my own psychic abilities.

The next morning at breakfast, I saw Katie King and Laura and Vincent Mangamelli, who were delivering messages the previous night. I went over to where they were sitting, excused myself, and asked if I could talk with them for a minute. They graciously said yes. I told them how thrilled I was to watch them read for people and stated that I pretty much knew what they were going to say to the people in the audience. I asked them if that was normal and they all just laughed and said something to the effect that, "For someone as sensitive and open as you are it isn't unusual at all." I then shared what happened with Suzanne's healing session with Henry Rucker and asked why I saw him as less than capable only to see this tremendous healing energy coming from his hands. When I told them about my meditation and seeing Henry's face smiling at me they just laughed. They confirmed that Henry was indeed a very powerful healer and when he does healing work, he himself does not have to be energized because he is not using his own energy to heal. He is using energy from "the source." Katie King then said that I too had healing potential if I chose to go that route, but that I must remember to be the *channel* not the *source* of the healing. I thanked them and went to meet Suzanne at an Astrology workshop.

At the end of the weekend conference, there was a final Q&A panel with all of the speakers and workshop presenters after which everyone was invited up to meet the panelists. As Suzanne and I went up to thank each member of the panel, David and Rosalind McKnight, Henry Rucker, Katie King and the Mangamellis were all standing next to each other and as we approached they gave us the *Namaste* sign. We returned the blessing. Katie King said they were pleased to have met me and wished me expanded awareness and to be sure to protect myself when I did future channeling sessions. The McKnights strongly seconded it saying, "Especially for someone who is as sensitive as you are." Henry then said, "Remember, don't judge by appearances alone." He then smiled that same smile I had seen in my mind's eye the previous day, and winked.

Our ride home to Delaware seemed very short as we listened to several tapes we had purchased and discussed everything we learned. It was one of the best Conferences I had ever attended. After we got home, Suzanne noticed that the "healing" lasted for about eight to ten weeks. It was a significant relief and when the pain and stiffness started to return, I felt it was directly related to Suzanne's unhappiness with her teaching job.

Returning To Reality – My Continued Studies

The next two years of college proved to be tough. However, with my newfound confidence in my ability to learn, my ability to call upon my Spirit Guides when I needed them, and my commitment to do the work necessary to get good grades, I continued to do well in my classes. Suzanne and I continued to enjoy our weekly meetings with our SFG Study Group and our Mediumship Group, and Suzanne enthusiastically pursued her study and work with her Astrology classes. I continued to use my psychic abilities to help members of our SFG Study Group and as I did so I found that I was becoming increasingly accurate, which increased my confidence. I began answering questions from friends regarding their health matters, work situations, or relationships, and spontaneously giving mini psychic readings. As a result, I learned a great deal about how psychic information was revealed to me.

The Death of Suzanne's Father

In the summer between my junior and senior years of college, Suzanne's father, Reynolds, who had been a Democratic State Senator in Delaware for several years, was diagnosed with lung cancer. The news of his diagnosis was devastating to Suzanne and even more so to her mother, Mae. Mae was a highly religious and proper Methodist and although she had heard about my psychic sensitivities, she told Suzanne that she did not believe in "that sort of stuff." However, as Suzanne's father became progressively ill, Mae became increasingly interested in what I *saw* and *sensed* and actually asked if I could do a healing on Reynolds the last few weeks before he died.

As Suzanne's father's illness became progressively worse, we arranged for him to die at home. During these last few weeks, I visited him a couple times a week, just to talk and hang out with him, even though I was still in school with a heavy course load. Reynolds loved talking about politics and baseball and he and I had some very good conversations. When it became obvious to me that he was not going to get well, I tried to talk to him about what he thought would happen when he died. Suzanne thought this was morbid and inappropriate, but I felt that he needed to have an opportunity to share his thoughts and possible fears.

About two weeks before he died, he opened up to me about his thoughts on death. We were sitting together in his study and he was watching a Philadelphia Phillies baseball game, which he loved, while I was reading one of my Engineering textbooks. I actually thought he was asleep because he would often nap while watching the game. But then he asked me to turn the TV off, which I did knowing that this had to be important. He became very quiet but quite alert and told me he knew he was dying and that his mother and a favorite aunt – Aunt Bee, both long since dead, had come to him in his sleep the night before. He said they told him he needed to "walk with them" and then he immediately woke up. He said that he didn't want to go with them because if he took that walk, it would mean he was dead and he was not ready to die. Not yet. I then noticed two energy forms, which I recognized as his mother and the woman I thought was his grandmother standing next to the TV. I *sensed* that he was also aware of them but did not want to acknowledge them. Risking that I might frighten him or be ridiculed, I asked him if he saw his mother and grandmother next to the TV. Surprisingly he said, "That's my Aunt *Bee* not my grandmother" and seemed sort of shocked at what he had just said. I then began talking to him about what I *saw*, and how they appeared to me, and what I was hearing in my head. He listened but said nothing. He then became somewhat glossy-eyed and very softly, as if in a whisper, began talking to them and saying he had forgotten how much he liked their perfume. At that moment I noticed the strong fragrance of what I thought was gardenias, which I had not noticed up to that point. His communication with them continued for several more minutes and I just sat there fascinated and thrilled at the fact that he had finally opened up. I could only hear part of what was being said, but I was aware of many of the thoughts or messages that were being conveyed. I learned later from my Spirit Guides that the messages that I did not pick up on or *hear* were not for me to hear – only for him. Another valuable lesson in how communication in that "domain" works.

Over the course of the next couple of weeks I spent as many days as my schedule would allow, just sitting with him and talking when he felt like talking. He occasionally asked me a question, often the same question as if trying to clarify the answer in his mind. He became much more accepting and even grateful for my "gift of sight." I can't tell you how many times he asked me how long I had known that I could talk to ghosts and how I knew they were not just my imagination. At one point I was sitting reading one of my textbooks and I heard a very loud voice in my head telling me to tell him that "Chauncey" was here. I had never heard that name before and so I very trepidatiously asked him, "Who is Chauncey?" He became very quiet and said, "Where did you ever hear that name?" I told him that I had just heard a voice in my head saying, "Tell him that Chauncey is here." He began to tear up and said that Chauncey was his childhood friend who was killed in a farming accident when they were only eight years old. He said that he had not thought about him in over fifty years and he knew that he had never mentioned that name to me before. Then he said, "I guess you really are psychic."

One morning Suzanne and I were both at her parent's home when Reynolds began having difficulty breathing. Mae called for an ambulance and when it arrived, there was only the driver and he asked me to drive while he attended to Reynolds on the way to the hospital. We were at the hospital about two hours when Reynolds' breathing became more labored and I knew he was in the process of transitioning. While standing by his bed I was very aware of how his energy pattern (Aura) was changing in intensity somewhat like a light bulb gradually going dim and then coming on strong again. Mae, Suzanne, and a nurse were also present when I noticed a flash in his Aura and I *saw* his Spirit leave his body and stand on the other side of the bed. As it did, I *saw* him take a deep breath, as if coming up from being under water a long time, and I *heard* him say, "I can finally breathe." I *saw* his Spirit take several more deep breaths and repeat, "I can finally breathe." He then looked at me and I *heard* him say, "Thank you for your *gift*. It helped me not be afraid of letting go, and tell them I'm OK now." He then simply disappeared.

The nurse noticed that he had stopped breathing, checked his pulse and said to Mae and Suzanne "He's gone" then she left the room to get a doctor for the official pronouncement.

As I was typing this story of Reynolds' death in my home in Tucson, Arizona, he came to me clear as day and reminded me to include the Chauncey story, which I had forgotten about. It really felt good to feel his presence and his energy again. I 'got' a real sense of approval and appreciation for writing my book and telling his story.

Suzanne and her mom struggled to make sense of his death. I told them of my experiences with Reynolds prior to his passing, including the appearance of his mom and his Aunt Bee, but nothing seemed to assuage their grief. However, when I mentioned Chauncey, Mae was totally shocked. Even Suzanne had not heard about him and Mae confirmed that Chauncey had been a young friend of Reynolds' who died when they were young boys, and said that she had not heard that name in over 40 years. As a result of that story, Mae began to believe in my psychic *gift.* One day during a meditation several months after his passing, I heard Reynolds' voice tell me that I needed to tell his daughter to stop grieving because he was fine and that she needed to look after her own health. I passed this information on to Suzanne but she seemed uninterested or unbelieving in my words, so I simply let it go.

Over the next several months Reynolds periodically came to me to offer a message of hope to Suzanne or Mae. He also came through to other psychics during the various Metaphysical gatherings we attended, but Suzanne seemed so filled with loss and grief that she just couldn't hear him. Finally, I suggested that Suzanne "cast" an astrology chart for her father to see if his death showed up in his chart. This seemed to capture her interest and she approached the task with enthusiasm. However, after casting several charts, she became somewhat discouraged because at times his death showed up and at other times she wasn't convinced. After one particular exercise, her father actually appeared to her in a dream and told her that he was OK and that she could stop trying to figure out whether astrology could show when a person was going to die. After that dream Suzanne became much more accepting of his death and shared her dream with her mother. Mae seemed to accept that Reynolds had actually come to Suzanne, which was a big breakthrough, and over time she became more believing and accepting of my psychic abilities. As time passed, she began to listen when I talked about the periodic messages I received from her late husband.

Loved ones will often appear in your dreams. Try asking them to come to you before you go to sleep. They will also use the radio to communicate so listen for yours or their favorite tunes on the radio.

Sometimes a TV will turn itself on as happened in my sister Kathleen's bedroom a few days after her husband died. Sometimes a picture will shift on the wall or a favorite perfume will permeate the room. For example, my partner Dotti's nephew Kevin has rung his mother's phone in the early morning hours of the anniversary of his death every year for the past five years. Every year she answers and every year 'no one' is there and she knows it's her son, Kevin.

Understanding Religions and Spirituality

In my junior year of college I took a Philosophy course called *The Religions of Man* using a book by Houston Smith, Ph.D. of the same title,[14] and I became fascinated with the Eastern religions, especially Hinduism and Buddhism. With my understanding of Karma, Reincarnation and other concepts from the Edgar Cayce readings, I devoured the reading assignments. For my term paper for the course, I wrote on *"The Atman-Brahman Concept of Indian Hinduism"* because it seemed, from a "Western mind set" or perspective, to be a concept that confounded most of my classmates. It was a great exercise for me and my professor commented that my paper was one of the best explanations of Indian Hinduism he had ever read and told me that he would be using it in his future classes.

As I continued to study the various Eastern and Western "orthodox" religions as well as many pagan religions, I had flashbacks of past lifetimes as an Egyptian High Priest, a Mayan Priest, a Rabbi, and a Catholic Priest. The Ancient Egyptian lifetime always felt very familiar and important to me. Over the years I have also remembered several lifetimes as a Native American Shaman or Medicine Man. As we read the tenants of the various religions presented in Houston Smith's text they all seemed very familiar to me, as if I had practiced them in the past. Additional details of those lifetimes were revealed to me in my meditations and dreams.

The study of religions was one of the most important classes of my college life because I became much clearer about what I believed about God. That course laid the groundwork for my continued and intense study of Spirituality and Religion. Years later I met Laura George who wrote an

---

[14] *The Religions of Man*, copyright 1958 by Houston Smith. First Harper Colophon Edition 1964 by Harper and Row

excellent book[15] on the five primary religions (Hinduism, Judaism, Buddhism, Christianity, and Islam). Her web site[16] indicates this is the first in a series of three books that will be published.

Fine Tuning My Sensitivities

When my mom decided to fly out from Detroit and spend a week with us for my graduation, I was delighted. We took her to our Mediumship and SFG Study Groups, which she thoroughly enjoyed and everyone was delighted that she was there.

Suzanne's mom and my mom got along quite nicely and Mom was always empathetic with Mae about Reynolds' death because my stepdad Tom had died some years before. However, Mae was a little uneasy with my mom when they went out because she was such a flirt. However, I watched Mae vicariously enjoy the attention Mom attracted because invariably Mea was on the receiving end of that attention as well. It was rather hilarious to observe these two old ladies enjoying themselves.

One memory that I cherish about that week was touring the buildings, grounds and labs of the campus with my mom. As we strolled through the halls and labs on campus, she made a hit with every professor she met. She was a charming and charismatic lady and several of my professors asked about her throughout the following year. That week she also became my teacher as she showed me how psychic sensitivities work and how to enhance them. As we walked around on campus she talked to me about the ghosts she *saw* or *sensed* and shared the information she picked up about a particular building or spot on campus. She asked me what I picked up and we compared that with what she was *sensing*. She helped me discern and better understand the more subtle energies I was only slightly aware of, and helped me to focus my attention and psychic sensitivities. The walks we took over the course of that week were incredibly helpful in fine-tuning my psychic gift. It was a marvelous learning experience, which has served me well throughout the years. I recall those memories with great fondness and much appreciation and have used that same process in teaching my students about their sensitivities.

---

[15] *The Truth: About the Five Primary Religions* by Laura George, The Oracle Institute Press, LLC, 2006
[16] http:// theoracleinstitute.org

Graduation occurred on a bright sunny day and I proudly received my diploma along with my fellow classmates. It was a real symbol of all of the hard work I had put in over the previous four years. After the ceremony, Mom took me aside and commented that it was through my own efforts and *in spite* of what my dad had done, not *because* of what he had done. I felt humbled and truly grateful to my Spirit Guides for helping me throughout the process, and I was delighted to have my mom be a part of it.

Graduate School

During my senior year at Delaware, I decided to stay in school and get my Masters degree rather than immediately go to work. Suzanne was definitely not pleased about that decision because she wanted me to go to work so she could quit teaching. The strain of her father's death and her worsening Rheumatoid Arthritis, which had been diagnosed a few months prior to her father's death, were making her very sick, and her attitude about her job simply added to the strain. In spite of her wanting me to get a job as soon as I graduated, I intuitively knew that to make myself eligible for the best jobs, I needed to get my Masters degree immediately rather than working and attending night school. I applied to several graduate schools including, the Universities of Arizona, Michigan, Florida, and Delaware. Because I loved Physics and Astronomy, I seriously looked into the University of Arizona to study Astrophysics. However, my logical brain kicked in and I realized that Astrophysicists do not get paid as much as Electrical Engineers and besides, I argued to myself, as an Astrophysicist I might have to wait a lifetime to make any significant find.

I chose to remain in the field of Electrical Engineering and was given a full Teaching Assistantship at Delaware teaching a Nuclear Physics Lab and a Basic Circuits Course

As I began my graduate work, I discovered that even though I was on a full teaching assistantship, graduate school was much easier than undergraduate school. I was taking fewer classes and they were all focused on Electrical Engineering, Physics or Mathematics. I quickly became friends with four East Indian graduate students who were very interested in psychic "stuff." We would often get together to talk about Metaphysics and Spirituality and they often joked that I understood more about their own religion, Hinduism, than they did.

As graduate school progressed, I took a course in the new field of Digital Signal Processing using the first textbook on the subject.[17] I thoroughly enjoyed that course, although like many first books on a subject, the text was incomplete with very few examples. As a result of that course, I chose a Digital Signal Processing thesis topic[18] involving a difficult theoretical mathematical problem. Although this discussion may all seem irrelevant to a story about a psychic, I want to share that unbeknownst to me, I was guided to study a new and important area of technology – Digital Signal Processing or DSP. Today, voice recognition and speech and speaker identification systems are all based on the work from the field of Digital Signal Processing. In fact DSP pervades more areas of the average person's life than they realize, from analysis of medical images and signals, automobile computers, as well as airplane, train and large ships' computers. Today's home video gaming technology is made possible by Digital Signal Processing algorithms. I truly believe that it was Divine guidance that led me to study and specialize in this incredibly important area of technology.

Solving An Unsolvable Problem

I am NOT going to go into a lot of details about my Master's Thesis other than to present a story about how "listening to your still small voice" can solve some unsolvable problems. Specifically, how my Spirit Guides provided me some incredible "insights" that allowed me to find a solution to a problem that multiple professors said could not be solved. I will be brief.

My Masters Thesis involved a theoretical mathematical problem of generating Poisson Transforms using Laguerre Polynomials and required me to find a solution for the Nth term in a matrix that defined the coefficients for each of the Laguerre Polynomials. After conferring with my thesis advisor, Dr. B., he sent me to speak with a Matrix Theory expert and a Complex Variables expert in the Math department about my problem. After about a half-hour discussion with both of those professors, I was told that the problem I was trying to solve was not solvable. When I went back to my thesis advisor with their analysis, he wisely encouraged me not to be discouraged. He said, "Sit on it for a few days. You might think of something unique."

---

[17] *"Digital Processing of Signals"* by Bernard Gold and Charles M. Rader, McGraw Hill Book Company, Inc., 1969

[18] "A Sampling Technique for Obtaining Poisson Transforms Using Laguerre Functions," University of Delaware MEE Thesis, Lowell K. Smith, 1969

Over the next several days in my meditations I asked my Spirit Guides to help me find a solution to my "unsolvable" problem. Meanwhile I had to continue with the rest of my Graduate School classes. One evening a couple of weeks later about 9:00 pm I was in my cubicle working on a difficult problem for one of my classes. All of a sudden I *heard* a voice in my head say, "Hey!" and then I *saw* in my head a blackboard and a set of equations. I knew I was *seeing* a different approach to solving the problem that had been stymieing me. I began writing down what I was *seeing* in my head, and began working out the details. By around 3:00 am I had completed the solution and I remember yelling, "I got it!" realizing that I had essentially completed my Thesis. I packed up my things and went directly home. Suzanne was in bed asleep and as I crawled in bed she mumbled, "Where have you been?" I excitedly told her that I had discovered the solution to my Thesis problem with the help of my Spirit Guides and had written it all down. As I lay there very excited, I asked my Spirit Guides to "Please help me sleep hard and fast." I had a class the following day at 11 o'clock and I needed my sleep. I went to sleep quickly and proceeded to have a dream showing me additional details about the solution I had "tapped into." When I got up I wrote down my dream and then explained to Suzanne how the solution to the problem had come to me. I told her, "I may have solved a problem that two math professors said did not have a solution."

When I presented my solution to Dr. Bolgiano he concurred that I indeed had found a solution and simply said, "Now all you have to do is document it, work out several examples, and run the computer simulations." A few weeks later I presented my thesis in an open forum with both math professors in the front row intensely following my presentation. Afterwards they came up and congratulated me saying, "Looks like there's a closed form solution after all – good job." I thanked them and mentally thanked my Spirit Guides.

A few days after I received a completed copy of my Thesis from the publisher, I remember feeling so relieved and grateful for all of the guidance and assistance I had received from my teachers, my Thesis advisors, my classmates, and of course my Spirit Guides. I was tremendously grateful for all the help I had received from "Spirit," for clearly I seemed to be guided each step along the way. I was also amazed at how one thing after another seemed to just fall in place. As I kept mentally saying, "Thank you Father" I *heard* in my head, "You asked, you listened and we provided you the information you were seeking. Remember you can do this with other things as well." The voice "smiled" and was gone. I did not recognize the voice, only the feeling, and it felt like a very old Spirit Guide I had not heard from in a very long time. One whom I would hear from again many more times in the years that followed.

The Early Years of Working and Learning

Following completion of Graduate School, I took a job with RCA in Moorestown, New Jersey working on the state-of-the-art AEGIS Phased Array Radar system. I soon discovered that although my Engineering education provided me with the knowledge to do well in my job, my psychic sensitivities came in especially handy. I found that I had the ability to *sense into* and correct complex software design issues and signal-timing problems. As a result, within a matter of a few weeks, I was able to uncover and correct several design problems that had stumped the Design and Testing team for months. I was learning how to use my psychic sensitivities in my work environment, while expanding my engineering knowledge, and was making significant contributions to our Design and Testing team. I was thoroughly enjoying my job.

However, six months after I started, RCA had a big layoff and "seeing the writing on the wall," I checked with the Central Intelligence Agency to see if they were still hiring. I had interviewed with the CIA when they came to the Delaware campus and they expressed a strong interest in my Thesis topic. However, I didn't pursue their offer at the time because they required a background investigation (BI), which would have taken about six months to complete and I did not feel I could wait that long without a paycheck, so I took the RCA offer. When I learned that the Agency was still interested, I submitted my application and waited for the BI to be completed.

Over the course of the next eight months I continued learning as much as I could and used my psychic sensitivities to continue to *sense* into and solve a number of complex problems that had stumped many others. I even received a letter of appreciation from a Navy COTR (Contracting Officer Technical Representative) for my efforts. When The Agency notified me that they had completed their Background Investigation and invited me to come to a job interview in Washington, DC, I jumped at the opportunity. Little did I know how much I was being Divinely Guided – again.

My CIA Interview

I took a couple of days off and took the train down to Washington, DC. My instructions were to show up at a particular building somewhere in Virginia. When I arrived, I was taken into a small room, asked a bunch of questions and told that the interviewers were waiting for me at another location. I was placed on a "Blue Bird" bus and the driver was told where I was to be taken and that he was to ensure that I got there.

The interview was conducted in an old building somewhere in downtown Washington in a room filled with about 20-25 people around a large table. The interview consisted of me reviewing my Master's Thesis in great detail and answering a lot of very specific questions, followed by a lunch break. After lunch, a second set of individuals came in and the leader, Dr. Bryan, asked me to draw a heterodyne receiver from memory. At first I didn't know if I could, but my Spirit Guides presented me with a diagram in my head and I simply drew what I was shown. I was impressed and so were the people present. Dr. Bryan then asked lots of questions about its design, waveforms at various points in the receiver, and the failure mode of various components. I had to rely heavily on my Spirit Guides because on my own I would not have been able to answer them, or at least it would have taken me a lot longer to figure out the answers.

My Spirit Guides would sometimes simply provide me the answer. Sometimes they would show me diagrams and symbols in my head. Sometimes they would tell me to pause and think about the answer before answering and to then trust that the correct words would come out of my mouth. I trusted and was able to answer most of their questions. At one point Dr. Bryan drew a circuit diagram of something I had not seen before and asked me what it was for. I initially had no clue, but then as I began to look at the diagram, I heard in my head, "It's a circuit for an optical laser control unit." As I told him what I thought it might be, I heard murmurs from the audience. A short while later he drew a second circuit diagram and before he completed it I heard in my head, "It's a trick question, it doesn't do anything." He turned to me and asked, "What is this for?" I looked at it for a few seconds to see if it made sense to me and again heard, "It's a trick question, it doesn't do anything." I then looked at Dr. Bryan and said, "I don't think it does anything?" He laughed and said I was right and announced that the interview was over. He thanked everyone for coming and thanked me for my time and patience. Several people thanked me and said that I had done a very good job. I was simply glad that it was over and so grateful for the help from my Spirit Guides. Dr. Bryan smiled as he said I would be hearing back from someone within a couple of weeks.

Following the interview, they took me to Union Station where I caught the train back to Philadelphia. Although I was mentally exhausted I had a well-deserved beer, relaxed, and enjoyed the train ride. Suzanne picked me up at the train station and we went to one of our favorite restaurants. I told her all about the interview and about my Spirit Guides talking to me and giving me words and ideas that I knew I could not have pulled from my memory on my own. It took me several days to process that incredible day. It was the most intense and concentrated interview I had ever experienced and it certainly boosted my confidence in my ability to listen and receive answers when I needed them. A couple of days later in my meditation, I *saw* Dr. Bryan saying that he highly recommended that the Agency hire me for their Technical Services Division.

Spiritual Development in New Jersey

During our stay in New Jersey, Suzanne and I continued our interest in all things Spiritual and Metaphysical and joined a local Search For God Study Group. We also became involved in several Metaphysical groups interested in Mediumship and other paranormal studies and practices and established very strong friendships with members in each of these groups.

As we began studying with this new SFG Study Group, Suzanne mentioned my channeling and other psychic practices I had carried out in our previous groups. However, we discovered the group leader, Alan, like Hugh Lynn Cayce, strongly discouraged practicing or exploring ones psychic sensitivities within the group. He stated that he felt we needed to concentrate on developing our spiritual understanding. The group was however very interested in Astrology and Dreams, so Suzanne continued her study and practice of Astrology and we both learned a great deal about dreams. In the other Metaphysical groups, I continued my study and exploration of Auras, and my communication with Spirits, discarnate and Angelic. As my awareness and understanding of the psychic world increased, I read about and began to understand that psychic information comes in different forms or modalities. They are identified as:

Clairsentience (clear sensing), Clairvoyance (clear seeing), Clairaudience (clear hearing), Claircognizance (clear knowing), and Clairgustance (clear taste or smell).

Although I had been psychic all my life, understanding this helped me recognize and clarify that I "picked up on" some things in one form or modality while other things were revealed to me in another form. For example I recognized that I *saw*, *heard* and *sensed* most things but occasionally I would "pick up on" scents or tastes as well. That increased understanding proved to be quite valuable to the development and expansion of my psychic sensitivities.

One night during one of our Study Group meetings, Alan, shared a dream he had regarding a possible accident due to "smoking" brakes on his car. Several members suggested the dream was about his brakes and that he should have them checked. However, I psychically *sensed* that it was heart-related due to his past smoking, his diet, and his lack of exercise, and told him so. I noticed that his wife Celia seemed interested in my interpretation but said nothing. Alan confirmed that he had smoked but stated that he had quit about five years previously and as far as he was concerned his diet and occasional yoga exercise routine was fine and he was in excellent health. He pooh-poohed my interpretation saying that I did not have enough information about him to know what I was talking about. I remember thinking, "I hope I am wrong, but I believe I'm right."

At our next meeting Celia informed the group that Alan had his brakes checked and they were fine. However, she reported that he had a slight heart attack the day before he was scheduled to drive to Ohio on a business trip and was in the hospital for some tests. She said that the doctors cautioned him that he needed to change his diet and get into a more vigorous exercise program. I simply listened and smiled. That experience increased the group's interest in psychic information and when Alan returned the following week, he apologized for being so adamant against exploring psychic sensitivities. From that point forward the group began discussing and exploring psychic sensitivities on a regular basis. We discovered that Alan's adamancy about exploring the psychic world was due in part to some very frightening psychic experiences he had as a kid as well as more recently. Having finally acknowledged those fears, he was able to move forward and became more open and curious. Suzanne and I became quite close friends with Alan and Celia because we enjoyed each other's company and loved to talk about and share metaphysical ideas and the new awarenesses we were all opening up to. We took several trips to A.R.E. conferences in Virginia Beach with them and thoroughly enjoyed our discussions during those long trips.

Moving To Virginia

Three weeks after my intense interview, I received a letter from the CIA offering me a job as a Technical Analyst. Suzanne and I agreed that I should accept the offer and give my two weeks notice to RCA the following Monday. That night I had a dream of being in the Washington, DC area enjoying myself and heard the words, "this is the next phase." When I awoke, I shared my dream with Suzanne and we both knew that accepting the job was the right decision. We began praying and asking for guidance to find the right buyer for our little log cabin, and to find the right house in our new location.

Everything manifested as we had hoped, and our move to the Washington, DC area became another powerful example of Divine Guidance. We found a small Cape Cod house in Falls Church, Virginia, which turned out to be the best area to live for SFG Study Groups, the Unity Church,[19] and other Metaphysical discussion groups, as well as being a short drive to work. We could not have known that information when we decided to live there. This was simply another one of those, "Thank you Father" experiences.

My Job At The Agency

There is not much I can say about my job at the CIA other than I worked as a Technical Analyst in the Signal Analysis Division, and that my expanding psychic sensitivities served me very well during my tenure there. Clearly there are many stories I could tell about experiences I had there, people I met, and examples of how my psychic sensitivities helped me solve problems and uncover mysteries. However, I am prohibited from doing so due to a secrecy agreement I signed when I joined the CIA. Suffice it to say that my psychic sensitivities, and my Engineering and Math skills played a significant role in carrying out my duties. My experiences there helped me to expand upon and increase my understanding of and the depth of my psychic sensitivities. That job also significantly enhanced my technical skills in Engineering and Mathematics as well.

After an interesting and fascinating six years, I left The Agency in February 1978 for personal reasons. They say you never leave the Agency, and in many respects that is true, because there is a special camaraderie in the Intelligence Community and I made many professional and personal friends there as well as within other Intelligence Community organizations. When I left, I took a job with IBM's Federal Systems Division in Manassas, Virginia.

Continued Spiritual and Psychic Development

As soon as we moved into our Falls Church home, we found a Search For God Study Group and made fast friends with people in the A.R.E. community. We also discovered the Unity Church in Fairfax and met several people who were involved in Mediumistic and Paranormal Groups, which we checked out and joined. I began doing technical consulting with the Spiritual Frontiers Fellowship (SFF) and other Mediumistic groups that were interested in recording voices of ghosts, photographing Spirits and investigating Kirlian photography. My technical expertise was being put to good use.

---

[19] Unity School of Christianity. See http://www.unityonline.org for more information

Our new SFG Study Group included a young couple in their mid-30's, Mack and Tanya, who also worked at the Agency. We really enjoyed being with them because they were very spiritual, very politically savvy, interested in organic farming, and were lots of fun to be with. When we first met them, they had two children and Tanya was pregnant with their third child. Other people in the group included a very dynamic lady in her mid-40's from New York, Helen Wentz, an older couple in their 60's, Jesse and Betty, who had been long time members of the A.R.E. and Unity, and several others whose names I cannot remember. The exciting thing to me was that they were all very interested in exploring psychic sensitivities and were all well read in the areas of Metaphysics and Spirituality. We all learned a great deal from each other.

Mack and Tanya were long time practitioners of Yoga and Meditation and we had many great conversations about many different Metaphysical topics. They were what I would call enlightened hippies who created an organic garden that included two beehives. Tanya made sunflower butter from their own sunflower seeds and kneaded their own bread. We delighted in being with them.

My First "New Age Kid" Experience

When Tanya's baby, Tabatha, was born she was a bright and beautiful baby with large penetrating dark brown eyes. However, almost immediately I noticed there was something about her *lights* or Aura pattern, which was fundamentally different from the *lights* or Aura I saw around her older siblings. Even though both of her siblings, who were about four and six, were very bright, their Aura pattern did not display the intensity of spirituality I saw with Tabatha. They did not seem to be interested in past lives, nor did they have a strong interest in psychic things even though their parents were steeped in it.

Several months after Tabatha was born I clarified what it was I was seeing in her Aura that was different. During a long conversation with Mack and Tanya I explained that Tabatha's Aura pattern was very different from any that I had ever seen up to this point, and that I was calling it a *New Age Kids* Aura pattern. I stated that her Aura had a lot of deep indigo blue as well a lot of violet and yellow in it, and I felt that she was very psychically sensitive, highly spiritually oriented – a very old and enlightened soul. They said that they were not surprised, since they believed they would naturally draw an advanced spiritual soul to themselves because of their ongoing spiritual work. I agreed but told them that I also believed she would be a very defiant little girl. I explained that I felt she would not follow any rules that did not make sense to her, much more so than her older siblings. They simply laughed. I told them that I felt that when she began to talk, she would probably talk about her past lives with each of her parents as if it were yesterday. I shared that I felt they were in for a real challenge because although Tabatha was very spiritual, she would be very demanding and impatient. They both laughed again and said, "Oh boy." Lastly I told them I felt that she would express knowledge and understanding of "things" (information) for which she would have no basis for that understanding, and that might cause her a great deal of frustration so they needed to be aware of that.

Sure enough, as she began speaking she told her mother that they were best friends in ancient Greece times "before the big war." These were the words of a toddler. Later I learned that little Tabatha was recalling a past life with her mother prior to a great war involving Alexander the Great. Several months later when her dad came in from working in their garden, she told her mom that "daddy used to bring me grapes when he was my daddy before." She loved grapes and whenever we knew they were coming to our house, we made sure we had some grapes for her. We later learned that this was a memory of a lifetime she shared with her father, Mack, when he had a large vineyard in southern France. As she grew, she became very self-willed and impatient, but was extremely bright, much brighter than her older siblings, and very spiritually oriented. By the time she was three, she would sit and meditate by herself or with her parents; something her older siblings would only begrudgingly do. Mack and Tanya discovered that life with Tabatha was much easier if they took the time to explain why they needed something done. She was expressing her defiance of rules that did not make sense. As I watched her grow and saw how patient her parents had to be with her, I realized more and more what her *lights* or Aura pattern meant. She taught me a great deal about what the *New Age Kids* Aura pattern was all about. I also appreciated the lovingness that was required to raise this little spiritual and psychic dynamo. It was a joy to watch Mack and Tanya work with her and gently guide her development.

Over the next several years as Tabatha began to grow, her Aura pattern increased in both intensity and complexity. When she was about 4½ years old, her parents brought her to an A.R.E. function and as one of the other women passed by them, I heard her say to her mom, "That lady's *lights* are bad and she doesn't like you, but your *lights* are nice" and then gave her mom a hug. She then came over to give me a hug and as she did, she said, "You look sad" even though I was smiling at her. About an hour before, my wife had gotten upset with me and said some very hurtful things. I guess I had not put that aside because she obviously picked up on it. I returned her hug and she ran off to play. As I told her parents, Tabatha obviously was able to pick up on my Aura and that lady's Aura, expressing her sensitivities to

Auras and her ability to "read" when people were not being truthful – a characteristic typical of sensitive *New Age Kids.*

Over the course of several years, I was told in my meditations to continue to watch for this *New Age Kids* Aura pattern because it signaled a coming of a new generation of spiritually oriented entities who could potentially change the consciousness level of human kind. I had no idea what the significance of this was at that time.

Unity and Teaching "Psychic" Kids

Shortly after arriving in Falls Church we found the little Unity Church in downtown Fairfax and discovered that many of our SFG Study Group friends also attended that Unity Church. We made several new friends as well. As I began learning about Unity's approach to Spirituality, I found that their teachings complemented the Edgar Cayce approach to Spirituality and included many ideas and practices from the Orthodox Eastern religions I had studied as well. As I studied Unity's Five Basic Principles, which I have included below, I realized that Unity held the same beliefs that both Suzanne and I shared. In the Unity Church we were not considered sinners or weird because we believed in Reincarnation, Auras or psychic things. Here was a place where church members understood and welcomed discussions about Metaphysical concepts and principles including Karma, Meditation, and psychic sensitivities.

Unity's Five Basic Principles

1. God is the source and creator of all. There is no other enduring power. God is good and present everywhere.
2. We are spiritual beings, created in God's image. The Spirit of God lives within each person; therefore, all people are inherently good.
3. We create our life experiences through our way of thinking.
4. There is power in affirmative prayer, which we believe increases our connection to God.
5. Knowledge of these spiritual principles is not enough. We must live them.

I began studying Unity's interpretation of The Bible, which is symbolic and metaphorical rather than literal, which made the Bible much more understandable. I also began avidly reading other Unity literature and taking classes to become a licensed Unity Teacher. I continued my study of other sacred texts such as The Bhagavagita, The Upanishads and the Vedas, as well as the Kabbalah to round out my understanding of sacred scriptures. As I had discovered in the *Religions of Man* class I took in college, I had a keen interest in religions in general. Many years later I learned about the origins and authors of the Bible[20] (J, E, P and D) and how the books that are included in the Bible (The Canon) were chosen. I ended up teaching classes on these subjects several years later.

A few years after I began going to the Unity Church and taking classes, I volunteered to teach the Uni-teens and Pre-teens. I very quickly recognized that many of these kids were quite psychically sensitive. Although they did NOT display the *"New Age Kids"* Aura pattern, several of their little brothers and sisters did. I taught them the Unity Principles but also shared with them the teachings of Edgar Cayce and the A.R.E., the concepts of Karma, Reincarnation, Meditation, and of course we talked about their psychic sensitivities and their dreams. I had their attention because of my openness and my ability to talk to them about their dreams, their psychic experiences and about things they knew but did not understand the basis of their knowing. I was usually able to fill in details they were otherwise unable to fill in for themselves. One of the early teens in my class who was especially psychically sensitive, would at times try to "psychically touch" my Aura. Her mom shared that her daughter remembered a past life with me in which I was her older brother. I was able to talk with her about that lifetime and what she (and I) could learn from that remembrance. She became very comfortable and receptive to learning about psychic stuff from me and her parents fully supported her.

One of the things I strongly emphasized in my classes was the power of Denials and Affirmations,[21] which involve "declaring not to be true a thing that seems to be true." and "affirming or positively asserting a thing that you desire to be true, even in the face of evidence to the contrary." I had learned that Denials and Affirmations could be a very powerful tool in one's life. These kids were quick to learn to create their own Denials and Affirmations for their own specific problems or difficulties. It helped them understand that they had the power and ability to take charge of their lives – a very powerful message, especially at that age. I learned as much from teaching those kids as they learned from me and it was a very mutually rewarding experience.

---

[20] As described in *Who Wrote The Bible* by Richard Elliott Friedman, J, E, P and D are abbreviations for the writers of the Bible. See also *How The Bible Became The Bible* by Donald L. O'Dell, and *The Lost Gospel – The Book of Q* and *Christian Origins* by Burton L, Mack.

[21] See lessons 4 and 5 in *Lessons In Truth* by H. Emilie Cady, Unity Books.

As I continued my Unity classes and Metaphysical studies I talked more and more about Auras and what I thought the colors and patterns in their Auras meant. I shared with my Uni-teen and Pre-teen students the differences I saw in their Auras vs. the Auras of their younger siblings who displayed the *New Age Kids* Aura pattern. As I began to identify and observe more and more children with this unique Aura pattern I became aware of the importance of these special kids.

Several other Metaphysical friends whom I knew were sensitive to and read Auras agreed with me that the younger *New Age Kids* had a lot of indigo blue in their Aura, which even the psychic kids in my class did not have. During this time period, I also began receiving confirmative information from my Spirit Guides and Angels that the soul's purpose of these kids, as a soul group, could have an effect on the consciousness of humanity. My Uni-teen and pre-teen kids were fascinated with this discussion and began contributing their own experiences and the differences they saw as well.

It wasn't until years later in the 1998-99 time frame that I discovered that several other sensitive people around the world were also identifying this change in Aura or energy pattern and, in fact, had labeled it *Indigo* based on the fact that they too saw the color indigo – a deep blue – as a prominent color in these kids' Aura pattern. Although I *saw* (and *see*) the strong deep blue indigo color in these kids' Aura, my interpretation was (and still is) based more in terms of what the energy "pattern" of their Aura looks like, than the color itself.

Becoming A Leader In The Local A.R.E.

Suzanne and I continued in-depth group discussions with various Spiritual and Psychic groups. We also participated in extensive experimentation with various forms of psychism including various divining processes such as telekinesis and automatic writing and various divining "tools" such as Tarot cards, Astrology charts, Numerology, pendulums, crystals, chimes, drums, and incense, etc. As a result, both Suzanne and I became quite knowledgeable about these subjects. In the early to mid-1970's we participated in the formation of an A.R.E. Council for the Northern Virginia area, and I became co-chair of that Council with Barbara Heiberg (now deceased). I remained in that role for several years.

Because our SFG Study Group was very active, well read, and understood much about the Edgar Cayce readings, one of our more outspoken members, Ms. Helen Wentz, suggested that we initiate a local monthly Mini-Lecture series. Her idea was to have members of our SFG Study Group and knowledgeable members from other SFG Study Groups in the Northern

Virginia area provide lectures on various "readings" topics to the public in libraries throughout the Northern Virginia area. Topics included various lessons from the Search For God material, such as Meditation, Cooperation, Love, Faith, Fellowship, and of course Dreams. Other topics included the Essenes, Karma, Astrology, Numerology, and health matters, etc.

Within a matter of months, the Northern Virginia Council began hosting weekend retreats, which we eventually called "Mid-Atlantic" retreats. Initially these retreats were Friday to Sunday weekend workshops drawing SFG Study Group members from throughout the Northern Virginia area as well as Washington, DC and Maryland. We also drew non-A.R.E. people interested in these Metaphysical topics. Like our monthly mini-lectures, the speakers were knowledgeable members from local SFG Study Groups including our own. We would meet at local "retreat centers" to keep the cost down, which allowed people who could not afford the Virginia Beach weeklong conferences to receive information from knowledgeable long-term A.R.E. Members. As these events became more popular, we decided to reach out to A.R.E. Headquarters to provide speakers. The Mid-Atlantic retreats became an annual event with major speakers such as Eula Allen on *The Creation Story*, Everett Irion on *Revelations*, Herb Puryear on *Jesus and The Second Coming*, June and Harmon Bro on *Call To Service*, Dr. Bill and Gladys McGarey on *Health and Healing*, Thea Alexander on *Creating Your Future Now* and many others.

During this time period, the Northern Virginia Council also hosted several other one-day events including Bill and Elsie Seachrist on *Dreams and Spiritual Development*, Mark Lerner and Zahi Hawass on *Egyptology*, Mark Thurston, Ph.D. on *Meditation*, Jeffrey Furst on *Edgar Cayce's Story of Jesus*, and Robert Krajenke on *The Bible*. Suzanne and I acted as the hosts for the speakers during this time period, which meant picking them up at the airport, welcoming them into our home, sharing dinners, and driving them where they needed to go. We thoroughly enjoyed getting to know many of them on a "first name basis."

Ghost Tours of Cemeteries

Many members of our SFG Study Group were interested in exploring their own psychic sensitivities. As an "exercise" we visited the Flint Hill Cemetery in Oakton to see what ghosts and things (information) we might *see, sense* or *tap into*. On this *outing*, almost everyone picked up some very strong Spirits that seemed to hang around trying to communicate with several of the group members. At our next meeting the presence of the Spirits that were still hanging around was a big topic. It became necessary to do some Rescue Mediumship channeling for the group to assist those Spirits to "go to the light." From that experience we learned that we needed to be more cautious when doing that kind of exercise.

To protect yourself from discarnate entities or 'remnant energies,' you can say the 'Robe of Light Protection Prayer' that I provided in Chapter 2. It creates a Robe of Light around you that 'repels' negative or draining energies. You can also make up your own prayer if you choose. But, deceased entities and/or 'remnant energies' see those of us who are sensitive, as lights that they are drawn to. So, whenever you feel or sense the presence of a disturbing energy or entity, simply repeat the 'Robe Of Light Protection Prayer' (or similar affirmation or prayer) over and over again until you sense that they (the disturbing influences) have gone, or at least are not causing you a problem.

The 'Robe of Light Protection Prayer' can similarly be used to 'disconnect' from a draining energy. For example, sometimes you may feel as if you are being 'drained' by a person or people in a crowd. It may be deliberate or unconscious, but you feel it just the same. Whenever you experience such draining sensation, just begin silently saying the 'Robe of Light Protection Prayer' over and over again because the statement, ". . . so that all who see it or come in contact with it (meaning Spirits or draining connections), will be drawn back to God and healed." will cause those draining connections to be broken.

When word of our "exercise" got out to other study groups, I was asked to conduct Ghost Tours for those groups at several other cemeteries as well. We quickly learned how to prevent members from being followed by discarnate entities and these outings became very popular and educational. We were able to confirm and validate several stories people "picked up on" during these tours, which was both gratifying and affirming for those people.

The Death Of Suzanne's Mother

After Suzanne's dad died it took a long time for her mom to heal. The last year of her life, 1972, she was beginning to come to terms with Reynolds' passing and even began going to dinner and enjoying the companionship of a man she and Reynolds had known. Suzanne and I both were happy that she was beginning to enjoy life again. Mae drove down to spend Christmas with us, which was a treat because we usually went to her home in Delaware for Christmas. My brother Terry, his Thai wife and their two little boys joined us for that Christmas and Suzanne and I were glad to share the holiday in our home.

Mae arrived on Friday and we went to her favorite restaurant and enjoyed a very good relaxing meal with lively fun conversation, which was a welcome change from some of our previous conversations. She appeared genuinely interested in how we were doing and actually seemed to enjoy our study group topics, which was highly unusual. However, that evening Mae became sick to her stomach and began running a high fever. Since there was a flu epidemic going around, we dismissed her condition as being the flu and began giving her Tylenol and lots of fluids. Meanwhile my brother and his family arrived the next morning and we told him to keep the little ones away from her because of her flu.

That afternoon when her fever spiked beyond 104 degrees we took her to the Fairfax County Hospital Emergency Room. After checking her over, the doctor determined that it simply looked like a bad case of the flu and recommended that we take her home and continue the Tylenol, give her lots of fluids, keep her warm, and keep the kids away from her. However, I was beginning to suspect that it was something more than just the flu because I noticed that her Aura pattern was becoming much weaker and more "discordant" but I did not know how to interpret exactly what it was that I was seeing. Throughout that night and the next morning Mae became more and more delusional and kept saying, "You need to let me go, you need to let me go," but neither Suzanne nor I realized what that really meant.

When we finally took her back to the emergency room late Christmas eve, she was completely delusional and her Aura pattern began separating, which I understood to mean that she might be on the verge of dying and I told Suzanne what I was *seeing*. When an Emergency Room doctor came in to examine her, he looked into her eyes with his light, looked away for a moment to talk to a colleague, and then looked back, and we heard him say, "Oh shit, they weren't that way just a second ago." What he had noticed was that her eyes had dilated, which indicated a serious brain abnormality. They immediately did some extensive blood tests to confirm what the doctor suspected: Meningococcal Meningitis, which is highly contagious and kills very rapidly! She was put on intravenous penicillin and placed in Intensive Care but within less than 24 hours she was gone. She died Christmas Day.

Suzanne greatly mourned the loss of her parents. For the next year and a half we spent almost every weekend at her parents' home in Delaware going through their collection of seventy-two years of accumulated "stuff." The strain of having to drive to Delaware almost every weekend to rummage through all of her mother's things was a tremendous strain on Suzanne's health, both physically and emotionally, as well as upon our relationship.

Unity Village Christmas

Because Mae had died on Christmas day, Suzanne and I agreed to go away the next year to the Christmas Conference at Unity Village near Kansas City, Missouri, which turned out to be a delightful experience for both of us. One night we were told to ask for a dream about Christmas and our relationship to Jesus' birth. That night I had a dream of walking on a beach with Jesus and we were simply talking. At one point I asked Him whether I had been "with Him" in a previous life and he said, "Yes." He then pointed to a grain of sand on the beach, which I understood to mean I was simply one who was there, just as the grains of sand made up the beach that He and I were walking on. It was a very powerful and affirmative experience. When I shared my dream with Suzanne she jokingly stated that she too had a dream and Jesus wasn't in it so she probably didn't know Him, and we both just laughed. That Christmas at Unity Village was one of the best Christmases Suzanne and I ever had together.

The Face of the Master

The next day Suzanne, myself and several other people were going down a set of stairs in one of the Unity Village buildings when I noticed a picture of the Master's face on the wall. I pointed and excitedly said, "Look, there's a picture of the face of Jesus."[22]

Everyone stopped to look where I was pointing. A few could see what I was seeing but Suzanne and several others could not. They just saw blotches of black and white. As indicated on the referenced web site, "The story that is told about this picture is of a Chinese photographer, who was deeply troubled religiously. He took a picture of the melting snow with black earth showing through. When he developed it he was amazed to see in it the face of Yeshua [Jesus] full of tenderness and love, and he became a believer. It may take you a long time to see the face, but that difficulty is perhaps a symbol of the effort that must be made to find Him in our world. Once found, however, as in the picture, He dominates the scene and one wonders how it was possible to miss Him."

---

[22] See http://www.prayerforallpeople.com

I was completely puzzled why everyone could not see what was so obvious to me. As soon as we returned to Virginia, I obtained a copy of that picture and began puzzling over it, trying to figure why Suzanne and others could not see the face of the Master. I decided to write to my friend Al Miner[23] who channels the entity *Lama Sing,* and ask for a reading about why so many people could not see the face of the Master in that picture. When Al's wife Lucy responded and sent me the reading tape, she said that Al also readily saw the face of the Master but she, like Suzanne could not see it until Al did a tracing of it for her. In the reading, *Lama Sing* said that Al and I had both been "with the Master" and "as such ye can easily *see* the Master even in very symbolic pictures." *Lama Sing* also stated that those who did not have personal contact would in general "have a more difficult time seeing the real in the abstract."

Moving To Loudoun County

Since Suzanne's father had left a substantial estate, which her mother passed on to her as the only child, we used part of that money to buy a larger home in Broad Run Farms in Loudoun County. It had a deep well with wonderful clean water and its own septic system on a little over an acre of land where we could now grow our own food. Another benefit was living away from the city lights of Falls Church, which gave me the opportunity to do some amateur Astronomy – planet and stargazing. Recall that when I was thinking about graduate schools, I thought about becoming an Astrophysicist.

A few months after we moved to Broad Run Farms, I quit my job at the CIA and took a job with IBM's Federal Systems Division in Manassas as an Advisory Engineer designing computer architectures and networks. I had mostly good memories of my days at the Agency, but I knew it was time to move on.

Although we loved our new home, being out in the country caused us to be less active in the Northern Virginia A.R.E. Council and I decided to resign as co-chair and handed my responsibility off to others. Also, we were unable to find a replacement SFG Study Group in the Sterling and Leesburg area. With the loss of our dear friend Helen Wentz a year before, and the move of our dear friends Mack and Tanya to a peaceful "hippie community" in Oregon, Suzanne and I both grieved the loss of our friends as well as the intense weekly Metaphysical discussions we had. We continued to attend the

---

[23] See http://www.lamasing.com

Mid-Atlantic Retreats, A.R.E. Conferences in Virginia Beach and our beloved Unity Church, but eventually we lost touch with our Falls Church Study Group members who did not go to Unity.

Past Life Regressions

Suzanne and I continued to share our interest in Metaphysics including a strong interest in past lives as a means of understanding current strengths, weaknesses and Karma. Shortly after moving to Loudoun County, we discovered a Past Life Regression Technique that was documented in a couple of small pamphlets[24] entitled *Awareness Techniques*. Curious as we were, we decided to try these techniques on each other. We had both had several readings by *Lama Sing*, which had revealed past life information and we were curious as to what else we could learn. One evening I put Suzanne into a hypnotic state and she went back to a lifetime in which she was a witch who was burned at the stake in Massachusetts. This was confirming information for some things that *Lama Sing* had told her about her fascination with things of the occult, yet a great reluctance to get involved in it. The information that came through in this regression proved to be quite valuable to her understanding certain urges, likes and dislikes, etc. and we found the "regression" process rather easy to do.

The next week Suzanne regressed me. As I lay on the sofa and she "induced" me, she asked me to come down to earth and describe what I was wearing on my feet. I said, "shackles." She then asked me where I was and I said, "I'm on the Rack, being pulled apart for heresy." As the session progressed she asked if anyone in my current life was with me and I said, "Yes, my dad (in this lifetime) is the executioner." I then stated, "And he loves his job" meaning that he delighted in pulling people apart. I told her that I was feeling the pain of my body being pulled apart. She told me to rise above the pain but it was too late. I could no longer feel my feet or legs and my butt was going numb. She brought me "out of it" but I laid there half paralyzed for about a half-hour. All I could do was lie there and experience the paralysis I was feeling. After another half-hour of Suzanne saying prayers, and trying to get me to release from that experience, I began regaining feeling in my backside, my legs, and finally my feet. Finally, after a little over an hour from the beginning of this journey, I was able to stand

---

[24] Awareness Techniques, book 1 and 2, by William Swygard; self published 1970

but was still quite shaky. From that experience we learned to be very careful when a person is experiencing his or her own death.

Subsequent Past Life Regression experiences went much more smoothly. We learned that my current father had killed me in several lifetimes, which caused Suzanne to ask, "OK, so if your dad has killed you so often and was so cruel to you in this lifetime, why did you come back with him into this experience – what was the Karmic lesson or tie?" Neither one of us were prepared for the answer, "To give him one last opportunity to do something differently – he failed, but your Karmic debt has been paid." It finally made sense to me, and I was able to release those past life experiences. A subsequent reading by *Lama Sing* confirmed this reason and the release of the Karmic tie.

Over the years I have used the *Awareness Techniques* to lead people to discover their past lives on their own, rather than me reading the *Akashic Records* for them. I like the technique because it is quite straight forward, and allows me to concentrate on helping the person heal the problem or problems and or relationships that are revealed in the Regression. Although the *Awareness Techniques* pamphlets say that it is not hypnosis, from my experience and perspective, it really is. I participated in a July 2008 weeklong Past Life Regression training by Brian Weiss, M.D. at the Omega Institute.[25] He uses clinical Hypnosis to take a client to a hypnagogic state from which they can tap into their subconscious mind and access the information they need. I find that his process is very similar to the *Awareness Techniques* processes but accomplishes it in a slightly different manner. When I do Past Life Regressions I interchangeably use both methods as well as information provided by my Spirit Guides.

Masters and Students – A Personal Story

The following story reflects how past life connections can show up in the strangest of ways, and how the roles are often reversed. As I have expanded my understanding of Metaphysics over the years, I have on several occasions met people in this lifetime who have been my students from a past lifetime. I have also met several people who were my teachers in a past lifetime. On a couple of occasions these past life Masters of mine were in this lifetime "biding their time" and my acknowledgement of their "significant" past life spurred them on to work on their Spiritual self and the process of "re-

---

[25] See http://www.eOmega.org for further details

awakening" to the work they have yet to do. I believe that my meeting the Swami in the following story was one such occurrence. At the time it truly humbled me, but I now recognize that he was simply being life's catalyst to spur me on to becoming a better me. For that I greatly appreciate that he remembered, so that I could remember. *Namaste!*

A Visiting Guru

The Unity Church invited an East Indian "Swami" follower of Yogananda to speak. I was an usher at the church at the time and as I sat down next to Suzanne, the Swami (who was on the lecture platform) stood up, bowed toward me with his hands clasped and then sat down. I did the same gesture to him and everyone just looked at me. Suzanne asked me what that was all about, and I told her I had no idea, because I really did not. I was as surprised and astounded as anyone.

Following a very inspirational talk by this Swami there was a "meet and greet" time in the lobby and the adjacent library. A lot of people were talking to him, asking him questions, and requesting his autograph. After a short time of just watching his magnificent Aura that seemed to fill the entire area around him, I began edging my way toward him to listen to what he was saying. I did not have a question; I just wanted to be close to his energy.

He was standing with our Unity Minister, David Davenport, and as I approached, he graciously excused himself from talking to someone and turned and bowed saying, "Greetings Master, do you remember?" I was totally stunned and flabbergasted as were those within hearing range. He proceeded to tell me that I had been his Master teacher in a previous life, and that he was glad to see me and recognize me, and that it was time for me to begin MY teaching – again. Although I felt somehow connected to him, I was very confused and embarrassed. I can honestly say that, at that moment, I did not remember him as my student and was extremely humbled and dumbfounded. However, something inside of me knew that what he said was true. I do not recall what I said, but I believe I just bowed in response and said *Namaste* and stood there trying to process this entire moment. He then said something like "Blessings, we will meet again on the inner planes," and then turned and walked with our Minister to talk with others who were waiting to talk to him.

Afterwards, several of my friends who had overheard him, asked me a bunch of questions that I had no way of answering. I was as curious as they were. At the time, I was a Unity Sunday School teacher but somehow I knew that was not what he meant. Several days later, I had an opportunity to talk with our Minister about the incident. He stated that he did not know I had an advanced spiritual past, but that he was really not surprised. I gave him a heartfelt "Thank you" and shared with him that I was still trying to understand it myself. That experience left an indelible mark on my consciousness and I continually pondered what that was all about for several years.

Channeling Archangelic Energies

Shortly after I moved to Loudoun County, an older A.R.E. couple I knew asked if I would try to tune into their little 8-year-old granddaughter who had recently died of leukemia. They were hoping I could tune in to her Spirit and bring forth a message that might comfort their daughter and her husband who were having a very difficult time coping with her death.

I told them that I was willing to try but that I felt I needed to channel rather than simply try to tune in to that young girl's Spirit. They agreed to "hold a sacred space" to allow the channeling to take place. When I met them and their SFG Study Group the next week, we sat in a circle and began to meditate. As I prepared myself to become a channel I asked that only the highest energy or entity that could provide the requested information be allowed to come through. As I held this thought, I found myself outside my body, and I both *saw* and *sensed* a very large and powerful yet loving energy envelop my body; my mind seemed to go blank.

Although I am "gone" when these sessions take place, I was told that the Archangel Michael came through first and blessed the gathering in a very booming voice that startled everyone. Several people later reported that as he made his presence known, they saw a flash of brilliant blue and white light. They stated that following the blessing, Archangel Michael declared, "Make way for Archangel Gabriel, for his is the energy most energetically appropriate for the entity Lowell at this time." The group reported that at that point my body became more upright and my voice changed to a softer and more loving energy. Archangel Gabriel then came through and stated that the young girl's short life was an agreement that she and her parents had made prior to her entering. He then stated that she would be returning through another "vehicle" shortly. Gabriel gave a blessing to the grandparents and a blessing that was to be passed on to the parents and said that they needed to pray for the return of their granddaughter. The next thing I knew, I was back in my body, with vague memories of what had been said, feeling extremely calm and relaxed. The grandparents thanked me for doing the channeling, said they felt that it was very helpful, and asked me to come back to their next meeting the following week. As I left that gathering, I felt very relaxed, calm and *knew* that I was doing what I had come here (the earth plane) to do.

The Key to the Akashic Records

Following that channeling session, I had a very relaxing night's sleep and had a very powerful dream. In the dream I was presented an ornate golden box with a lock on the front that opened as soon as I looked at it. I was told that the box represented the *Akashic Records* and that I was ready to "read the records" any time I chose to look at them. I was also told that "the records" were the source of much of the information provided in readings I had done in the past. I then saw myself holding a full key in my right hand. As you may recall in my first Guided Image Meditation experience (back in the mid-1960's) I was shown that I had one-half a key and was told that I needed to develop the other half. This dream meant that I had, in fact, done that.

In my meditation the next morning, I was told it was time to do more channeling sessions and spontaneous readings and that I would be shown and told when and how to "read the records." I went to the next SFG meeting and as I entered that couple's house I felt a very powerful calming and loving energy. When everyone was gathered, the grandparents talked about Gabriel's message that the granddaughter would be returning shortly through another "vehicle." I told them I felt that within a matter of a few months another of their daughters would become pregnant and that it would be very unexpected. I said that I felt that their recently deceased granddaughter would be coming through that daughter and they would recognize her because she would be born with a scar on her left shoulder exactly where their granddaughter had a scar due to an accident she had when she was about two years old.

Much to the grandparent's and their daughter's surprise, sure enough, one of their daughters who had her tubes tied, got pregnant and when the baby was born she had a scar on her left shoulder exactly where their deceased granddaughter had a scar. She had come back.

Going Our Separate Ways

When Suzanne and I first moved to Broad Run Farms, I really liked the large spacious yard and the two-car garage, which I did not have in Falls Church. Also, once a farm boy, always a farm boy, and I really enjoyed the two large garden areas we lovingly created. However, when it became clear that I was to do all of the plowing, planting, weeding, and tilling, etc. while Suzanne simply "picked the crop," it became quite burdensome and I became resentful. I also began to resent the fact that Suzanne refused to help mow the lawn even though I had a very nice riding mower. She said, "That's man's work."

After several long and difficult conversations over the next three years, it became increasingly evident that Suzanne felt that she should not have to work in the garden or yard, and her Rheumatoid Arthritis made that especially difficult. She simply wanted someone who could be empathetic and take care of her physically ailing body and support her financially. She felt that since she worked while I was in college, she should not have to work now. We agreed that our life style desires had become much more disparate in spite of our common interest in Metaphysics and Spirituality. We decided to separate to see if we could get a clear sense of what we each wanted and needed from our relationship.

We had purchased a house on 67th Street in Virginia Beach next to the A.R.E. Library about six months previously, and Suzanne decided to go live there while I lived in the Broad Run Farms home. I thoroughly enjoyed the quiet time and the lack of conflict. Every couple of weeks I drove down to the beach and spent the weekend working on that house while discussing what we wanted and needed from each other. It became increasingly clear that we both needed to go our separate ways. When the Broad Run house sold about six months later, I moved into a rented townhouse in Manassas, which was close to my work. I threw myself into my new life. I became a social recluse withdrawing from many of the Metaphysical groups in which Suzanne and I had participated. However, I started a daily morning Yoga exercise program followed by a structured Meditation, which I found to be very relaxing and uplifting. I was achieving a real sense of peace within myself. I also began working long hours focusing my energy on my Engineering career.

Since Suzanne had received a substantial estate from her parents, as well as the house in Virginia Beach and half of the proceeds from the Broad Run house sale, and we had no children, I felt that I should not have to pay her alimony. However, she adamantly insisted that I support her for the rest of her life. After a two-year bitter and expensive court battle, she won and we went our separate ways, but she remained bitter about the settlement.[26]

Shortly after my divorce from Suzanne I met a woman at Unity and quickly and unadvisedly remarried. Although it only lasted fifteen months, it

---

[26] Seventeen years later she took me back to court and won a four-fold increase in alimony. When she finally died about 5 years later, I thought how sad that our relationship had gone from a very supportive and caring relationship to such bitterness.

turned out to be a disaster and was emotionally and financially devastating. The only positive thing that came out of that marriage was that I got into psychotherapy with an excellent therapist shortly after we were married. He helped me process my childhood traumas and helped me recognize that I needed to end that marriage for my own mental health. After another two-year bitter and expensive court battle, I was again ordered to pay lifetime alimony! This experience caused me to completely shut down my *psychic sensitivities* since they had not been helpful in "picking" my second wife. I also withdrew from all my Metaphysical studies, including my studies to become a Licensed Unity Teacher. Only occasionally did I attend the Unity Church since that is where I had met my second wife. My focus again became my Engineering career.

The New Beginnings Years

A few months after my second divorce I discovered and joined a separated and divorced men and women's support group called *New Beginnings.*[27] Although I was not interested in "getting involved" with anyone any time soon, this group helped me re-establish a whole new set of friends – a new social network. I learned that I could establish healthy loving friendships without getting "involved." I was also learning how to play again. A few months after joining, I met my Soul Sister Angie at a *New Beginnings* event and we immediately *knew* that we had known each other before – in many different settings over many lifetimes. Although we became very emotionally and spiritually close, our relationship was not a romantic connection but a true soul mate connection. This was something new and wonderful for both of us.

Since Angie was very interested in Metaphysics and developing her own sensitivities, I began re-opening up to mine as well, although I did so cautiously. One day as we were driving to a movie, Angie complained about a tremendous pain she was experiencing in her left hand which had been crushed in a sliding glass door accident several years previously. She told me that the pain never abated and many times it actually woke her up in the middle of the night. As she talked, I placed my right hand over her left hand and, almost immediately, my entire right arm began "burning with severe pain." It hurt so much that I wanted to pull it away, but something inside me told me to continue holding her hand, and I did so until we stopped at the movie. As I held her hand, my arm continued to burn so severely that the pain made it difficult for me to concentrate. After the movie we went to a restaurant for a bite to eat. As we sat down, Angie kissed me on the cheek and said, "Thank you so much," and then began to cry. She told me that for the first time since the accident she felt no pain in her hand. I then shared with her that when I placed my hand on hers, my entire arm began burning and remained burning throughout the movie. I told her that only now was the pain starting to abate. She began laughing and stated that when I had first placed my hand on hers, her hand also began burning "worse than ever," but she somehow knew that this was part of the healing process. She shook her hand in the air with tears of joy and gratitude, something she said she could

---

[27] See: http://www.NewBeginningsUSA.org

not have done before. Her pain was gone. When I recently checked with her and told her I was writing this story, she told me that the pain has never returned, and again thanked me.

Past Life Recall

Angie had a keen interest in Reincarnation and a strong curiosity about where we might have known each other. Over the course of the next few months we began filling in many details of our shared past lives as we experienced dreams and spontaneous recalls of experiences in various lifetimes. One in which we had actually been brother and sister. When Angie learned that I had done past life regressions with Suzanne, she asked that I regress her using the *Awareness Techniques* process. We were at my apartment and, as I hypnotized her, she began speaking of a past life where we were fellow monks. She stated that I baked incredible bread, which she got fat from eating and was lovingly resentful for my being such a good baker. We were inseparable in that lifetime. As the regression continued, she stated that one day on our way to the village, I tripped on my robe belt and fell in front of an ox cart and was run over and killed. The amazing thing about this regression experience was that although I was talking her through the event and scenes, I was right there with her in my mind. I could *see* what she was *seeing* and could *hear* her as she yelled, "You stupid jerk, you went and got yourself killed. Now what am I going to do?" I remember *seeing* myself leaving my body. Keep in mind I am the one who is regressing her, yet I am *seeing* myself being run over and am experiencing my own death, not hers – a very strange experience.

As she was coming out of her hypnagogic state, we continued recalling what happened, including memories and scenes of other events in that lifetime even though neither one of us was "under." As we processed information from that lifetime, we "spontaneously" recalled another lifetime where I was her ten-year-old little brother who was sickly and died. She then recalled another lifetime where we were again monks together and again I ended up dying and leaving her. She reached over and grabbed me by the shoulders and said, "Not this time, you can't leave me this time!" meaning that I was not allowed to die before her in this lifetime, and we both laughed. Angie and I both recognized that she is truly my Soul Sister, and I am truly her Soul Brother. Only time will tell who goes first this lifetime, but if I do she will be very pissed.

As Angie and I continued to explore various Metaphysical topics and began opening up to our psychic sensitivities I began to again become more aware of Auras, ghosts and other *psychic phenomena.* Angie also began opening up to and developing her own sensitivities, and we mutually supported each other as we continued to grow. We went to various local Psychic and Metaphysical conferences and workshops and met many new friends at these events.

NB Weekend Getaways

Throughout the mid-1980's and 1990's, I was very active in *New Beginnings* support group activities. I joined the Board of Directors, began facilitating NB Discussion meetings, and trained other facilitators as well. One of the fun and very helpful activities that *New Beginnings* created was organized 3-day weekend getaways to places like Seven Springs, Pennsylvania, Berkley Springs, West Virginia, and Wintergreen, Virginia. We would have around fifty-to-eighty participants with five or six men and the same number of women in each house or cabin. The residents in each cabin or house had to share responsibility for cleaning, cooking the meals, preparing parties, and organizing activities like tennis and golf; and it had to be done with cooperation and respect for the opposite sex. This was a great learning experience for newly separated and divorced individuals, as many were not too excited about starting the dating game all over again. These long weekends were great for building and practicing new social skills.

As I became more aware of my Aura reading abilities again, I began to spontaneously *read* for many NB members telling them what I *saw*, sometimes giving guidance on a relationship or whether a couple's energy pattern seemed compatible, etc. Angie and I had a lot of fun with that, and I would often receive feedback confirming what I said in my readings. My *New Beginnings* friends became my extended family and in many respects I became closer to these people than I ever was with members of my own family. We were there with loving support for each other during the crazy times and many of those friendships remain today. It also provided a safe environment to reopen my psychic sensitivities following my two devastating divorces. Whenever I was asked why my psychic sensitivities did not warn me about my second wife, I had to admit that I received dreams of caution but had to acknowledge that I was not paying attention to them.

Exploring Sensitivities

As Angie and I became more explorative with our sensitivities, and our ability to read and interpret Auras, we would often sit in a shopping mall and observe people to see what we could *see*. Sometimes we got the courage to actually ask our *targets* if what we *saw* or were *sensing* was valid. In a few cases we were way off but we discovered that most of the time we were quite accurate. The following pages document examples of several of our outings and experiences.

The Old Lady In The Restaurant

Angie and I had gone to the Tysons Corner Mall and sat near an escalator watching people come and go, reading what we could from their Auras and comparing notes. After about an hour, we went to a restaurant in the mall for a bite to eat and to talk about what we had picked up. An older couple was sitting in the booth behind Angie when we sat down, but neither one of us really paid much attention to them as we were seated. However, when the older couple got up to leave, Angie watched as my mouth dropped open. I turned ashen white and said, "I think I am going to be sick." I was responding to what I *saw* when the old woman stood up. I could *see* that cancer was eating away at her internal organs and although she was not in a lot of pain at that time, I *knew* that she was going to die. I also *knew* that she had not yet told her husband.

After they left I shared what I *saw* and *picked up on* with Angie so that she could understand my strange reaction. That was a very disturbing scene for me but my Spirit Guides later told me that I needed that experience so that the next time it happened, I would be fully aware of how to deal with it. I was also *told* that there was nothing I could do to change the outcome, but that I needed to pray for her and send her light and healing energy and do the same for anyone else I would *see* with a similar condition in the future.

The Dead Little Girl

One day, Angie and I visited the old *YES Metaphysical Bookstore* in Georgetown near Washington, DC to look for some books and crystals. *YES* had a reputation for having the greatest selection of religious, spiritual and metaphysical books, as well as audio and video tapes, CDs, crystals and minerals. I always felt at home there.

We spent about an hour looking around and after I found what I needed, I told Angie that I was going to the Grace Episcopal Church down the street, which had a small memorial garden out front. I felt drawn to that church for some reason and was curious about what I might *sense* or *see* there and wanted to explore it. After about thirty minutes, I picked up several interesting entities (ghosts) who were "hanging out" there and wanted to be acknowledged. Sometimes all they want is to be noticed. As is normal for me, they would appear in my mind, sometimes telling stories about how they died. That day, I became aware of one little girl about five or six years old who appeared in a very torn and tattered dress holding a dirty rag doll. I *understood* that she had been molested and then drowned in the nearby canal back in the early 1950's. I got the feeling that her murder was never solved but I also got the image that her killer was struck by a car and killed within a few days of her death. Although she did not *say* anything to me, all of this information came from her. I told her that her mommy was waiting for her in the light, but she seemed to just stand there not aware of the light that I *sensed* was all around her. I repeated that she needed to go to the light to find her mommy. Then she turned and disappeared. Several years later when I went back there, that little girl appeared to me again. This time she was holding her mother's hand and I saw her wave before they both simply disappeared. I have been back there several times over the years but have never seen her again.

The Hanging Priest

When the little girl disappeared, I turned and walked to the church. As I entered, I noticed four or five people near the front on the left-hand side talking in hushed tones with a priest. As I was watching them, I suddenly saw another priest hanging from one of the open rafters near the front of the church on the right. As I focused on the hanging priest, I realized the people near the front did not seem to notice the hanging priest and I knew I was seeing a past event. As I walked past the people engaged in conversation with the priest, he acknowledged my presence and said something like, "Blessings my son." I nodded and continued walking toward the front of the church. The priest who was hanging then opened his eyes and began to talk to me in my mind. Although most people would think they were totally crazy to have a dead person talk to them, I had gotten used to this. The hanging priest *told* me he had hung himself when one of his parishioners killed herself following the breakup of their affair. He said that he could not live with the guilt and shame. Somehow, I *knew* this happened in the mid-1950's. As I began to speak to him in my mind, he floated down from where he was hanging. I told him that he was dead, that he needed to move to the light, and to forgive himself as well as ask for forgiveness from the young girl he had harmed. As I was standing there *talking* to the dead priest, the other people turned and walked toward the entrance and left and the living priest began walking toward me. The dead priest then disappeared. The priest asked if he could help me and, being somewhat irreverent, I asked him if a priest had hung himself in this church in the mid-1950's. He was initially taken aback but then nodded, "Yes, why do you ask?" As I was explaining the hanging priest's story to the living priest, Angie entered the church and I motioned to her and said, "Come 'hang out' with us."

I smiled as Angie approached and told the priest that she *saw* dead people too. The priest laughed saying it was unusual for someone to openly tell a priest that they *saw* dead people. He said he understood because he also *saw* dead people but he did not usually reveal that piece of information to others.

Angie overheard our conversation and said "Oh one of us" and we all laughed. The priest was very interested in what the dead priest looked like and I described him as being a Polish man in his early 30's, with reddish brown hair and a rather stocky, but not fat, build. The priest laughed and said, "You did see him." And I replied, "Yeah, he was right here," and pointed to where he had been standing next to me. We thanked the priest for being honest and not reprimanding us and told him we looked forward to seeing him again sometime. As we said goodbye, I told Angie about the hanging priest and about the little girl I saw out front.

Over the next several years, I periodically visited the *YES* bookstore and would sometimes go to the church. I often *saw* the dead priest either in the chapel or in the memorial garden area in front but I never *saw* him hanging again. At some point, I stopped seeing him. I also saw the living priest who saw ghosts and he was very gracious to me, always inquiring if I saw any other dead people. At some point I stopped seeing the living priest and do not know what happened to him. I'm grateful to have met him and I appreciated being able to share my experiences with a priest who understood.

As a result of Angie and I expanding our Metaphysical understandings and psychic sensitivities, Angie started her own Spiritual Discussion Group called "Kindred Spirits"[28] in the early 1990's. She held the meetings in her home in Silver Spring, Maryland helping others expand their sensitivities. I started my own Spiritual Discussion Group a couple years before that in the Fairfax area. Several years after Angie and I first explored our past lives using the *Awareness Techniques* process, she became trained and Certified as a Past Life Regression Therapist[29] under Roger Woolger, Ph.D. Over the years she has used her knowledge from her training, her own insights, and those that we learned together in our shared experiences, to help others. Angie has become a truly gifted PLR Therapist.

NB Lecture On Auras

As I began to read Auras for *NB members*, I became known as *New Beginnings'* very own Psychic, and was asked to give a formal talk on Auras as a special guest lecture event. I realized that many of the NB members had probably never heard of an Aura, so I went to the *YES* bookstore to find a book that would explain what an Aura is. As I stood in a room stacked to the

---

[28] See: "http://metaphysics.meetup.com/335/calendar/9772348"
[29] See www.SoulBridge.net for further information or to make an appointment.

ceiling with Metaphysical books, I began praying, "Father, help me choose a book that will help me talk about Auras to this group." Almost immediately a book entitled *The New Clairvoyance: Deeper Perspectives On The Aura and Reincarnation* by Rev. Mario Schoenmaker literally fell off the fourth shelf, which I could not have reached without a ladder. I got the message and needless to say as soon as I got home I devoured the book.

New Beginnings meetings were normally held in a member's home with typically five to fifteen people at each meeting. However, when the Auras lecture was announced in the NB Newsletter, some fifty responses forced the hostess to move the meeting to a larger home to accommodate everyone. When I heard about the *"sell out"* I was compelled to acknowledge the incredible interest in this subject.

When the meeting began I asked if everyone understood what an Aura was and was not surprised to learn that several people had never heard of an Aura. There were also several skeptics in the audience who didn't believe Auras existed much less that someone could actually read them. Although the skeptics were not real vocal, some of them were somewhat antagonistic about what I was saying. It became fun for me when a skeptic would make a negative or sarcastic comment and I was able to tell them something about themselves that I could not have known. When I did so, they became quiet or asked, "How could you have known that?" For one of the attendees, I read information about a past life that was influencing her current situation and it was fun to see her skepticism transform into genuine curiosity.

Due to the tremendous interest this topic generated, I was requested to repeat the topic several times. During one of these talks, I was *picking up on* a guy sitting close to me in the circle. I told him about the scars on his right arm and pointed to where the scars were on my arm to correlate with his. He immediately stood up and started taking off his shirt. Of course all the women in the group joined in "take it off, take it all off" and everyone laughed. However, as he wiggled out of his shirt and revealed the scars just as I had described, there was a lot of murmuring. Spirit sometimes gives me an example, which helps validate what I'm *seeing* to help those who doubt.

Reading The Wrong Aura

In another one of my NB talks to about thirty people, I was reading for a member named Jim. As I read what I was *seeing* and *sensing*, he said that he could not relate to almost anything I said, which greatly puzzled me. After I had made several statements that he said were not true, I gave up, figuring I was just wrong for some reason, and went on to accurately read another person in the group. I then read for several others and was accurate for them as well. However, I left that meeting very puzzled as to why I was so wrong with Jim.

The next day, Judy called me and said she was sitting next to Jim, the guy I was so off with. She said, "Everything you said about him was true for me, but I didn't want to speak up because I couldn't believe it." She went on to say that prior to that night's meeting, she did not believe in all this "stuff." However, I was so accurate with her and with so many others at the meeting that she had to reconsider her position. I subsequently did an individual reading for her and provided her additional information about her family, including messages from her father who had died several years earlier. She later told me that my reading helped her to understand her father's premature passing, and changed her outlook on life and on psychics. She had become a true believer, and her Aura indicated that she had become a much softer and gentler person from the time I initially met her.

What I learned from that experience was that sometimes information is presented to me but it is not about the person I'm reading for. So when I find that I am way off with someone, I now know to ask the group "Who is it that I am reading for here?" That usually prompts someone to speak up and then I can proceed to read that person as needed. I do not have an explanation as to why that happens but other psychics have told me this occurs with them as well. Even well known psychics such as James Von Prague and John Edwards report in their books and on their TV shows that this sometimes happens to them as well.

Another case of reading the wrong Aura occurred several years later while facilitating an SFG Study Group in my home. One of my young students, Sonia, had brought a friend, Neal, whom she wanted me to "read" for. Neal indicated that he was skeptical but was sort of interested in what I could pick up. As we introduced ourselves to our new guest, I got the very strong sensation of a female entity who wanted to come through with a message – for whom I did not know. After everyone had introduced themselves, I began to read for Neal and received an image of a hand dipping him in "multiple vats of spirituality" as he was growing up. I told him what I *saw* and that my interpretation was that he had been exposed to spiritual and psychic material throughout his growing up years. He laughed and stated that in fact his parents were members of the A.R.E. and had been interested in this "stuff" for as long as he could remember. And yes indeed they had taken him to several A.R.E. conferences as a child and he was "exposed" at meetings his parents held in their home.

I read several other things for Neal and then was overwhelmed when the woman who had been trying to come through me earlier came to me with this great sadness, and I had to hold back the tears. I explained to the group what was happening and told Neal that this lady who was his aunt had died when he was about six years old and that she had left behind a young two-year-old son. However, Neal indicated that he had no idea what I was talking about. He had a blank stare and did not identify with anything I was saying. Finally, I simply let it go and moved on to read for others in the group but remained very puzzled and aware of that lady's presence.

The meeting went on as normal and broke up at the usual time. After almost everyone had left I told Neal and Sonia that I was very puzzled by what had happened. Then I *heard* the lady telling me her name. I said, "This lady is telling me that her name is Alice, or Ah-lee-c-ah. She keeps repeating her name over and over again." Sonia suddenly burst into tears. "Oh my God, Oh my God, that is my Aunt Alicia." She explained that her Aunt Alicia had died in a plane crash sixteen years previously when her son was two years old and Sonia was about six. That son was now eighteen and Sonia said that she had just spent the previous day with him. That connection brought Alicia into Sonia's subconscious, Sonia came to my meeting, and Alicia was allowed an avenue to come through. That is how it often works. Sonia said that when I was reading for Neal, she had not connected to the information because she thought it was for Neal. She never thought it might be for her. Thankfully, Alicia was persistent. What a beautiful and wonderful connection for both Sonia and Alicia and a tremendous confirmation for me.

Over the next several months, additional information was brought forth from Sonia's Aunt Alicia. One evening, Sonia brought her mom and several other family members with her. One of the women mentioned that her husband had passed away a year or so previously. I described the small town where they had been together and several other things about their relationship. When he came through, he was speaking Spanish, which I tried to repeat. The tears flowed as she knew I was talking about experiences I had no way of knowing about.

Thea Alexander – 2150 AD

In the spring of 1988 I was given and read a book entitled *2150 AD*[30] by Thea Alexander, a very psychically sensitive woman who was a longtime student of the Edgar Cayce material and very knowledgeable of Unity and other New Thought material. Her book is a marvelous story about a graduate

---

[30] *2150 AD* by Thea Alexander; Warner Books, Copyright 1971, 1976

student who goes forward in time during his meditations to the year 2150 AD. There he discovers a society of spiritually and psychically advanced people referred to as the Macro Society. In the book, the Macro Society consisted of highly evolved individuals who had extraordinary psychic gifts, and their societal theme was *"Let Go and Let's Grow"* meaning that you need to accept and allow rather than fight life. There was neither jealousy nor envy in that society, only love and acceptance. All children were raised to use their innate psychic sensitivities and there was a hierarchy within the Macro society starting with the lowest level of awareness called *"Aton"* to the highest level of awareness called *"Macro"* as indicated below.

1-Alpha, 2-Beta, 3-Gamma, 4-Delta, 5-Aton, 6-Zton, 7-Kton, 8-Muton, 9-Maxon, 10-Macro

The Macro Society also had a very large computer referred to as CI (Central Information) that you could talk to and which would provide verbal answers. CI knew everything and was the avenue through which you were quizzed to determine what level (Aton –> Macro) you should be included in. When you had advanced to the next level you did so through testing by CI and other advanced guides and leaders.

After reading her book I was so impressed with the metaphysical content and the story that I wrote to Thea stating that I thought writing a book like that must have changed her life. Little did I know how true that statement was. Shortly after I sent the letter, I received a phone call from Thea stating that she was coming to the Washington, DC area the following month and she would like to meet with me. She also told me about a Macro Society Group that had sprung up as a result of her book and she invited me to join it, which I did.

When Thea came to DC I went to the meeting but arrived about five minutes late. The room was almost filled, with only a couple of seats left in the back. As I entered the room, Thea stopped her talk in mid-sentence and said, "You must be Lowell?" I was embarrassed but said, "Yes." As I went to the back to find a seat she continued, "I have been expecting you," which made almost everyone turn around to see who I was and made me even more embarrassed. She then continued where she had left off. Following her lecture, a question was asked about *life's lessons* and why we come to the earth plane, and why certain people seemed to come in with advanced knowledge and psychic abilities, like people in the Macro world from her book. Thea answered the question then explained to the group; "For example, Lowell here (I had not told her anything about me in our previous phone conversation) came in for a post doctorate study program." She went on the say that "he has been here many times before as an advanced teacher and he retains, or is beginning to open up to, a lot of those memories." She continued, "We have met in the past (meaning a past life) but he has not yet connected to when. That will come in due time." I was floored. Thea then said to the group, "Oh by the way, Lowell and I have never met each other in this lifetime prior to tonight and I have not discussed this with him." There was that quiet murmur that flows throughout an audience.

After the program and some very interesting Q&A, several participants talked with Thea and I stayed in my seat trying to figure out what all had been said and what she had meant. Thea motioned for me to come to her, and introduced me to her husband Michael. She thanked me for the letter I had written, and talked to me about her upcoming annual Macro Society retreat. She said that she was glad to finally make contact with me and that I would be hearing from her. She told me that I should look for her on the "inner planes" and in my sleep. I thanked her, purchased several tapes and books and left.

A week later I saw her whole body, not just her face, in one of my meditations and in one of my dreams. She seemed to be telling me to remember this contact. She told me something, which I wrote down at the time. About two weeks later Thea called me asking me to contribute an article to the Macro Newsletter and asked me if I had seen her about a week previously in my dreams or "on the inner planes." I read my Dream Journal to her, which stated in the dream that we would be collaborating on something in the near future. She confirmed that she had attempted to communicate this in my dreams and that I should pay attention. I continued to *see* her on the inner planes and in my dreams.

Shortly after my meeting with Thea, I shared one of the books I purchased with my soul sister Angie. She devoured it and also became very interested in the Macro Society.

As I learned more about the The Macro Society groups I discovered they have a *Creed*, which I found to be particularly appealing and in alignment with the way I desired to live my daily life. I have included it on the following page. It can also be found on the following website.

http://www.donalexander.com/MacroSociety/Pages/MacroSoc.html

The Macro Creed

I Believe in the Macrocosmic oneness of all,
and in myself as a perfectly functioning
aspect of that Macrocosm.
I Believe that I, and only I,
have the honor and the power
to determine, to design and to alter
whatever my daily life contains,
for it is the result of my own thoughts.
I Believe that there are as many paths
as there are people to walk them,
and that each person is the best judge
of which path they will most effectively walk
at any given time.
I seek the adventure of interaction with others
knowing it is the classroom of my evolution.
I joyously receive this and everyday
knowing it is the canvas upon which
I am painting my life.

Macro Society Retreat in Colorado

A few months after I met Thea in DC, I attended the Annual Macro Society Retreat in the mountains of Colorado where Thea introduced me to a lot of other people. She explained that I was psychically sensitive. I soon discovered that although many were interested in the same things I was, most of them were not psychically sensitive like myself. They just wanted to learn more about it. The focus of the retreat was on what it meant to be *"Macro"* and how one would go about creating a similar environment in the current time frame.

One evening a male and two female Native American Shamans came and performed a Drumming Ceremony for the retreat participants. We lay on our backs on the floor in several circles, with our heads at the center of the circle. There were about ten people in each circle. The Shamans began drumming and chanting while we all tried to tune into whatever we could tune into. As the drumming began, I began chanting along with the leaders and soon found myself out of my body looking down at the scene, while my body was chanting. Somehow I knew the words, the tune, and the rhythm.

As the chanting increased in volume and intensity, I *saw* myself in a past life as a minor Native American chieftain. My teenage son had been killed by the white men while he was out hunting game. It was a useless killing. Never having been a parent in this lifetime, I was totally surprised at how *"into"* the feeling I got. I became consciously aware of a deep physical pain in my chest as I lay there going through this experience. I then apparently let out a cry that startled some people and began speaking in a voice and language that was clearly not mine.

The drumming stopped and the Chief Shaman began recording what I was saying. Apparently I was speaking in an ancient tongue they recognized but did not completely understand. This went on for several minutes and then I began chanting again and they picked back up on the drumming. When they stopped the drumming and I came out of whatever state I was in, I felt completely drained and very sad. When they played back the recording, the male Shaman explained that I was speaking in an ancient language and stated that this was a powerful expression of my connection to my past. He asked me about my ancestry and smiled when he learned of my Native American heritage. He said something to Thea about my being one of the Ancient ones – the Anasazi.

NV Mid-Atlantic Retreat – 2150 AD

When I was on the Northern Virginia A.R.E. Mid-Atlantic Retreat Committee with my Soul Sister Angie, I suggested that we invite Thea Alexander as our guest speaker for the following year, and have her talk about the Macro Way of thinking. Angie and I explained that she was a long-time A.R.E. member and had written an extremely powerful metaphysical book. The committee liked the idea and thought it would be a nice shift from the usual A.R.E. speakers.

The following week I contacted Thea and learned that she was available, her fee was reasonable, and she would be delighted to be our guest speaker. She then said, "Remember your dream? I guess this is what we were to be collaborating on." The Committee Chairperson was grateful to have a New Thought person as a speaker, and we began planning our weekend retreat around the *2150 AD* theme using the title, *"Creating Your Own Future Now."*

As part of the preparation each of the committee members read Thea's book, really liked the concepts presented, and everyone was looking forward to meeting Thea. In an attempt to incorporate the Macro Society principles into the retreat, the committee decided to use the Macro Society levels (1-Aton through 10-Macro) on each workshop attendee's name tag. However, there was some concern about people being assigned to a lower Macro level than they thought they should be, so we chose to make it a random drawing by the attendee when they checked in. That way they (and their subconscious) were the ones to choose what level they would be associated with that weekend.

Holographic Macro Symbols

The committee met once a month at various committee members' homes, including my apartment. One meeting as we were sitting on my L-shaped sofa discussing how we could use each of the Macro Society levels (1-Aton through 10-Macro) as part of the nametags, I began seeing a 3D holographic image of a symbol for each of the Macro society levels.

Note to the reader: The book, 2150 AD, does not specify any symbols associated with the Macro 'levels' so there was no way of 'checking' whether what I 'picked up' was valid or not. I simply went with what I was presented.

As the rotating 3D holographic images began to appear, I excitedly pointed to where they were and asked if anybody could *see* what I was *seeing*. Everyone said, "No." I then described what I was *seeing* as the images continued to rotate and pulsate. For those familiar with the *Star Wars* movie, the images appeared very similar to the images that R2D2 robot projected. They were so real and powerful to me that I became frustrated that nobody else could *see* them. I kept saying, "Can't you see them, can't you see them?" However, in spite of some members seriously trying to look to see what I was *seeing*, nobody else could see them – not even Angie.

The rotating and pulsating 3D holographic images continued to appear and as they appeared, I *heard* what each image meant and began writing it down. As I drew the image and wrote the meaning of each symbol, the next image would appear and its meaning would come to me. This lasted for well over an hour. When I had drawn all ten images and wrote down what they meant, the hologram simply disappeared. Over the next few months following that initial appearance, I only *saw* the images that way a few more times as I created 4" x 6" cards of them. After the retreat I tried to recreate that experience several other times, but could not.

When I told Thea about my experience with these 3D holographic symbols for the various Macro Society levels and provided her with a set of the 4" x 6" cards of them, she told me that they were fascinating, but that she could not validate whether the symbols accurately portrayed the levels. I have included these images and their meaning in an Appendix to satisfy the readers' curiosity.

Playing CI

At Angie's suggestion, the *2150 AD* Retreat Committee decided that as part of the *"entertainment"* on Saturday evening we would offer to have people dress up as they thought they might dress in 2150 AD. Angie also suggested that I play CI (Central Information). Her plan was for me to go into an altered state and allow participants from the audience to ask questions – any questions. Since everyone knew I was psychic, we all thought it would be great fun. We put a pillow on top of a coffee table with a white sheet hanging in front of it. I sat behind the sheet on the pillow and with our creative back lighting all the audience could see was my shadow. I was dressed in a white monk's robe and wore a white headband. Angie acted as moderator, taking questions from the audience. We agreed not to share our plan with Thea or anyone outside the committee. We simply told everyone that Saturday evening was to be a "come as you would dress in 2150 AD," and that there would be some *"unique"* entertainment.

When Saturday night arrived, Angie kicked it off by explaining that The Mid-Atlantic Committee had brought CI from 2150 AD into the present, and they turned the backlight on. I sat on the table and had already prepared myself to channel – I was in an altered state. Since many people were not familiar with CI, Angie explained what CI was and then opened it up to questions.

People began asking questions, some very personal and some very grandiose like, "What is the meaning of 2012?" I was amazed that I was able to give answers, many of which I had no cognitive knowledge. After several questions were asked and answered, to the amazement of the questioner and others in the audience, Thea asked a serious question which I apparently answered accurately. As it became obvious that CI could answer all kinds of questions, the questions became more pointed, intense and important for everyone present. It ceased to be entertainment and became an adventure in learning. When Angie stopped the questions, I came out of trance and emerged from behind the sheet to a rousing applause and the evening then proceeded with snacks, dancing, lots of talk and just plain fun.

Shortly after the channeling session, Thea and her husband Michael approached Angie and me and said that she knew I was sensitive, but that she had no idea that I was capable of doing what I did. I laughed and said, "I didn't either." She was very appreciative and said she would reference my psychic abilities in her remaining talks the following day. She said over and over, "How did you guys come up with that great idea?" Angie's response was precious, "Well we have the real thing here and he's not a computer," at which point Michael burst out laughing.

The lesson I learned from that experience was that I was capable of channeling information if I just allowed myself to *"get out of my own way"* and simply let the information flow through me. That was a very valuable lesson. A few days later, my Spirit Guides told me that much of the information came from *"the records"* meaning the *Akashic Records*. It was a very positive and valuable experience, and was actually a lot of fun.

Following the successful 2150 AD Mid-Atlantic Conference, I became re-energized about my Metaphysical and Spiritual/Religious studies. I continued my active involvement in *New Beginnings* and continued my communication with Macro Society members throughout the United States. I also contributed several short articles for the Macro Newsletter. However, my focus remained on trying to succeed in my job.

Meeting Dotti

As I continued making friends in *New Beginnings* I met several people with whom I felt particularly close. One such lady was Dee (now deceased) who had a rather large house in Springfield, Virginia and often threw great parties. When I first met Dee I was very impressed by her wonderfully bright (mostly white) Aura that indicated a strong Spiritual connection. However, I later learned that she was somewhat reticent about spiritual matters. She was clearly curious about my psychic sensitivities and always respectful of them, but she was also somewhat afraid of them. I can still see her as she "rolled her big blue eyes" at some of my "other world" comments.

In the spring of 1995, Dee was in charge of the NB Memorial Day Weekend Get Away held at the Wintergreen resort. As such, she got to decide who would be in her cabin. Dee included me as well as several other NB friends she knew, and a new NB friend of hers named Dotti Maraney (now McKee). I later learned that Dee decided to play "match maker" and told Dotti that I was going to be in the cabin and that although I was a little "weird" she thought Dotti might like me.

As a tradition, a couple of weeks before the weekend retreat the cabin members got together at someone's house to iron out the cabin details: plan the traditional cabin party, decide who would bring what food, who would bring what music and what games, who would cook, clean up, and plan the sleeping arrangements. It was a hard rule that there was absolutely no sleeping around.

The day of the cabin meeting, I had gone to a doctor to get the results of an MRI. Some earlier blood tests indicated the possibility of a brain tumor, specifically a pituitary tumor. The MRI showed a non-malignant pituitary tumor that was increasing in size. The prognosis was that although it was not cancerous and thus not terminal, unless it could be shrunk through medication or operated on and removed, it could possibly impinge on the optic nerve and cause me to go blind. I was really not concerned about dying, in fact I felt that perhaps I could do more good on the other side than I was doing on this side. My two ex-wives were draining me financially and trying, whenever they could, to otherwise disrupt my life. They were constantly telling me "I owed them" so at the time I was just not enjoying life very much, and I related more with "the other side" than I did with this side. However, the prognosis that I might go blind was unacceptable to me. The doctor gave me a lot of literature to read about pituitary tumors and a prescription to shrink the tumor and reduce its side effects. Following my doctor's appointment, I headed straight for the NB cabin meeting.

When I arrived, everyone was already partying, so even though the doctor told me to hold off on the alcohol, I immediately "popped a cold one" and drank it down. A couple of beers later I was feeling better and loosened up a bit. I was introduced to my cabin mates, most of whom I did not know but was open to listening to them and learning "their story." As an NB Facilitator, I had learned to do that very well. Although I was feeling a little down I tried to put my feelings in my back pocket, but "darling Dee" *sensed* that I was a little depressed and in an attempt to cheer me up told everyone, "Lowell here is a psychic and can answer all of life's questions!" and then just chuckled. This of course pulled me into the center of the conversation and I had to concentrate on the questions my cabin mates began to ask. What was going to happen with their pending divorces? With their ex-spouses? With their lawyers? On and on and I just answered as the information came to me. Toward the end of the evening, Dotti said, "I just want to know if I will have a companion in my life." I responded, "You've already met him, you just don't know him yet" and went on to answer someone else's question. At the time I had no idea that it might be ME that "Spirit" was referring to.

After the sleeping arrangements, meals, housekeeping and other details were completed and I had eaten and drunk enough, I left the party to try to figure out what I was going to do about this damn pituitary tumor thing.

Dotti's Dilemma

I later learned from Dotti that following that cabin get-together, she drove past her old family home in Annandale where her ex-husband still lived. She had been thinking that perhaps they should try reconciliation. She later told me that since I had told her "You've already met him" (which was the only part that she heard), as she drove she went through the names of every guy she ever knew. She couldn't think of one guy that she had already met that she would be interested in as a future companion, including her estranged husband. What she realized was that what she wanted was the financial security and the house and the family togetherness and the mutual friends and the history and the good times she and her ex-husband had shared. When she told me this, I reminded her that my full statement was "You've already met him, you just don't know him yet!" She said that hearing only part of my statement helped her clarify that what she really wanted was a compatible and loving relationship.

Following the NB Memorial Day weekend, Dotti and I recognized that we were attracted to each other and decided to get together to see if we were at all compatible. After a couple of dates we learned that we had a great many interests in common. On our second date, I told Dotti that I was being sent to Orlando, Florida for six months to begin working on a proposal for my company. Although most people would say, "I'm out-of-here," Dotti and I looked upon the move positively because it would allow us to explore a romantic relationship slowly. That next Monday I drove my van to Orlando and rented a small condo in a gated community. I spent the next six months there working and flying back to Northern Virginia every couple of weeks. Dotti would fly down alternate Fridays and spend the weekend, then fly back to DC early Monday morning returning to her job at a DC law firm. That arrangement allowed us to be together and more slowly explore whether we wanted to continue in our relationship.

Dotti's Dad

One Saturday morning Dotti and I woke up in my Florida condo and I began talking to Dotti about her father, who had died a couple years before we met. She had not yet talked about her dad so I knew nothing about him. However, that morning I woke up with him talking to me incessantly. We had plans to visit the Epcot Center at Disney World that day, and as I began telling her what he was telling me, she told me that her dad had always wanted to go to Disney World but her Mom couldn't walk very well and wouldn't use a wheel chair, so he never got to go there. That morning he was excited about going with us and began telling me all kinds of things in a stream of communication. At some point I heard him say the word "Dort" several times. When I asked Dotti what the name "Dort" meant, she told me that was her dad's nickname for her! She knew then that I was talking to her dad. Her dad told me that he loved to invent things, and that he was, "really looking forward to going to Disney World." So that day, Dotti and I enjoyed taking her dad to Disney World! When we got to the Epcot Center, her dad was right there with us telling me all kinds of things all day long, which I shared with Dotti. I got to know Dotti's dad through my experiences that day and Dotti got to see how Spirit expressed though me. A few months later, Dotti and I attended a James Von Praagh event in Baltimore, Maryland and as we sat waiting for the event to start, Dotti sensed her dad's presence and stated that she *felt* that he had brought us together.

Becoming A Metaphysical Teacher

Shortly after I returned from my assignment in Orlando, I went to a reunion of former SBS (Satellite Business Systems) employees with whom I had worked for about five years. I was expecting to simply go, introduce my new girlfriend, Dotti, to a few of my former colleagues, and just stay a short while. However, Dotti bumped into and struck up a conversation with my former second line manager, Alan T without knowing who he was. When Alan told her about his new interest and study of Spirituality and Metaphysics, Dotti told Alan that she was also interested in Metaphysics and that her "partner" had been involved in Metaphysics for a long time and, in fact, taught Metaphysical classes. She also told him that I was a psychic. She brought Alan over to where I was standing and told me about his new interest. I said, "That's great" and he replied, "I never knew that about you?" I responded, "Well, it wasn't something that I really talked about at work."

Alan then told me that a mutual friend from SBS, Alexa, who was not there that evening, was having a very difficult time because she had lost two husbands, both named Ted, within the span of about a year, and Alan wondered if I could talk to her and see what I could *pick up*. I arranged to meet with Alan and Alexa that following week. I went to Alexa's place with Alan and after some introductory conversation, I began *reading* for her and bringing forth information from her two deceased husbands – things which I could not have known. I was grateful for the information that came through, and she appreciated being able to talk to someone who could actually communicate with her late husbands. It gave her a great sense of comfort to *know* that both of her husbands were OK.

Starting A Spiritual Discussion Group

Shortly after I helped Alexa "communicate" with her deceased husbands, she and Alan asked if I would begin to teach them about Spirituality and Metaphysics and help them develop their own psychic sensitivities. We formed a Spiritual Discussion Group with Alexa, Alan and his wife Connie, Dotti, and myself. We began meeting once a week in Alexa's home since it was a central location for all of us, and agreed to read and discuss the Edgar Cayce Search For God material, as well as other Spiritual or Metaphysical books. Both Alan and Alexa were fast and voracious readers and although I had a hard time keeping up with their reading, my Spirit Guides made sure that I was always able to help the group with difficult concepts they had read in their books.

One meeting Alexa showed us an interesting book that she was reading and handed it to me and asked me what I thought. I looked at the title, table of contents, and then flipped to a couple of pages when I *heard*, "Hold it to your forehead and we will help you *read* it." I thought, "What the hell" and held it to my forehead and *got* or *knew* what the book was about. I began telling the group what the book was about, how it was written – the style, important information it was trying to convey, etc. Alexa confirmed that what I said about the book was true and just shook her head. I thus learned that I could put a book to my forehead and *read* it – at least pick up the general theme, etc. That process helped me a great deal when they came to a meeting with a new book. It became a joke within the group that they would read a book and I would put it to my forehead and learn what they had read. I pointed out however, that my *reading* was not the same as their reading. I still had to struggle through a book and it was a significantly slower process for me – it still is.

Spontaneous Channeling

One evening Alan invited a lady friend visiting from California to the group discussion. She was a former employee of Alan's when he worked at Oracle, who was very interested in Metaphysics. Alan was constantly asking very complex questions but I could usually follow him and provide an answer that satisfied him and the group. However, on this particular evening, Alan asked a particularly difficult question and as I began thinking about how to answer it, I found myself being pushed out of my body and feeling this different energy "take over." I began speaking in a very different voice. That entity then very pointedly yet gently answered Alan's question.

Although the communication only lasted 3-4 minutes, it was very powerful and focused for all members present. I then snapped back into my body and my consciousness, shook my head, and asked, "What was that all about?" Everyone just laughed. I described to the group what I had just experienced and they in turn described to me what had been said. We all realized that I had been pushed aside because a Master Being/Entity needed to answer the question for Alan and the group. We all agreed that the power of that entity's presence was palpable.

That type of *Spontaneous Channeling* process has continued periodically during group meetings (my SFG and my *Indigos & Sensitives Groups*) and we usually keep a recorder present to capture the information because I usually do not remember what is said, only the general gist of the information that is delivered.

The Be Your Own Psychic Conference

In the spring of 1996 I was drawn to attend the *Be Your Own Psychic Conference* at A.R.E. headquarters in Virginia Beach, which was taught by Carol Ann Liaros and Dr. Henry Reed. This conference was designed to teach attendees how to tap into and recognize their own natural psychic sensitivities, and as I later learned, was a required course to become a field-tested Psychic for the A.R.E. My primary interest in attending was to learn what Carol Ann and Dr. Reed had to say about the subject, as well as hear about their own psychic sensitivities and experiences.

As I drove to the conference I thought back to the days when I first met Hugh Lynn Cayce and how strongly he had discouraged me from exploring my psychic sensitivities and how Eula Allen had told me to ignore Hugh Lynn's advice, but to "work on developing both" – my spirituality and my psychic sensitivities. Here I was going to an A.R.E. conference that was specifically designed to help people explore and develop their psychic sensitivities. I just smiled internally at the irony.

Carol Ann and Henry began the conference by stating that all of us have some psychic (beyond our five physical senses) sensitivities, but that most people either ignore them, discount them, or don't know how to interpret them. They explained that without training, most people don't know what those sensitivities or experiences look or feel like. They indicated that psychic experiences can be categorized as *Clairsentience* (clear sensing), *Clairvoyance* (clear seeing), *Clairaudience* (clear hearing), *Claircognizance* (clear knowing), or *Clairgustance* (clear tasting or smelling) and combinations of these senses, which I had learned previously. Carol Ann and Henry designed the conference and exercises to help the attendees recognize the psychic sensitivities and experiences they *do* have, and provided them with techniques to help them expand and develop their awareness of those experiences. They explained that intuition and the awareness of synchronicities[31] were forms of psychic sensitivity.

I have a slightly different view on this. From my understanding, intuition is the 'sixth sense' whereas psychic sensitivities such as

---

[31] Synchronicity is the experience of two or more events that are seemingly unrelated occurring together in a meaningful way. To count as synchronicity, the events should be unlikely to occur together by chance.

seeing Auras and seeing and communicating with ghosts, Spirit Guides and Angels are examples of the 'seventh or higher' senses.

Carol Ann shared that her own remembrances of Hugh Lynn were not unlike mine. She also told of the difficulties she and Dr. Reed had in coming up with a format for a conference that would be well-grounded in Spirituality while helping people understand, experiment with, and develop their own psychic sensitivities. I found the conference to be extremely well designed, with many experiments to help conferees expand their awareness and understanding of their own sensitivities.

One of the highlights of the conference for me was a video of Carol Ann teaching blind people to *see* using their natural and developed psychic sensitivities.[32] Part of the video was a documentary experiment conducted in a Buffalo, New York studio with Carol Ann and a young blind girl. The blind girl was asked to describe a "target" location and the detailed interior of a house at that location (a Remote Viewing experiment). The video documented what she described or *saw* there, along with film footage of what was actually at the location. Carol Ann then explained to our group that when they did the interview and filming, she thought that the film crew would tell her and the blind girl how she had done. But they told her that they couldn't do that because they had not been to the "target" location yet and had not seen any pictures of it. Carol Ann said that the film crew left immediately following the interview and went to the "target" location and began filming. The resulting video that we saw was created by dubbing the young girl's words describing what she *saw* with the video the crew shot from the actual location. It was amazingly accurate in almost every detail, and where she was "off" Carol Ann explained the components that were "inaccurate" and why, which was very helpful in understanding how *psychic* information is presented. The video was truly amazing.

Throughout the conference I heard my Spirit Guides periodically say, "Pay attention" and "Notice the energy differences of each of the other attendees." Although I did not fully comprehend exactly what I was to be noticing, I did pay attention and wrote down in my journal what I *saw, felt, heard* and *sensed*. Only later did I come to more fully recognize and understand some of the more subtle energy differences that I *saw, felt, heard* and *sensed*. By concentrating my awareness on the single sensitivity

---

[32] See Carol Ann Liaros' web site:
    http://www.creativespirit.net/CarolAnnLiaros/2005/cal.home.html

modality that was being talked about, (i.e. *Clairsentience*) and consciously ignoring all the other modes of awareness, (i.e. *Clairvoyance and Clairaudience*) I became much more aware of the subtle energy differences that I was picking up with each individual sensitivity. Then when I combined the different modalities, I was much more accurate in my readings of other attendees. When I shared this with Carol Ann and a couple of other psychics, they said they found this process to be very helpful as well. Several months later when I developed the exercises for my own *Spiritual & Psychic Development Workshop,*[33] I based them on the information I picked up at the *Be Your Own Psychic Conference*, but included more consolidated, concentrated, and detailed instructions that I received from my Spirit Guides as I developed that workshop.

As the conference progressed, I periodically *heard* Hugh Lynn say that he was pleased with how the conference seemed to be helping people integrate their spiritual understandings with their psychic sensitivities. On the last day, as I left the conference and proceeded to drive home, I again thought about the many conversations I had with Hugh Lynn and noted how his Spirit had become much softer and accepting. It was clear to me that Hugh Lynn's Spirit approved of A.R.E.'s successful conference on psychic sensitivities.

Following this conference, I intensified my exploration and development of my own psychic sensitivities and discovered that as a result of this conference I had indeed increased my sensitivities in each of the individual modalities I experienced. I would highly recommend this conference to anyone interested in exploring and expanding their psychic sensitivities.

Becoming A Metaphysical Teacher

As word spread that I was leading a Spiritual Discussion Group, several additional people joined and we began meeting at the Unity of Fairfax Church in Oakton. We continued to study various Spiritual, Psychic, and Religious topics while using the Edgar Cayce SFG material as the primary focus of our group discussions.

I re-joined the Northern Virginia A.R.E. Council and was asked to speak at an *SFG Study Group Inquirer's Meeting*, which introduced the Edgar Cayce SFG principles to potential members. When it was my turn to speak, I talked about what our SFG Study Group was studying, and about the *Indigos*

---

[33] See Spiritual & Psychic Development Workshops in Chapter 7

& *Psychically Sensitive Teens and Adults Support Group* I had started a short time earlier. I then did mini Aura readings for several members in the audience. I identified several young adults in that meeting who expressed the *Indigo* and *Crystal* energy patterns and suggested that the *Indigos & Sensitives Group* might be helpful to them. From that Inquirer's meeting, several people joined the *Indigos & Sensitives Group*, several joined our SFG Study Group, and some joined both groups.

At that Inquirer's Meeting I received a lot of intense questioning about Ghosts, Auras and energy patterns, Dreams, Karma, the Archangelic Realm, and Meditation, and realized that there were no workshops on these topics available in the Northern Virginia area. I decided to develop some in-depth workshops on these topics to help address this interest. The next day in my meditation, I *saw* Eula Allen's face and realized that I was being called on to be a Metaphysical teacher just as she and that Swami that I met at Unity so many years before had told me I needed to become.

Over the next few weeks I created workshops on: *Auras – What they Are & How to Read Them, Spiritual & Psychic Development, Discovering Your Soul's Purpose, Indigo & Crystal Children, Meditation – Pathway to Enlightenment,* and eventually a workshop on *Past Life Regression.* I continue doing many of these workshops.

An Egyptian Book of the Dead Ritual

A year or so after I started the SFG Study Group, several people in our group expressed an interest in how the Ancient Egyptians approached and prepared for death, so we decided to study of *The Egyptian Book of the Dead.* After looking at several different texts, we chose Dr. Ramses Seleem's book[34] as our text. I mention our study of this text not because I want to talk about the Egyptian Book of the Dead, but because of a specific ritual that we read about in that text.

As we were reading about how the Ancient Egyptian High Priests selected the students who were ready for advanced training, I experienced a past life recall where I was one of those high priests making the selection of students. I *saw* myself hold out my hand – palm up, in which I created a ball of light about 8"-10" in diameter. The Ancient Egyptian test was that if the students held out their hand and also created a ball of light they were ready, if they

---

[34] *The Egyptian Book of the Dead* by Dr. Ramses Seleem, copyright © Godsfield Press, 2001

didn't they were not ready. I excitedly shared my experience with the group and then attempted to repeat that exercise and discovered by concentrating I could in fact produce that ball of light. As I held my hand out and created the ball of light, some in the group said that they saw a light emanating from my hand, but on that particular evening nobody in the group actually *saw* the ball that I had created. However, when I would periodically repeat this process in the group, several group members reported that they were beginning to *see* and sometimes just *sense* the ball of light.

Some time later, I was conducting an *Indigo & Crystal* Children Workshop and was talking about Auras to a young *Indigo/Crystal* girl about twelve years old. As I was talking to her, I heard in my head, "Create the ball of light." I held out my hand and began creating the "ball of light" and asked her, "What do I have in my hand?" In a very low voice, she very sheepishly said, "A ball of light?" and I said, "YES, now you create one." She bravely held out her hand and as she concentrated, sure enough, a small ball of light began forming in her hand. Her energy became much stronger and she smiled as she realized that she could do it. The *Indigo* girl next to her repeated the same exercise and was also able to create a small ball of light. I then explained to the entire audience what had just happened and that this was an exercise I used as a High Priest in Ancient Egypt to select which students were ready for advanced study. I said, "They are obviously ready," and everyone laughed.

I have repeated that exercise many times in my various workshops and almost always the *Indigos* and *Crystals* can *see* or *sense* the ball of light. Some are able to reproduce it, which to me is very encouraging. When I repeated this exercise in my *Indigos & Sensitives* class, Kat, a 20's something *Indigo/Crystal*, found that she could produce a small ball of light. I suggested that she to go home and repeat the exercise for her 6-year-old psychically sensitive *Crystal* son, Colton, and report back to the group what his reaction was. At the next meeting, she excitedly said that the next day she held her hand out to her son and he responded, "What is that pyramid doing in that ball in your hand mommy?" She was both shocked and pleased. I sometimes repeat this "exercise" with children I meet in a library, a church setting, or just in a store, and enjoy seeing a child creating a ball of light in their hand spontaneously. This *ball of light* exercise makes a significant and lasting impact even though it kind of freaks out some of the parents.

Auras and Energy Patterns

For me the Aura has always presented itself as a constantly changing pattern of colors, or "blotches" of color, and *"bands"* of color that overlap and interact as they come to the front and then fade to the back forming what I call Energy Patterns. When I concentrate on a color or area of colors that are present, they typically increase and/or decrease in intensity and complexity as I read the information. Only when I concentrate on what is being presented do they "distinguish" themselves as being information about the Etheric, Astral or higher levels of consciousness information. My belief and experience is that a person's Aura reflects what that person is thinking about or experiencing at that moment (their physical and emotional state) as well as what is going on with them psychically and perhaps spiritually. Although I constantly hear people ask, "What color is my Aura?" I have never experienced a person with only one or two colors. From my perspective, everyone has a large array of different colors that are constantly changing as I interact with them. Their Aura colors and patterns may be muted or bright but, from my observations, everyone has this multi-colored Aura pattern.

When I read the book, *The New Clairvoyance: Deeper Perspectives On The Aura and Reincarnation* by Rev. Mario Schoenmaker, which I mentioned in the last chapter, my awareness of what information is contained in an Aura expanded greatly. I had never really thought about Auras in terms of layers or levels, but Rev. Schoenmaker's three-layer model provided me a framework that I could relate to.

Armed with this "model," as I read for *New Beginnings* members, people within our SFG Study Group, and attendees at other A.R.E. functions, I began to distinguish various patterns in and levels or layers of the Aura and thus began to more fully understand that there was a great deal more information in a persons Aura than I previously recognized.

A Three Layer Aura Model

The three-layer Aura model described in Rev. Schoenmaker's book, made a lot of sense to me. However, as I have studied and examined the Aura patterns of many people over the past few years since I read that book, I have a greater understanding of what each of those layers or levels relate to, and what they tell us.

Rev. Schoenmaker lists the Aura layers as: the **Etheric Aura,** the **Astral Aura** and the **I Am Aura,** which he refers to as *"bodies."* In the following discussion, I describe what Rev. Schoenmaker says about each Aura level or "body" and include my experiences about what I *see* and believe about each of these Aura expressions. I have included some specific examples of each of these Auric fields, because I believe examples are one of life's best teaching tools.

The Etheric Aura

Rev. Schoenmaker states that the **Etheric Aura** or "body" consists of an energy field that extends about two to three inches around the entire physical body, and that all living things – plants, insects, animals, and humans – have this Aura. He says that this Aura consists of a striated energy field and is the one that Kirlian photography captures. See the photos of Kirlian photos of a hand, and an Apple I found on the following web sites.

> http://www.webpan.com/dscinclair/kirlian-fingerprints.jpg
> http://www.swordmagick.com/images/kirlian/apple.jpg

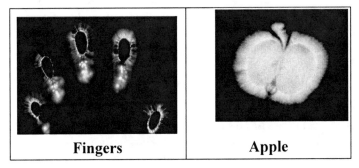

| Fingers | Apple |

My experience agrees with Rev. Schoenmaker's explanation. However, I have come to believe that this field (or Aura) is generated as a result of *"life force"* passing through a body's neural system, much like an electromagnetic field is generated when electricity passes through a wire. Although, Rev. Schoenmaker does not state this in his book, I believe this explanation is true because from my experience whenever I see someone with a missing limb – a finger, hand, leg, I usually see the Etheric Aura of the missing body part. Also, these people report that they have *"phantom pain"* or feelings associated with the missing body part. I have concluded that although the physical body has been healed, the **Etheric Aura** (or body) has not been healed. I have also discovered that when a healing has been performed by an acupuncturist or Reike Healer, etc., the person being healed no longer experiences pains or sensations AND I no longer *see* the Etheric Aura associated with that missing body part.

Most everyone can *sense* or sometimes *see* the Etheric Aura and I include an exercise in my *Auras Workshops* and my *Spiritual & Psychic*

Development Workshops to help participants awaken this ability. From my experience, all *New Age Kids – Indigos, Crystals* and *Star children*, are able to *sense* and often *see* the Etheric Aura once they know what to look for and learn how to *sense* into it.

My Grandma Hazel's Father

When I was a small boy about six or eight years old, we would visit my grandma Hazel's father who lived in Detroit. The first time I saw him, I was very taken aback because he had a *"peg-leg"* just like in the pirate movies. He was an avid Snooker player (a game similar to pool) with a table in the upper part of the house and sometimes he would take my brother and me up there and let us shoot. Although I did not understand what I was *seeing* at that time in my life, I am fairly certain that much of my curiosity about my step-great-grandfather's peg-leg revolved around why he would rub the outside of his leg near his knee and sometimes tap and/or try to scratch his peg-leg with his Snooker cue. Sometimes he'd comment that his missing lower leg hurt, and I would say, "I'm sorry" as if I could do something about it, and he'd say "thank you" and continue rubbing. Based on that memory, I am convinced that he had *"phantom pain"* or sensations, indicating that his **Etheric Aura** was not healed. Too bad I did not have my current understanding; perhaps I could have helped him heal.

> *If your child, or you, sees someone with a missing body part, allow them, or yourself, to be curious and question what it is you or they are 'seeing' or 'sensing.' It will help validate the experience, whatever it is. Then send light and love to that person with the missing body part.*

The Young Man With The Missing Arm

At an A.R.E. conference in Virginia Beach, during a break I was standing in the crowded lobby along with many others, when a young man in his early twenties walked past me. Although I did not actually see him or pay attention to him as he passed by, as he did so I saw this full motion video in my mind's eye. He was a Roman soldier/senator whose name was Plautius (or something similar to that) who had just returned from a foreign war and could not locate an item he was looking for. He accused one of his young servants of taking it. When the young servant denied the theft, Plautius demanded the servant get his sword, which he obediently did. When he returned, Plautius again accused the servant of stealing what he could not find and the young servant again pleaded his innocence. Somehow I believed the servant. However, I *saw* Plautius take the sword and chop off his young servant's left arm next to the shoulder. The scene was a flash in time and went away as quickly as it had come. As I turned toward the young man I noticed he was missing his left arm at the shoulder. I knew that what I was *seeing* was a past life Karmic debt being paid by this young man.

When I glanced over at the young man, his **Etheric Aura** associated with his missing arm was very prominent and seemed to throb or pulsate with pain energy. I *"understood"* he was in pain most of the time. When I went to talk to him about what I saw and to ask about how he lost his arm, and hopefully help him with his pain, he was not open to hearing it and walked away from me. However, two other young people he was talking with were very interested. When I expressed to them my concern about his constant pain, they confirmed that indeed his missing arm constantly hurt. They told me that he had lost his arm in a car accident a little over a year previously and was still very bitter. Hopefully this young man will one day come to grips with his past Karmic debt and begin to heal. All I can do is pray and send healing light of forgiveness to him and the one he injured.

The Little Girl With The Missing Leg

This past year (2008) when I was in Costa Rica visiting a Unity Church in San Juan, I noticed a little six-year-old girl on crutches with one leg missing below the knee. As I looked at her I was puzzled because I did not *see* the **Etheric Aura** of the missing limb. As I continued to study and ponder what it was I was *seeing*, I felt that she was born with a deformed leg, not that her leg had been injured and amputated, but I was not sure.

Following the service I talked to the Unity Minister and a man who was obviously either her father or taking care of this little girl and her little female friend. I told the man and the minister that I saw *lights* or Auras, and was curious about what happened to the little girl with the missing leg because I suspected that she was born without a full leg not that it was amputated. The man seemed quite amazed that I had picked that up but confirmed that was indeed the case. That confirmation was very validating, because initially I could not tell exactly what it was that I was seeing that was different. That is often how it is for me. I don't always know or understand what it is I am *seeing* or *sensing* unless I ponder on it, try to figure it out and then make the effort to try to validate it. I did not ask about nor did I *see* or *sense* what Karmic debt might be at play with that situation. I don't always want to or need to know. My experience is that when I *need* to know, I am shown or told.

> *Allow yourself and your children to be curious. As in the above two examples, explore exactly what you may, or may not, be picking up on. Don't miss the opportunity to explore your children's and your*

own subtle sensitivities. These opportunities can be very educational. And always say a prayer for that person.

The Astral Aura

Rev. Schoenmaker states that the *Astral Aura* or "body" consists of an energy field that extends as much as three to four feet around the physical body, and carries past life Karmic memory information. He also states that all humans and animals have this Auric field, but insects and plants do not. He further states that newborn babies do not have this energy field until several months after they have been born, and that the Astral Aura is the *"energy"* that was painted as halos around saintly people by artists in early Christian times.

I agree with Mario's explanation that this field is only around humans and animals, and not around plants or insects. I also agree that halos depicted by artists around saintly people are an attempt to portray this Aura. However, I do not agree with Rev. Schoenmaker's statement that newborn babies do not have an Astral Aura or energy field until several months after they have been born, because I often *see* an Astral Aura, or at least an energy field associated with the fetus, around women who are pregnant.

Although Rev. Schoenmaker does not state this, I have come to understand that the Astral Aura is the energy field or "body" that we experience when we dream, and the body in which we "Astral travel." Further as Mario states, the Astral Aura contains or carries past life memories and Karmic information that can be tapped into or sensed by many psychics. For me, the Astral Aura is a primary component of the complex yet beautiful pallet of many bright and changing colors. As I explained previously, for me the Aura is a constantly changing pattern of colors and the Astral Aura component reflects not only what the person is thinking or experiencing at that moment but past life Karmic information as well.

Just as almost everyone can learn to *sense* or sometimes *see* the Etheric Aura, many people can be taught to at least *sense*, and sometimes *see*, the Astral Aura as well. However, for most people to consistently *see* or even *sense* the Astral Aura requires that they commit to meditating on a regular basis and learn how to *see* with their inner eye, their Third Eye Center. Almost all *New Age Kids – Indigos, Crystals and Star children,* are able to at least *sense* this aspect of the Aura and once they know what to look for, many are also able to *see* it as well.

The Psychic Who Knew I Was Psychic

Many years ago at an A.R.E. conference on Meditation, I met Mary, a lady whom I *knew* was psychically sensitive and was struggling to understand her sensitivities and what to do about them. For me, a big clue was that whenever we were in the same area, her Aura literally "reached out for me" and she told me that mine did the same. She was happily married with two little girls who were very sensitive themselves and I was happily married at the time as well. She and her husband and my wife, Suzanne, and I became close friends.

When I first met Mary, I told her that I *saw* her Aura. At the time, I was not really distinguishing which "band" or pattern it was I was seeing. But what I saw surrounding her were a lot of bright yellows (indicating high intelligence), light and bright greens (indicating healing), and forest greens (indicating a love of the forest and gardens), and she confirmed that she was interested in healing and had a "green thumb." I also *saw* dark streaks of purple (indicating deep religious ties and understanding). I later learned she had a past life as a nun in Bolivia South America; she was always fascinated with that country. There were multicolored violets (these are indicative of high spirituality, high integrity and great curiosity) in her Aura as well. The deep blue in her Aura (which indicates depth of knowledge or wanting to know) also indicated to me that she was a voracious reader (as was my wife Suzanne) and probed into information. Sure enough you would find her in the library during most breaks researching something that had been said in the conference. She also had a lot of very bright orange (indicating energy) in her Aura and she was indeed an inexhaustible individual. Sometimes Suzanne was drained just being in her presence because Suzanne was not a high-energy person. One of the things I specifically noticed about Mary was that her Aura indicated that she had almost no bright or broad bands of red. She would have streaks of red in her Aura periodically, but they soon dissipated. As we got to know each other over the years I learned that her mother was a very angry person and that Mary had learned to redirect her own anger. She was determined that it would not rule her as it did her mother. Thus, her Aura showed very little red.

As I picked up on *(saw, sensed, and heard)* Mary's Aura pattern, I learned that I could tell by how her *"lights* played" as to what frame of mind she was in and sort of what she was thinking about. One afternoon, we spent the entire time at the beach just sitting and talking about and reading what each of us could *see* in the other's Aura. We also talked about what we *saw* in the Auras of the lecturer's and other conference participants. That conversation proved to be very helpful and instructive for both of us because we realized that the Aura pattern we were *seeing* in each other and what we *saw* around other people (what I later came to understand as the Astral Aura) told us what people were thinking and feeling and provided us information about what past life "stuff" was being brought forward for them at this point in their life.

My Angry CIA Co-worker

Not all Auras are positive or beautiful. When I was first introduced to Ray who was a contractor in our Signal Analysis division at the Agency, I recognized that he was someone who was extremely bright, but someone who carried a great deal of anger. Ray's Aura first struck me as somewhat like a flamethrower – it seemed to spew out lots of intermixed bright and dark reds that had a very cutting effect. I wanted to stay away from him because I did not know what he might do; he seemed that angry. He was known to throw things like erasers and pens and would straighten out a large paper clip and throw it, trying to make it stick somewhere. I really tried to stay out of his way. He also had a very serious stuttering problem, and the more stressed he became the worse he stuttered.

It took me several months, working with him on a daily basis, hearing his extremely negative and cutting comments, before I began to understand what his energy pattern (his Aura) was telling me. When I would talk to him about his anger, he would deny it and just say that I didn't understand and begin to stutter. As he did this, his Aura would become "puffed up" and begin to "roil" which meant that I needed to back off. I recognized that his anger was primarily at himself and his inability to express himself due to his stuttering. However, it took about two years before I was able to have some conversations with him to help him acknowledge that his anger was a real problem, for himself, his family, and everyone he worked with.

As I wrote this story I tried to analyze exactly what I *saw* and experienced with Ray and his Aura through those years. Ray's overall Aura pattern was quite prominent (large or expansive) and seemed like a broiling caldron of roiling clouds of reds, yellows, deep blues, and dirty grays. It consisted of both bright reds and dark reds with streaks of dark gray (indicative of current and past anger experiences as well as suppressed anger) interspersed with lots of yellows (both pale yellows – indicative of immature intellect, and golden yellows – indicative of a deep intellect). It also included bands of very deep blues but with streaks of dirty grays and reds, which is indicative of a deep probing mind but one that is not clear. It also indicates a lot of unresolved anger, which I believe was about his inability to express that deep understanding.

Ray was indeed a brilliant mathematician and when we talked about some deep mathematical signal processing problems, we had some very good conversations and his Aura reflected a much smoother pattern. However, that Aura pattern was short-lived because he was always very conscious of the fact that he did not have a college education. He claimed that college was a waste of time and suggested, "BS, MS and Ph.D. simply means Bull Shit, More Shit and Piled Higher and Deeper!" Although I recognize that statement is somewhat humorous on the surface, it was simply his way of covering up for this lack of education. However, we all recognized that in certain areas, he was a lot smarter than many of us.

Ray's Aura pattern seldom showed any purples (religious understandings and interest) or violets (spirituality) but had some very deep greens (different shades of greens, which indicated to me that he enjoyed the forest, but again with streaks of grays and reds. He later told me that he loved to take walks in the woods, but that he would usually use those walks to vent his anger at his parents and curse God for his speech affliction. He told me that I was the only person he had ever shared this with. I later learned that his anger at his parents and God was what the gray and red streaks in his Aura represented. When I left the Agency, Ray gave me a profound compliment. He told me that I was one of the few people he had ever met that he felt I deserved my degrees, and that he felt I never held them against him. From him that was a great compliment and I humbly thanked him. He also gave me the gift of a t-shirt on which his daughter had drawn a perfectly colored Agency Seal – this was when you could not find them anywhere. I proudly wore that t-shirt for many years.

My point of relaying this example is that a person's Aura reveals a great deal about what is going on with that person, and it isn't always a positive experience for those of us who are sensitive to those energies.

Parents need to be aware of how their kids are responding to people. If you see that your child is drawing back from or becomes frightened by another person (or even yourself), be aware that they may be experiencing something akin to what I experienced with Ray, but may not know how to interpret what it is they are 'seeing,' 'sensing,' or experiencing. So as a parent, try to question them; draw it out of them. Proactively ask them what it is they are 'seeing' or 'sensing,' and be open to what they might tell you. Teach them to send light and love to that person because they do indeed need it.

The I AM Aura

Rev. Schoenmaker states that the *I AM Aura* or "body" is the God Essence that expresses in each person. He further states that only humans have this Aura or "body."

I agree with Rev. Schoenmaker that this Aura pattern represents the God Essence of an individual. However, as my understanding and sensitivities to all levels of the Aura around living creatures has increased, I have begun to question whether the I Am Aura or Energy Field is only associated with humans. I have begun to wonder whether other highly evolved creatures such as primates, dolphins and whales might express this energy pattern as well. Although I have not *seen* the I AM Aura pattern with primates, dolphins or whales the way I do with humans, I seriously look when I visit a zoo or aquarium or walk on the beach. As I have looked, I have become aware of an energy field that has a God Essence quality that makes me question whether these beings might simply express a different kind of God Essence that I have not yet identified or categorized. I am pondering that possibility.

My First Conscious Encounter With The I AM

One of the first times I consciously (and spontaneously) *saw* and experienced the *I AM Aura* of another person (as an adult) occurred in the early 1970's, long before I had read about Rev. Schoenmaker's model. I was working on the "discipline" that our SFG Study Group had selected for the week, which was to, "try to see the God Essence in another individual." I was at work at the CIA and had just completed my noon-time meditation and had repeated the request, "Father help me see Thee in my fellow man, and help me reflect Thy presence in me so that others might see Thee in the things I do." I had gone to the restroom and was on my way back to my office when a man I knew and had seen many times before was walking toward me in the hallway. He was about ten feet from me when all of a sudden the entire hallway lit up with a brilliant light that seemed to be all around this person. It lasted perhaps five or ten seconds and then simply disappeared. I stopped in my tracks. My mouth was open. I was stunned. As he approached me he asked if I was OK. I stammered, "Yes" and continued on to my office. When I got back to my desk I sat for a few minutes puzzling over what had just happened and what I had seen. I realized that I had seen the God Essence of that individual as I had been asking, and I heard a voice in my head say, "You asked and you have been shown." I replied "Thank you Father" and continued to contemplate what I had experienced. That night I shared my experience with Suzanne and she simply smiled and said, "That's really something, you need to share that with our SFG Study Group."

As I have re-examined how I *saw* Aura's as a child, I am fairly certain that I *saw* the I AM Aura around some people and I believe those were the people whom I experienced as being very loving. For example, my mom when she was being loving and caring, and Mrs. Anne when we lived at the foster home. Today, whenever I tap into the *Akashic Records*, as I do when I do a psychic reading, I have the privilege of seeing the I AM Aura or God Essence of each person I read for. Seeing this Aura is one of the most awesome experiences and spiritual gifts one can have.

Although I have been able to teach people how to *see* or become sensitive to the Etheric Aura and the Astral Aura, I have not yet discovered how to help people *see* or *sense* the I AM Aura. However, as I state in my Auras workshops, I do believe that each individual is capable of becoming aware or sensitive to this I AM or God Essence Aura, because this essence is a part of everyone. When I talk to the *"New Age Kids"* at my various workshops about this Aura pattern, it is encouraging to me that some of them believe they have seen it.

A Seven Layer Aura Model

In an attempt to be complete in my description of Aura models, there are several books that describe several other models of the Aura. Some claim that the human Aura has seven layers, while others claim that the Aura has many more layers. The most prominent model of an Aura in the literature appears to be a 7-layer model[35] (similar to the one on the following page). For example, Barbara Brennan, Ph.D. talks about a 7-layer model of the Aura in her book *Hands of Light*[36] and teaches this "model" of the Aura in her *Barbara Brennan School of Healing.*[37] Her book is an excellent text for those who are interested in learning how to heal, and I have heard great things from students who have gone to her school.

---

[35] The Spiritual.com.au web site: http://www.spiritual.com.au/articles/auras/human-aura.html provides a picture and explanation of the 7-layer or level Aura.

[36] *Hands of Light: A Guide to Healing Through the Human Energy Field* by Barbara Brennan and Jos. A. Smith

[37] See: http://www.BarbaraBrennan.com

PHYSICAL PLANE	
Layer 1 Etheric Body	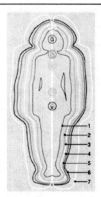
Layer 2 Emotional Body	
Layer 3 Mental Body	
ASTRAL PLANE	
Layer 4 Astral Body	
SPIRITUAL PLANE	
Layer 5 Etheric Template Body	
Layer 6 Celestial Body	Picture of a 7-layer model of
Layer 7 Ketheric Body	the human Aura

Although I have known of some psychically sensitive people who say they see *at least* seven layers in the Aura, I have not personally been able to distinguish the seven layers as depicted in the above figure. However, according to my Spirit Guides, the additional layers that people claim to perceive are simply refinements of the dynamically changing multicolored patterns that I *see* in the *Astral* and *I AM* Aura.

A Twelve Layer Aura Model

Very recently, I came across a 12-Layer Model of the Aura presented by Pamela Nine Martinez, Ph.D. from the *Nine Wellness Center™* in Knoxville, Tennessee, which she has graciously allowed me to reference here. On her web site[38] referenced below, she talks about a 12-layer model of the Aura as indicated in the figure on the following page.

You will notice that the description of the first 7-Layers of Dr. Martinez's 12-Layer model correspond directly to Barbara Brennan's model, but Dr. Martinez's model includes five additional (or higher vibrational) levels. Both models list the first three levels or layers as related to the *Physical Plane*, the next layer to the *Astral Plane*, and the next three layers to the *Spiritual Plane*.

---

[38] See http://www.ninewellnesscentre.com/ivwc_auras.html

Dr. Martinez's model then states that the next three layers correspond to the *Cosmic Plane* and the last two layers to the *Universal Plane*. I would like to point out that the Aura pattern shown in Dr. Martinez's figure is not in *layers* as depicted in the Barbara Brennan model but *"multicolored blotches"* of color, which corresponds more closely to what I *see* in the Aura.

PHYSICAL PLANE

Layer 1	Etheric Body
Layer 2	Emotional Body
Layer 3	Mental Body

ASTRAL PLANE

Layer 4	Astral Body

SPIRITUAL PLANE

Layer 5	Etheric Template Body
Layer 6	Celestial Body
Layer 7	Ketheric Body

COSMIC PLANE

Layer 8	Memory Body
Layer 9	Soul Body
Layer 10	Integrative Body

UNIVERSAL PLANE

Layer 11	Eternal Body
Layer 12	Universal Body

Copied from the following web site:
http://www.ninewellnesscentre.com/ivwc_auras.html

Although my sensitivities have not yet allowed me to distinguish the twelve layers that Dr. Martinez identifies, I remain open to the possibility that as I study her model more and work at trying to distinguish these layers in the Auras of people I know or meet, perhaps my sensitivities will increase to allow me to make such distinctions.

In thinking about the 12-Layer model that Dr. Martinez specifies and what I experience when I *see* an Aura, I continue to believe that the layers or levels beyond the Astral in her model correspond to aspects of the constantly changing, multicolored Aura patterns that I see in what Rev. Mario Schoenmaker would refer to as the *Astral* and *I AM* Auras. As my Spirit Guides have been telling me, I simply do not separate out the individual layers; I just interpret what they mean.

Aura Cameras – My Experience

Although there are Aura cameras that supposedly take a picture of the Aura, from my experience the Aura photographs that these cameras produce usually does NOT correspond to the Aura that I see around people. As an engineer/scientist, this still puzzles me greatly.

The first time I saw an Aura camera was at a Pathways Natural Living Expo show in Maryland in the mid-1990's. Dotti and I were walking around the show enjoying various displays of crystals, jewelry, herbal essences, psychics doing readings, etc. and came upon a display where they were taking photos of peoples' Auras. This peeked my curiosity, so when a lady asked to have her Aura photo taken I thought, "Great, let's see what this shows," thinking I could compare what I saw to what the camera captured. I took a close look at her Aura, and *got* that she had a fight with her daughter that morning – her aura showed streaks of bright red with shades of browns and grays, which is what anger usually looks like to me. It also had broad streaks of yellows (which normally indicates high intelligence in specific areas) but her yellows were intermixed with muddy greens in an interleaved and overlapping pattern, which implies deceit. In general her Aura did not indicate a spiritually aware soul but more of a spiritual "wannabe" who was gullible, lazy and did not practice what she knew or talked about.

When they took her Aura photograph it showed a lot of white, green and purple in it and they told her that it indicated she was a highly evolved Spirit, a healer and an advanced Spiritual soul. She was delighted; I was completely depressed. As an engineer, I thought the machine does not lie, it must be right and what I was seeing must be wrong. I remember leaving the show feeling confused and depressed. Throughout my meditations that week, I kept asking why my view was so different from what the camera showed, and why the camera operator's translations were the antithesis of mine. My Spirit Guides told me that I needed to trust what I was *seeing*. They stated that what I *saw* with her was accurate and valid but that the Aura camera was taking a picture of what she was trying to project to the world and that I *saw* through that. Not very encouraging to an engineer, but I have learned to trust my Spirit Guides and remain curious about exactly what it is the Aura cameras are taking a picture of.

A short time after that Pathways Natural Living Expo show, Dotti and I "worked" another Metaphysical show – The Festival of Lights show – which also had an Aura camera booth. Out of curiosity, I decided to do an experiment and asked the people who had their Aura photograph taken to hide their photograph. I told them I was doing an experiment and wanted to read their Aura without the benefit of their photograph and compare what I saw to what the camera showed. Everyone was curious and agreed. I read what I saw in their Aura pattern, told them what I thought it meant, and then asked them if it was correct. They provided me feedback on what I said and then pulled out their picture and shared what they had been told by the camera expert. In every case, I was told that my reading of their Aura (and them) was more accurate than what they were told. Yet, when I looked at the photograph, only in a few cases did it show what I saw, which was puzzling for all of us.

There are, of course, exceptions to every rule and my dear friend, Dee, who "set me up with Dotti" was one of those. As I indicated previously, Dee's Aura had a lot of white light in it, which denotes a high spiritual being, and we were all well aware of her strong intuitive abilities. Well, Dee had an Aura photograph taken while we were at a conference in Ocean City, Maryland and her Aura photograph showed a large band of White light all around her – very similar to the white bands I saw in her Aura.

Over the years I have asked many other psychics about this discrepancy, including Nancy Anne Tappe (the lady who coined the term *Indigo Children*). When I asked Nancy Anne what she thought about Aura cameras and the photographs they create, she stated that she did not see the same thing that the Aura photographs showed either. As an Electrical Engineer, I clearly understand that the Aura cameras do indeed capture some sort of energy, but what it captures I do not know.

If you have had your Aura photo taken and you feel that it accurately represents what you believe is true, then go with it. However, if your Aura photo does not accurately reflect what you believe about yourself, just recognize that many of us psychics do not *see* what the Aura camera *sees* so you might also want to check with your own intuition, or with a reputable psychic.

Medical Intuitive Readings

During the mid to late 1990's I was becoming more and more aware that I could *see* health problems with people. I recognized that in addition to what I *saw* in the Aura, I was able to *see* images of their various systems (skeletal, circulatory, endocrine, gastro intestinal, etc.) and tell them what I thought it meant. I did not have a lot of confidence in my ability to interpret what I was *seeing* or *sensing*, so I always told them to share the information with their doctors and to tell their doctors that I was open to talking with them. Often what I *saw* proved to either be accurate or a symptom of some other problem, which caused the doctor to further investigate something they would normally not check out, and possibly discover an underlying cause.

I am still somewhat reluctant to do Medical Intuitive readings because of the tremendous responsibility I feel when doing such readings. However, I have been right enough times and helped enough friends, family members, acquaintances, and other people, that I continue to do them as I am called upon by Spirit. The following stories show how medical intuitive information comes to me, and how these readings have helped the individuals I *read* for.

Lana's Thyroid Problem

Shortly after I returned to Northern Virginia from Florida, my friend Dee and her partner John invited Dotti and me to meet them at a New Beginnings friend's house in Ocean City. Lana's place was on the beach and we were all looking forward to the weekend getaway. Lana's partner was one of the guys in our Wintergreen cabin when Dotti and I first met. As we arrived, Dee and Lana were in the kitchen talking about a medical condition that Lana had and my ears perked up when I heard the big "C" word. Lana was expressing some real fear as she talked about an upcoming cancer surgery her doctor had scheduled on her thyroid.

Having never met Lana before, I was not sure what to say. But when I heard her talking about cancer, I automatically did a *medical intuitive scan* of her throat area and did not see the cancer the doctors told her she had. Dee had told Lana that I was a psychic and that she felt I was a "good one." Lana then asked me what I *saw.* I told her, "Well I don't see cancer but I do see scar tissue that should be taken care of." I then drew a picture of what I saw on a napkin. I stated that there were several small pieces of scar tissue that I *saw,* and that these "shadow" areas that the doctors suggested were signs of spreading cancer, were simply scar tissue from a previous surgery. Lana confirmed that indeed she had thyroid surgery many years previously, which could account for the scar tissue but she was still a little skeptical. I encouraged her skepticism and told her that she should take the napkin to her doctor, tell him what I saw and what I thought the "shadows" were, and see what he said. She put the napkin in her purse and said, "Well, I sure hope you're right," and then said, "Let's go eat." We all went out to eat and proceeded to have a very nice weekend. Nothing much else was said about Lana's upcoming surgery.

The following week Lana told her doctor about this "crazy" psychic person she had met, and that I had told her I did not feel she had cancer. She showed him my drawing and told him what I said the "spots" were. Her doctor pulled out her X-ray and the spots on the X-ray exactly matched what I had drawn on the napkin. He told her that although those "shadows" could indeed simply be scar tissue, they could not be certain unless they did a biopsy. Because the biopsy would have been invasive and could potentially cause nerve damage, Lana chose not to have the biopsies done. She has neither had problems with, nor worries about them since. Lana recently told me that her thyroid checks for cancer over the years have all been clear.

Rebecca's Inner Ear Problem

One afternoon while I was working in my home office, Dotti received a phone call from a friend and former co-worker at a law firm. Rae shared with Dotti that her daughter Rebecca was feeling very sick and had been for quite some time. She had headaches, stomach nausea, and dizziness and the doctors did not know what it was so they recommended an upper and lower GI series of tests. Dotti suggested that I might "pick up" or figure out what was going on and asked if I would talk to Rae.

While Dotti was talking to her friend, I *felt* or *sensed* that the problem with her daughter was related to the inner ear. As I took the phone I also *sensed* that there was some kind of cyst or growth (non-cancerous) on the inner ear that was causing pressure, some pain, and dizziness. I told Rae that I felt like I was on a rolling ship and trying to get my sea legs and I actually felt a little nauseous as I talked to her. I recommended that before they do the GI series, she should take Rebecca to see an Ear, Nose and Throat Specialist. She took my advice and much to her and the ENT doctor's surprise, they found an inner ear growth that was indeed affecting her balance and causing the nausea and possibly causing her headaches. Unfortunately, an MRI revealed that it was not something that could easily be removed. However, it did cause her doctor to also check the daughter's standing *and* resting blood pressure and thereby discovered a problem known as Postural Orthostatic Tachycardia Syndrome (POTS).[39]

Although I was grateful for correctly *seeing* the inner ear problem, I was not pleased with the diagnosis. However, I also realized that when I tuned into Rae's daughter, I was *sensing* a blood flow imbalance between her daughter reclining and her daughter upright but did not recognize it as such. I actually got an image of one of those red liquid gel-filled lights that rock back and forth, but this one went from horizontal to vertical and there did not seem to be enough fluid when it was upright. At the time I simply ignored the image, thinking that it was completely unrelated to her daughter's condition. This is an example of being presented with the correct information, but not knowing how to interpret it. Whether that information

---

[39] See http://home.att.net/~potsweb/POTS.html

would have made a difference in helping the doctor interpret the daughter's condition I cannot say, but it represents a significant oversight on my part and I am presenting it here to help other psychically sensitive readers realize that you have to pay attention to ALL of the information you are given, even if you don't comprehend it. The following is an email Rae sent to me, which she has graciously permitted me to include here.

Hi Lowell,

It was very kind of you to put this experience [Rebecca's inner ear problem] into writing for me. It also gave me insight into the images you were given to interpret. It is so very interesting and I'm glad that helping us figure our Rebecca's medical issues also gave you some insight into your work.

Lowell, you ARE the reason we found out about Rebecca's medical issues as quickly as we did. Even though you didn't realize what your images were telling you regarding her blood flow disorder (POTS), your diagnosis of the growth deep in Rebecca's inner ear put us in touch with a neuro-otologist who is treating her for that growth, but who also is knowledgeable about POTS and took the time to run some preliminary tests on Rebecca that confirmed to him that we should have her checked out for POTS. He put us in contact with a POTS specialist who we see on an almost monthly basis to treat this disabling condition. Without you tuning into Rebecca and what she was feeling, it could potentially have taken us years – as it does so many people who suffer from POTS – to obtain a diagnosis. With your help we were able to obtain a diagnosis within a couple months of the beginning of her illness.

You were so very instrumental in the quick diagnosis of what was/is causing the issues from which Rebecca suffers and every time someone asks us how we found out about her condition, I don't hesitate to tell this amazing story.

Thank you so much for using your God given talent to help people – especially my daughter.

Most sincerely,

Rae T

The above experience is an example of, "sometimes psychics say things after the fact" and unfortunately as a result, the information is often not considered valid. Although I did not tell Rae what I saw at the time, I did *get* the information at the time I did the reading, but I just didn't understand that what I was *getting* was related to what was happening with her daughter. So when you *get* or *pick up* on information and only after the fact are you able to make sense of what you *saw* or *sensed*, don't discount it; learn from the experience.

But Do I Have Cancer?

Following the formal lecture part of an *Advanced Auras Workshop*, several people asked me how to see a potential medical difficulty in another person. I explained that this was not something I could teach in a class, even an advanced class like this one, but required training to learn how to discriminate the energies and then learn how to interpret the information. Several people requested medical intuitive Aura readings and I told them what I *saw*, what I felt it meant including any Karmic reason for the difficulty that I *saw*, and told them to share the information I had given them with their doctors.

After I had done this for several individuals, a young oriental lady in her late 30's stood up near the front of the room and asked me to do a medical intuitive reading of her Aura. She simply told me her name. I "tuned into" her Aura and began telling her about the strong yellows, violets, and deep blues that I *saw*, which indicated that she was a spiritual-seeking individual with a strong intellect and a deep probing mind, but someone who had little patience or compassion with herself or others, which she acknowledged. Then she blurted out, "But do I have cancer?" The room immediately went still and all eyes were on me. I had to answer her honestly. I turned my back to her to "retune" into her Aura and what it was telling me. I fervently prayed that God would give me the right words, not only for her benefit but so that everyone present could hear the love and caring that comes when the answer is from the Source. I turned around, re-scanned her body, and confirmed for myself that she did indeed have cancer. However, I was told that it was treatable. I then said, "Yes you do and here is where it is." I described a growth in the right portion of her upper torso from her breast down into her upper intestine area. I described it as an elongated bundle of fibers or connecting tissue that had cancer cells throughout. I stated that I believed that it had manifested about a month after she had a mammogram about seventeen months previously and that I thought it was operable, but that it would require multiple surgeries.

She thanked me for being honest and told me that she had known for several months that she had cancer, and that she did indeed have a mammogram several months previously. She then said that she was scheduled to begin what the surgeons said would be multiple surgeries, the following week. She told me the surgeons were not sure about the prognosis because they felt her breast cancer had spread from her liver. I told her that I believed that the elongated fibers I saw from the upper portion of her intestine area to her right breast area could be indicative of this.

I thanked her for having the courage to ask the question and thanked everyone present for holding the space to allow me to tune in and honestly respond to her. I asked that everyone say a prayer for her full recovery and I gratefully thanked God for guiding me. Many people in the audience later reported to me that they could feel the loving and caring energy in the room for this lady. That experience was both draining and yet rewarding beyond expression.

Consciously Reading The Akashic Records

Throughout the 1990's while I was doing "mini" Aura readings, my Angels and Spirit Guides were pushing me to do more readings. They suggested that I become a "professional" reader. However, I just didn't have the confidence to do readings like a "professional" psychic. My Spirit Guides had shown me that I had the ability to read the Akashic Records in the late 1970's and as I explored that ability throughout the 1980's and 1990's, they were teaching me how to "read" the highly symbolic information. However I still did not feel that I could do "professional" readings. However, as my spontaneous readings became more complex and involved and I became more conscious of the information I brought forward, I began to feel that perhaps it was time I follow what my Spirit Guides had been pushing me to do.

With perfect timing, Kate from our Unity Church asked me if I would do a professional "Medical Intuitive" reading for her. She was having a number of medical difficulties that her doctors were unable to figure out and she felt that by "reading the records," an answer might be revealed. Although I was initially very reluctant to do so, my Spirit Guides encouraged me and said they would help. On the day of the reading, I felt surprisingly comfortable and was intuitively guided as I prepared myself. When Kate arrived, I thanked her for coming and led her into my sun-filled kitchen where I was set up to do readings. I was guided to ask her to print her full name as it appears on her birth certificate as well as the name she was currently using and then held the paper in my hands. As I did so, I *sensed* into her energy and was immediately shown what I knew to be the Akashic Records, but in a much clearer manner than I had ever seen them in the past. As I became aware of the "records" being opened to me, a very large egg shaped orb of white light began to form behind her. I intuitively knew that I was looking at her "God Essence." As I started to speak, something took over and I began speaking in a much more forceful manner and tone than I normally would. I have no idea what possessed me to say the things I did, but as I was "reading" from these records, it was as if I had done this many times before. Everything just seemed to flow.

As I focused on her "God Essence" I was immediately *shown* two significant past lifetimes that Kate had experienced – both of which directly related to "issues" she was facing or had faced in this lifetime. Following a review of those lifetimes, I was drawn to the current lifetime and *saw* her (as an Essence) standing before her parents and was *told* why she chose to come in through them. I was also *shown* certain important events in her life from the time she was born until she graduated from college. The information included the people involved, what happened, how she felt, etc. I spoke in a continuous monologue, simply relaying the information I was *shown*. After about fifteen minutes, I was *told* to stop and ask her for feedback on the information I had just provided. I later learned that the process of asking for feedback helps me refine my attunement to that individual's energy and allows me to more easily and clearly *read* the Akashic Records for that person.

I was totally amazed at the information that came out of my mouth, as was she. She told me that the lifetimes I told her about and the Karmic lessons from those lifetimes really resonated with her. She also confirmed several significant events in her early childhood, her relationship with her parents, as well as several classmates and teachers and a couple of boyfriend relationships. I opened the reading up to answer any questions that she might have. As she asked questions or made comments, I *knew, sensed, saw* and *heard* information that I simply passed on to her. Most of the information was presented to me in a symbolic language, which I somehow knew how to interpret. Kate told me that the reading was accurate and very helpful, and she felt much more confident about why she was experiencing her medical difficulties as well as how to deal with them. She took the information to her doctors and they were able to more accurately target their therapies. Over the next year or so, her health improved significantly and she has become a knowledgeable Metaphysical Teacher and intuitive psychic reader in her own right.

After Kate left I tried to take in and make sense of all that had transpired. I had been talking and answering questions for about an hour and a half and could remember very little of what I actually said. I thanked God and my Spirit Guides for helping me access the records and for helping me interpret the symbolic information presented to me. I knew I had done an accurate and helpful "professional" reading for Kate and I realized that I had been guided in how to read the Akashic records in a more complete and clear manner than ever before. I felt humbled and blessed.

Since that initial reading, my readings process has followed this general format and over the past year or so, I have also learned how to carry out this process via the phone. I am now able to do readings for people around the world. I find that, during a phone reading, when I hear the client's voice and the client tells me their name, I am provided a mental image of them and am able to "tap into" their energy and then "tap into" their Akashic Record. As I tune into the client's energy and ask that I be allowed to open their record, I see the client's "God Essence" (the large orb of white light) appear behind the mental image I am holding, just as I do when the client is sitting in front of me. I then know that I have tapped into the correct "record" associated with that client. Interestingly, based on photos that various clients have sent me, my mental image is not always photographically accurate. I do not understand why.

Repeat Readings

When I do repeat readings for clients, I have an interesting and reassuring experience. As I tune into the client's energy and *see* the records, a delightful "little old man" comes out from the records and says, "We have seen these records before" and then proceeds to lay out a series of card like objects with information relating to what has transpired in that person's life since the last reading. There is also information related to that client's present understanding and Spiritual development. This delightful entity is a similar energy to Yoda from Star Wars but he does not look like Yoda. There is always a sense of great wisdom and peace with him even when he "scolds" the client for not doing what they have been told to do. He is a reassuring figure for me and sometimes shows up in my dreams as well as in my meditations.

My Mother's Passing

In July 2002 my mother had carotid artery surgery, which went very badly. When my sister Kathleen notified my brother Robert (Terry) and me that our mother had slipped into a coma following her surgery, she said that we needed to come see Mom and "say our goodbyes." As Kathleen said those words, I heard Mom say, "Not just yet" and I thought that perhaps she was just resting for a while and would wake up in a few days or so. However, as Dotti and I drove to Detroit, something inside told me that she was not going to last long and I was glad that we were going to see her.

When me met Kathleen and Robert at the hospital and went to Mom's room, I was immediately aware of several deceased relatives hanging around including our younger half-brother Chris, a Vietnam veteran who had died from Agent Orange several years earlier. When I commented to Robert and Kathleen, "Look at all our relatives!" the nurses just looked at me strangely. However, my brother simply made an off-hand comment to the effect, "So what" and went on to talk about something else. I realized that he *saw* them to but preferred to simply ignore them.

After a long conference with the doctor about what our options were, we all agreed that Mom would not want to be kept alive like this so we told him to simply keep her comfortable and let her pass.

Sadly, at the same time that Mom was in the hospital, Robert's wife Pamela was suffering from lung cancer and while we were at the hospital with our mom, he received a phone call to return home. Pam, who had been having dizzy spells, had fallen and was being admitted to the hospital for a possible brain tumor. Robert left that evening to drive back to his home in Marysville, Ohio to be with his wife.

Mom's Grandmother Appears

A couple of evenings after we first arrived, Kathleen and I were sitting at the foot of Mom's bed just talking and being with her when all of a sudden I began to *see* a mist or cloud begin to form at the head of her bed. As it began to form into the shape of an older woman I pointed to it and asked Kathleen, "Do you *see* that?" At first she wasn't sure and then she said, "I think so?" The mist formed into the shape of an older woman with a long full brownish pink dress with a lace collar and long sleeves with lace on the end of the sleeves. She was a tall thin woman with long, middle of her shoulders length, gray hair pulled into a ponytail. As she appeared out of this mist, I intuitively *knew* that she was my mother's grandmother, although I had not remembered ever seeing a picture of her. I then *heard* her say, "It's time to go Hattie" and *saw* her reach out for Mom. I *heard* the name Sara and then I *heard* the name Blank. I half expected to *see* Mom die or *see* her Spirit be taken or something, but the lady just turned her head and looked at me and my sister and then simply disappeared. Mother continued to breathe normally as if nothing had happened which really confused me. When I asked Kathleen if she *saw* her, she said, "I think so but I'm not sure." I then asked her, "Who is Sara, and what does blank mean?" My sister said, "I think that is the name of Mom's grandmother." We stayed a short while longer and then went back to my sister's house. When we got there, I shared my experience with Chach, Kathleen's husband, and Dotti. Kathleen went to her bedroom to try to find a photograph and emerged with an old faded picture of a tall, thin and elegant looking lady with long hair pulled back. The lady in the picture was the one I saw appear beside my mother's bed. When I turned it over it said Sarah

Blanks. It was a picture of my mother's grandmother and she was wearing a brownish pink dress!

When we went to bed that evening, I told Dotti that I thought Mom would probably not last through the night, and I half hoped she wouldn't because I knew she would not want to be kept alive that way, even though she did not seem to be in pain. When we awoke the next morning and learned that Mom's condition had not changed, Dotti and I decided to drive down to see Robert and Pamela on our way back to Virginia, knowing that Kathleen would let us know when Mom passed. None of us, except the grandkids were really distraught. We all knew that Mom was going to die and that she surely didn't want to be kept alive in her current condition. I said my goodbyes to Mom on the inner planes and told her that I would stay in touch with her and ask for her help whenever I thought it was appropriate. We left and drove to Marysville, Ohio to be with my brother and his wife Pamela.

When we arrived at the hospital where Pam was being cared for, we learned that, as I had suspected, the news was not good. Several months earlier Pam had quit smoking after thirty-five years as a heavy smoker. The current news was that the lung cancer had spread to her brain, and they suspected that it might have also spread to her breasts. The brain tumor they removed was the size of a small orange and was located near the occipital lobe, a very bad place to have a large cancerous tumor. We had a rather short but pleasant visit, as pleasant as one can have under the circumstances, and continued our drive home to Virginia. Pam struggled with her cancer for about and year before she lost her battle.

My mom made her transition August 8th about ten days after we returned home. Per her request Kathy had her body delivered to the University of Michigan Medical Center. Several months later she was given an urn containing Mom's ashes with a very nice note of appreciation. Kathleen flew out to California and per Mom's request spread her ashes in Mom's beloved Pacific Ocean just outside her favorite town, San Diego. Although I miss her physical presence terribly, I am still able to communicate and interact with her psychically. I bless her every time I think about her, and as I did when she was alive, I constantly thank her for having been my Mom in this lifetime.

Mom's Dimes

Several months prior to my mother's surgery and ultimate death, she and I made an agreement that in the event of her death, she would find a way to let me know that she was still around. Although this may sound strange to readers that two psychics would have to do something like this, but you need to understand that almost all psychics still question their own "correctness" because the information that we often pick up is not as straight forward or definitive as "physical" evidence.

Anyway, about a month after my mother had passed away, I noticed that I was finding a lot more pennies than was usual. Dotti and I had this habit of picking up coins and affirming, "I'm a Money Magnet." One day it hit me that perhaps it was my Mom sending coins and I said to Mom's Spirit, "If this is you Mom, I want to see dimes, not pennies!" The very next day when I went into work, I found five dimes on my desk under a piece of paper next to my laptop docking station. I knew they were not there the previous day and I immediately knew that was my Mom's way of saying that she was with me. However, being the Engineer that I am, I still asked all of the other people in the office whether anyone had left some dimes on my desk. Everyone looked at me as if I were from a different planet and said, "No" and questioned why I asked. I explained that the previous few days I had found an inordinate number of pennies and had told my deceased mother that if she was leaving pennies, I wanted her to leave dimes instead and I would know it was her. I said, "I guess she answered my request," to which several people retorted, "Boy Lowell, you sure are weird. Why didn't you ask for one hundred dollar bills?"

Ever since then, Dotti and I find dimes everywhere – on the floor, on the street, in the closet, on counters, even in the little plane I fly. We just say "Hi Mom, thanks for being here." My mom continues to watch over me.

Loved ones who pass often try to get their family and friends' attention by playing a favorite song on the radio, moving objects in the home (e.g., shifting pictures on the wall, creating a special fragrance, etc.). A dear friend and co-worker of Dotti lost here grandmother and was missing her terribly. When Dotti learned what was bothering her, she told her about my Mom's dimes and this young lady 'asked' her grandmother for buttons. The next day she found several buttons on her desk and that experience helped her know that she could still communicate with her grandmother, which comforted her greatly.

My Dad's Passing

Almost a year to the day after my mom died, I received a call from one of my half-sisters saying that our dad had died and that the funeral would be held in the town of Gwinn, Michigan where my stepmother, Henrietta, had been buried several years earlier. I flew into the Marquette Airport, rented a car, and drove straight to the funeral home. However, when I arrived the funeral home was not yet open so I went to a local park to relax and wait until it opened. As I sat on one of the benches, I was immediately aware of many Native American Spirits as well as Spirits of English and French explorers and hunters. It was as if I had been transported back to several different time periods simultaneously and they all seemed to overlap. It was simply another interesting experience that often happens to me. After a short while I walked over to the nearby docks where my dad had kept his fishing boat, and thought about the last time I had been there with him and wondered where he was and what he was doing now. Although I did not *see* him, I did *sense* his Spirit but did not receive an answer.

Shortly after the funeral home opened, I went in and told the greeter that I wanted to spend some time alone with my dad's body. He ushered me into the room where my dad's body was and left me alone. As I entered the room, I half expected to *see* my dad's Spirit but alas it was not present - only a U.S. flag, a number of very nice flower arrangements and my dad in full dress uniform laying in the coffin. I grabbed a nearby chair – one that was high enough that I could sit beside his coffin and look down at him and I just sat there talking to him, both aloud and in my mind. I felt the need to have this *verbal* and *mental* conversation with his Spirit.

After about a half-hour of this one-way conversation – I never *heard* a response from his Spirit – my dad's face appeared to me in my mind. A much younger face than the one in the coffin and he appeared more gentle than I ever remember him. I *heard* him say, "So now what?" At that point, I knew that somehow I had to forgive him and bless him in order to be released from him. Similar to the story in Genesis 32:24-32, where Jacob had to be blessed by the "Angel" he wrestled with. Even though my *Lama Sing* readings and my own Past Life Regressions had indicated that my Karmic ties to him had been broken, I felt the need to go through this forgiveness process. After several minutes of trying to figure out how to even begin, I came up with the following prayer, which I repeated for perhaps ten minutes or so.

> *I now bless and release you to the Karma that you created, and release myself from any and all ties to you. I forgive you for the things you did to me while under your care, and I ask forgiveness of any hurts or harms that I might have caused you. I send the healing light of the Christ to heal and seal all past connections. I bless and release you to your own Karma, and demand that your Spirit bless and release me from any ties you have to me. Through the power, love and grace of God, all is forgiven and released.*

At some point I felt a release of bondage from his Spirit, and when I opened my eyes and looked down into that coffin, all I could see was this very sad looking old man in a military uniform who was *dead*. As I sat there, my *Angel Lady in White* appeared to me in my head and I *heard* her say, "It is finished" then she disappeared. I left the funeral home feeling calm and peaceful – not excited, not down, not "I told you so," just calm and peaceful. I knew that I had completed what I had needed to complete, and as far as I was concerned I could have gone straight to the airport and flown home. However, my dad's funeral was the next day and even though I didn't want to go, I knew that my older brother and other siblings needed me to be there.

The next morning I attended the service at the Baptist Church in Gwinn. As I sat there in the front row with my brother Robert and other siblings, I thought to myself, "You're psychic. Why aren't you picking up on anything?" Just then my dad's mother, Alethea, who I only knew from pictures of her, appeared at the foot of my dad's flag-draped coffin with her arm on the shoulder of a young reddish-haired girl. I instinctively knew she was a deceased daughter of my dad's – a child none of us knew about. Then both of them just disappeared. I thought, "That was strange, could that be true?" Just then this demonic skeleton, like the skeleton that appeared at the end of the movie *The Golden Child*,[40] sat up out of my dad's coffin and turned it's large horned bull-like head toward me, gave me a menacing look and then promptly disappeared. I was not frightened, only somewhat startled. I thought to myself, "What the hell was that all about?" I did not say anything to my siblings about this experience. I am weird enough to them and I didn't need them to be able to validate my craziness. It wasn't until several weeks later when I went to a therapist friend and related my experience to him that I got a *sense* of what that was all about. My friend listened to what I had to say and after a bit, he said, "Well your dad was indeed the devil to you, so it is not surprising that he appeared to you in that form." He continued with a laugh, "I don't think you will be seeing him that way again." I had an answer I could live with.

As the rest of the funeral service continued, a young man who apparently knew my dad many years after I had left home, got up to speak. This young man in his early 30's spoke glowingly about my dad being this wonderful

---

[40] *The Golden Child* with Eddie Murphy, 1986 Paramount Pictures. In the movie, Satan appears as a flying skeletal figure with a bovine like head with large curved horns.

positive influence in his life. My mind raced as I thought, "He couldn't be talking about the same person I grew up with." Immediately a voice in my head said, "He isn't, your dad changed, and that is something you are just going to have to accept." Following his talk we proceeded to the gravesite for the 21-gun salute and burial. We then went back to the church to eat and I introduced myself to the young man who was so high on my dad. I told him, "The person you talked about is not someone I recognize, but I can assure you *that* person was *not* the person I or my other siblings grew up with as a dad. My dad was deliberately mean and vindictive and physically and verbally abusive *all the time*!!" I found his comment to be very interesting. He simply said he was truly saddened by my experience, and that it was a shame I never got to know the person he experienced. That was a touché. It was an interesting experience to stand there and hear that and not feel angry, simply an acknowledgment, "You're right!"

I learned later from several of my other siblings that at some point our dad did indeed change, and became a significantly different person. They say that he treated his last two children completely differently and apparently was a much gentler person. I have heard his later grandchildren talk about him as a loving caring person, and I am glad they experienced that person, not the one that I grew up with.

Becoming A Professional Psychic

In April 2006, almost nine years after I took the *Be Your Own Psychic Conference* training, I received an email from Dr. Henry Reed asking me if I was interested in becoming a Field Tested Psychic for the A.R.E. I of course jumped at the opportunity. The process consisted of passing a "psychic test" prepared by Dr. Henry Reed, a "test reading" for Carol Ann Liaros, and then serving as a psychic for participants at the annual *Be Your Own Psychic Conference* and receiving positive evaluations from all those I read for.

Dr. Reed sent his "test" material which consisted of three sealed envelopes marked #1, #2 and #3 each containing a serious question that required an answer. These were questions he did not know the answers to, not just questions to see if I could figure them out. The instructions were to "psychically read" the question in each sealed envelope and record my answers on tape. I was to then open each envelope and read the actual question. If I felt I had *gotten* the question and answered it properly I could record additional information I might have picked up once I actually read it. If I had not *gotten* the question, then I was to "read" what I could for the actual question and explain why I felt I had not *gotten* the question before I opened the envelope.

When I did the reading for Dr. Reed, I was able to clearly *see* the question that was being asked in envelope #1 and #2, but had a more difficult time *seeing* the question in envelope #3. I finished "reading" all the information I could without opening the envelopes. Then I opened envelope #1 and *knew* I had not only read the question correctly but was satisfied with my answer. I opened envelope #2 and again was satisfied with both my reading of the question and my answer. When I opened envelope #3, I realized I had not answered the question being asked but instead answered a slightly different question. I recorded this and then "read" what I picked up regarding the actual question. I explained that the question I "read" and answered was in fact related to the question he actually asked and that I felt that the answer was important. I then answered the "original" question, and sent the recording to Dr. Reed and waited for his reply and feedback.

Carol Ann Liaros' test was very different from Henry's test. Per her instructions, a couple of weeks after completing Dr. Reed's test, I called Carol Ann at her home in Buffalo, New York. After a short introduction, I started her reading as a normal reading. However, as I opened the "records" and began the reading, Carol Ann stopped me and told me she wanted me to do a Medical Intuitive reading. I then told her that I needed to refocus and I remotely tuned into her "physical body" to *see* what I could pick up.

I did a "psychic scan" of her body and described what I *saw* with each of her systems as I had learned to do so many years before. I started with her skeletal structure. I scanned for abnormal formations (or deformities), what past breaks, strains and when they most likely happened and whether I *saw* any "osteoarthritic fuzziness" in her joints, etc. I then described what I *saw* about her muscular system, her circulatory system, then her endocrinological system (pineal, hypo-thalamus, pituitary, thyroid, parathyroid, thymus, adrenals, pancreas, and ovaries), and the smoothness (or lack there of) with which her endocrine fluids were flowing.

For me, when I do this type of body scan, I can *see* (Clairvoyance) each of the organs involved both physically and energetically, and am *told* (Clairaudience) or sometimes just *know* (Claircognizance) what is going on with the body. If there is a condition that needs to be corrected I am *shown* that as well. I have learned to tell the client what it is I am *seeing*, *sensing*, and *hearing*, etc. and tell them what I believe it means. This information usually comes to me in a symbolic manner and does not always indicate a medical condition. Throughout this process, Carol Ann was very helpful (not withholding yet not leading), in that she let me know when I was right or not interpreting something correctly. After about forty-five minutes, we talked about what the information meant for her, what she needed to do about it, and whether she should have her doctors perform certain tests to confirm (or refute) my information. When we were through, she told me that the medical intuitive information was very accurate and thanked me for the reading. I thanked her for the feedback, said I looked forward to seeing her at the beach, said goodbye and hung up.

It was clear to me that I had done very well with Carol Ann's reading, but I was not so sure about my accuracy with Henry's reading because of my experience on the 3rd envelope question. I thought and felt that I had done well but had not received any feedback from Dr. Reed and so I really did not know for certain. After about five months, I wrote to Dr. Reed and asked for feedback on his reading and explained that Carol Ann had told me that I had "passed" her test, but I was not clear whether I had passed his test. About a week later, Henry informed me that I had passed both tests, and reminded me that I still needed to be chosen to participate as a psychic in the annual *Be Your Own Psychic* conference. He stated that once I had completed and passed this third test, I would become acknowledged as a "Field Tested Psychic of the A.R.E." and that my name would be added to their list of approved psychics.

In the spring of 2008 I was selected for the *Be Your Own Psychic* conference and gave readings to about twenty conferees. Throughout the conference I was able to interact with the conferees and help them with subtle energy differences that I would *see* and *sense* but *knew* they could not yet distinguish. What a wonderful experience for me. I appreciated the positive feedback from those I read for and for those I provided feedback to throughout the conference. At the end of the conference, Dr. Reed told me that I had done very well and that my name would soon be added to A.R.E.'s list of approved psychics.[41]

Not so surprisingly, on the last day of the conference when I was up in the Meditation Room in the library building, I *saw* Hugh Lynn and Eula Allen standing near the front curtain smiling, and I *heard* them say, "Well done, well done" then they simply disappeared. I thanked them both for challenging me and for supporting me along my path.

Becoming A Priest/Minister

Throughout the 1990's, in addition to my Spirit Guides pushing me to do more readings, they also began urging me to become a Priest/Minister. In my meditations, and sometimes in my dreams, I would *see* myself in a monks robe, or with a priest's white collar and *heard* a voice saying that I needed to become a priest again. Throughout this period my Spirit Guides showed me several past lives as a Priest: in Ancient Egypt, as an Essene Priest, a Catholic and Greek Orthodox Priest, and in the Mayan/Aztec period as well. In several of these lifetimes I was shown that in spite of being a "man of the cloth" my understanding was somewhat flawed. I was *shown* that I had some negative Karma to address as a result – for example my life as an Aztec Priest in which I cut the hearts out of some sacrificial "victims" was particularly graphic. Those recall experiences caused me a great deal of regret and anguish, for which I continue to ask for forgiveness every time I think about that lifetime.

In early 2002 I began to seriously check into what I needed to do to become a Priest/Minister. I knew that I did not want to go to a Baptist or Methodist seminary and suffer through the "hell fire and damnation" lectures. I also was not drawn to become a Unity Minister even though I had

---

[41] As of this writing, one has to call the A.R.E. at 1-800-333-4499 to receive a copy of the list of approved psychics. Hopefully this list will soon be published on their web site; http://www.edgarcayce.org

accumulated several credits toward becoming a Licensed Unity Teacher. I was *told* by my Spirit Guides that my Religious, Spiritual and Psychic studies were to form the basis for my education and training and that I would be ordained by a *Priest of the Order of Melchizedek*. Although I had heard a great deal about Melchizedek over the years, and knew that according to Edgar Cayce, he was one of the incarnations of the Master energy that became Jesus the Christ, at the time I knew of nobody associated with that order.

In the fall of 2004, I was volunteering at Unity when I *synchronistically* bumped into a lady who asked me where the ordination class was. I didn't know anything about it, but *heard* in my head, "Tell her it's being held in the other building," which I did. It turned out that a class and ordination ceremony was being conducted by Rev. Dan Chesbro in the Mildred Park Center on Unity's property. I later learned that Rev. Chesbro is an ordained Baptist minister who had become a Metaphysical minister, and that he was ordaining attendees as *Priest's Of The Order Of Melchizedek*. The next week I looked up Rev. Chesbro's website[42] and found that he would be doing an ordination in Cleveland, Ohio in early March 2005. I flew to Cleveland to take the necessary training to become ordained during the weekend of March 13, 2005.

When Dan and I first met I had an immediate recognition of a past life with him and said, "I believe we have done this in the past because I see us as fellow Priests." He responded, "So that's what it is, but I think the roles may have been reversed." I then shared with him how I had been studying for this for many years, studying about and then teaching Metaphysical classes, the Bible, the Kabbalah, as well as Eastern Religious classes. I explained that I had taken a number of Unity classes, and that my Spirit Guides had told me a couple of years previously that I would be ordained by a Priest Of The Order Of Melchizedek. He just smiled, nodded and said, "I know" leaving me to wonder what he really knew.

In the training, Dan talked about Melchizedek and the Early Christian teachings, as well as about the Edgar Cayce readings and emphasized the need to have a strong understanding of, not necessarily religious studies, but Spiritual and Metaphysical principles. Dan stressed that each participant must have a strong desire to become a Priest, be willing to undergo a sacred initiation process, and actively carry out the responsibilities of the

---

[42] See http://www.sanctuaryofthebeloved.com/index.html

Melchizedek Priesthood, which we were about to be inducted into. As he was talking, I experienced a past life recall scene of becoming a priest in Ancient Egypt and taking a vow to commit my existence to helping others with their psychic sensitivities and their connection to their Source. I then *heard* in my head, "Your commitment continues."

Dan ordained each person individually and instructed each of us to "observe" and make a note of whatever we could, as each person was ordained. As Dan pronounced the words of ordination over each person, I *saw* most participants' energy pattern change in a very positive way; their Aura seemed to get lighter in feel and brighter in intensity. Some people's energy seemed to simply be absorbed or dissipate, and their Aura did not really change. When it came my turn, I sat in the "honored" seat with Dan at my back, and as I did, I had another flashback to another past life in Egypt. I knew it was Ancient Egypt because I could see the pyramids of Giza and the Sphinx in the distance. However, their appearance was significantly different than what one sees in pictures today. It was as if they shined and there were many other building structures around them. In this scene I saw myself being ordained into the Priesthood; what I understood to be The White Brotherhood, by a High Priest figure I recognized as Dan. As Dan proceeded with the current ordination ceremony and spoke the words of ordination, I felt this "energy blanket" descend upon me and I heard in my head, "Now you are to begin your ministry as the priest that you have been in the past and are meant to be again." Afterwards I felt the presence of what I recognized were several "Masters" who appeared in my mind wearing long white robes with hoods. The feeling and awareness of their presence remained with me for several days. A couple of years later when I was doing some work with the "Council of Archangelic Energies" I recognized that those Masters were associated with "the Council."

When I got home I shared my experience with Dotti, my SFG Study Group, and my *Indigos & Sensitives Support Group*. My dear friends Gerry and Siobhan Rice both said, "To us you have always been a Priest and teacher. This just makes it official." The following week I flew my rented Cessna C-172 to Winchester, Virginia to file the necessary paperwork and received my certification as a licensed Minister in the state of Virginia. As a licensed Minister I could now legally do weddings, baptisms, preside at funerals and do Spiritual Counseling – Psychic readings for clients. Reflections In Light, Inc., a 501(c)(3) supports this work.

Metaphysical Weddings

Shortly after I was ordained and received my certification as a Minister, I was asked to do a Metaphysical wedding in Maryland for some friends. It was an older couple whom I had met in *New Beginnings* and although I had serious concerns about whether they were matched (based on the energies I *saw*), I agreed to do the wedding. My primary concern was that there was a lot of contentious energy I *saw* around them, both individually and as a couple. Despite my reservations, I checked with the Maryland authorities to learn the process for obtaining, signing and sending in the necessary documentation to make the marriage legal. The process of helping them work through the wording of their vows was both a pleasure and a new challenge. One of the things I recommended was that they use "as long as love abides" rather than "until death do ye part" in their marriage vows because I suspected that was much more appropriate, which they agreed to and greatly appreciated. Surprisingly I was not nervous on the day of the wedding. I knew what I needed to do and say and knew the bride's desires for the wedding ceremony and subsequent reception dinner. Everything went as planned. I had performed my first "official" ceremony as a Minister. Although the wedding was a joyous and beautiful ceremony, that marriage did not last. Just as I had suspected, there were too many things that they disagreed upon, and when "love was no long abiding" they chose to go their separate ways.

A few weeks after my first wedding, my soul sister Angie asked if I would perform a marriage ceremony for a young couple who were the children of a couple of her friends. Here again, I encouraged the young couple to put their own words of love into their wedding vows, thinking and talking over what they wanted to say to each other on this very important day. I enjoyed a "counseling session" with them and was assured that they truly loved each other, and that they understood the implications of getting married. But the most important part for me was to "see how their lights played together." I spent time talking with them about marriage from a Metaphysical perspective, and learned to my delight that they both felt the same about waiting to start a family, about finances and financial responsibilities, and about family relationships, etc. I was pleased that they both felt the importance of establishing a Spiritual connection with their Source and with each other. Following this discussion, I felt much better about their ability to make their marriage work than the previous couple I had married.

The wedding day was gorgeously bright and sunny, and everything went extremely well. Just prior to my leaving I took "the kids" aside and thanked them for allowing me to perform their ceremony and I blessed them as I had remembered from a past life as a Catholic Priest. As I did so, I was aware of a Highly Charged Spiritual energy (which I believe was the Holy Ghost), descend upon them as I did this blessing. The groom commented that he felt an energy come from my hand that somehow enveloped him. The bride said she felt the energy too and was surprised at how peaceful she felt after I did that blessing. The groom quickly added, "So did I." I left, feeling I had done a good job.

The mother of the bride later called me and commented on how grateful the family was for such a beautiful, open, and inviting ceremony. She said "the kids" were pleased and seemed unusually peaceful, loving and caring toward each other, which flowed to all of the guests. She reported that their honeymoon went unusually smooth and that they were very happy together. She thanked me again and I told her that it was an honor and privilege. More than four years later I understand that they are still doing very well.

The Monroe Institute (TMI)

Just prior to my becoming a Minister/Priest, I decided to take the TMI training, as my friend and former boss Alan T had been pressing me to do for several years. Alan had read Robert Monroe's book entitled *Journey Out of The Body* and was fascinated with his accounts about his "out of body" experiences. As Alan explained to me, Robert Monroe experimented with binaural audio tones and discovered that certain binaural tones and tone combinations allowed him (and others) to reach different levels of consciousness or awareness much more rapidly and easily than without these binaural tones. His "work" was to categorize the binaural tone combinations, which he termed *Hemi-Sync*, as well as categorize the consciousness or awareness "levels" that the *Hemi-Sync* binaural tone combinations helped students reach, which he called *Focus Levels*. The Monroe Institute (TMI)[43] was founded to carry on Robert Monroe's work and continues to do so to this day.

Because Alan knew that I could tap into the Akashic Records and do spontaneous channeling of Archangelic energies, he felt I could most likely tap into the most advanced Focus Levels. He urged me to attend TMI, take their initial class, *Gateway Voyage* and see if I could "gauge" what level I naturally tapped into as compared to the Focus Levels categorized by TMI. I took Alan's challenge and thought, "This was going to be interesting." In January 2005 I took the *Gateway Voyage* training at The Monroe Institute. I found the instructors to be competent and the training to be very informative and helpful. I also found that the *Hemi-Sync* music that is played with each

---

[43] See The Monroe Institute web site: http://www.MonroeInstitute.org

"exercise" or experiment truly helped me rise to different levels of consciousness more readily than without it.

During the training, the instructors told a story about a pair of elderly Buddhist Monks who had taken the *Gateway Voyage* training several years previously. One was in his mid-60's and the other one was in his early 90's. They said that in the afternoon of the third day, the 90-year-old monk stated, "with your *Hemi-Sync* technology and training techniques you are able to get students to the level it takes us about fifteen years (of meditation) to achieve." That is a phenomenal affirming statement about the power of *Hemi-sync* and the TMI training, but I understand why that monk said that. I too found that the *Hemi-Sync* music played for each exercise did seem to facilitate getting to the desired Focus Levels very readily for almost all participants.

During the last few *Hemi-sync* sessions in the *Gateway Voyage* course, I asked my Spirit Guides what "level" I attune to when I do readings of the Akashic Records. I was told that I attuned to the equivalent of Focus Level 39, but that I did not maintain that level once I opened and began reading the records. I then asked what "level" I achieved during some Meditative exercises I had done when I asked my Spirit Guides to, "Show me what I look like to you." My Spirit Guides told me that when I did that exercise, I was raised or attuned to a level that does not have a Focus Level equivalent. I thanked them and noted the information in my journal and then told Alan the next time I saw him. When I had done that exercise (several years previously) I found myself outside my body observing just my Spiritual Essence in a body-like form yet without any real features that one could identify as me. I was simply aware that I was experiencing my Essence as my Spirit Guides *see* or *experience* me; simply a "cloud of energy."

Remote Viewing Course

A year after I took the TMI *Gateway Voyage* training class, I took the *Remote Viewing* course taught by F. Holmes (Skip) Atwater and Joe McMoneagle, both of whom are long-time Remote Viewers who participated in the U.S. Federal Government's Stargate Project.[44] In the early 1970's I had done many Remote Viewing experiments. Also, shortly after the book *Psychic Warrior*[45] by David Morehouse came out, I read it and thoroughly

---

[44] See the following web site: http://en.wikipedia.org/wiki/Stargate_Project
[45] *Psychic Warrior* by David Morehouse, St. Martin's Press, Copyright © 1996

enjoyed it. I then met David at a book-signing event and we had a long talk. David signed my book "To a fellow psychic warrior."

In this course, both Skip and Joe talked about their experiences with Remote Viewing and discussed various paradigms they had experimented with over the years. I talked to them about my early Remote Viewing experiences and the experimental paradigms we used, and noted how much more complex the Remote Viewing paradigms had become. As in the experiments we did those many years previously, I learned that just because one is psychically sensitive does not necessarily mean they are the best Remote Viewers. From a Remote Viewing perspective, several people in our class were far better at this than I was. However, others did not have the ability to do Psychic Readings nor were they sensitive to Auras.

This is a course I highly recommend if one is really interested in exploring and developing their Remote Viewing capabilities.

Everyday Psychic Experiences

Over the years I have come to understand that we are not simply physical bodies with five senses, but Spiritual Beings expressing in a physical form – a Multisensory human being. Our purpose on this earth plane is not simply to enjoy that which our five physical senses allow us to experience, but to become aware of the other realms of existence that we are a part of and which we co-create or contribute to via our intentions, our actions and our reactions.

As I have continued to do readings from the Akashic Records, taught classes, conducted Ghost tours, and conducted Religious and Spiritual ceremonies as a Minister, I have continued to have many interesting and fascinating experiences. To give the reader a sense of the scope of these experiences, I have included a few additional "stories" to help the reader understand how psychic information is presented to me, how I deal with it, and how I use my psychic gifts, on an every day basis, to help clarify information for others.

There are literally thousands of other psychic experiences I could write about but hopefully, the few I have included here will help the reader remove the fear some of you might have with your own psychic experiences, or the psychic experiences of others. For some readers, these will simply be interesting stories, but others will be able to relate to the information presented here and perhaps learn how to deal with their own psychic awarenesses, intuitive experiences and/or synchronicities, and be encouraged to further explore their own sensitivities and how they might be enhanced or expanded.

Seeing My Own Pituitary Tumor

As I indicated previously, in May of 1995 I learned that my life was being challenged with a little but rather scary brain tumor. After about nine months of trying unsuccessfully to shrink the tumor with both medicine and Essiac Tea, I made the decision to have the tumor removed and chose Dr. Edward Laws at the University of Virginia in Charlottesville, Virginia. My research revealed that he was considered to be "the best doctor in the country for pituitary tumors." During my pre-surgery exam, I told Dr. Laws that I was "psychically sensitive" and could *see* my pituitary tumor, and drew a picture of it for him. As I did so, I pointed to a spot on the backside of the tumor and told him that although I *knew* he would normally not look at that area, he needed to because there was "a problem" there as well. Dr. Laws humored me and noted what I said, but one of the residents, George, listened intently to what I was saying. As they left, George took the piece of paper that I had drawn the tumor on and winked at me as they left.

Following the surgery, Dr. Laws reported that the surgery went extremely well. Then he graciously stated that my diagram was surprisingly accurate and that there was indeed "a problem" on the back where I had indicated and that they removed it. George just winked at me and smiled.

The hospital was awesome in that Dotti was given a cot next to my bed and the nurses greatly appreciated the help she was able to give, even though she usually passes out when she sees blood. Unfortunately, two days after the initial surgery I began leaking spinal fluid from my nose and Dr. Laws' team had to rush me back into surgery to seal the leak.

> NOTE: In case you must ever have this surgery, please know that this is very rare.

When I asked my Spirit Guides why this happened, I was *told* that this was done for Dr. Laws' and George's learning and that I had agreed to be the guinea pig. It took me six weeks to fully recover and gratefully I have had no recurring problems.

The Impulsive Driver

For several years in the late 1990's Dotti and I actively participated in several Metaphysical shows selling our Alpine Air (EcoQuest) Purifiers.[46]

---

[46] See my web site: "http://www.ReflectionsInLight.org/Health"

Following those shows we typically went out to dinner to talk about what we learned, what we earned, who we met, and how the day went. On this one occasion, we were at the Outback Steak House in Vienna sitting in a booth when all of a sudden a full motion video appeared in my head. Dotti could see that I was quite distracted and having seen me do this several other times, knew I was "tapping into" something and patiently waited while I processed what I was *seeing* and experiencing.

In my mind's eye I *saw* a scene of a young man in his early thirties impulsively and carelessly driving onto a freeway without looking. As he did so, I saw his wife and a young boy about three years old standing alongside the road crying. As he drove out onto the freeway his car was broadsided and run over by an eighteen-wheeler, then the scene disappeared. I *knew* I was picking up something from someone in the restaurant so I turned around to see where it might be coming from. Seated at a table about twenty feet from us were the young man, his wife and the little boy I had seen in the vision. I pointed them out to Dotti and told her what I had seen and said to her, as well as my Spirit Guides, "Now what the hell am I supposed to do with this information?" I knew that I couldn't just walk over to them, and tell him to be careful the next time he drives onto a freeway! That would simply scare his wife and child and he would probably have thought I was weird and called the cops. Yet I knew that I was being shown this for a reason and that I had to do something.

My Spirit Guides told me that he was a very impulsive driver and if he was not careful, what I saw would occur! I was told that I needed to make contact with his Higher Self and warn him that he needed to be more attentive and less impulsive because he had a wife and a young son to care for. I did as instructed. Hopefully his Higher Self got the message and that he will listen to his intuition whenever he is driving or otherwise in danger. I will, of course, never know whether I was successful in preventing a possible accident, but I felt better for taking the action I could. My Spirit Guides told me this was just an example of how I needed to pay attention and be of service as I was called to be. That kind of experience happens to me a lot.

Although Dotti is not psychically sensitive, she is very intuitive and has become very aware of and sensitive to synchronicities in her life. As she often points out to people, you can expand your intuitiveness just by becoming more aware. For example, if you *sense* a problem with one of your children, listen to that still small voice. If you find that you missed a car accident because you took the "wrong" road, know that synchronicity is at work. "Mother's intuition" is very real. Know it and honor it!

Raphael's Death and Appearance

In the late 1990's, a neighbor, Raphael, whom I knew casually and liked, passed away from pancreatic cancer after a rather long illness. Although I knew he was ill, I did not realize that his illness was terminal. The morning after the ambulance came and took him away I was sitting in my study working on my computer. As I did so, a dove landed on my windowsill and walked back and forth, cooing. It repeated this several times but I was oblivious to it. When I finally noticed it, I thought that it might be Raphael trying to send me a message. As I looked at the dove, I said, "If you are from Raphael, please stop and coo twice then turn around and coo twice again." It did it! The dove then flew to the tree in front of Raphael's home, and continued to coo. When I told Dotti about this incident, she stated that she heard a lot of Doves cooing from several trees nearby. Our neighbor Terri also reported hearing a number of Doves cooing in her back yard that day.

Later that day, Raphael's oldest daughter saw me at the community mailbox and asked me to say a few words at her father's funeral. I had been the President of the Board of Directors for our Homeowners Association for several years and had helped Raphael out with several matters. The day of the funeral, Dotti, our neighbor, Terri, and I attended the memorial service at a local funeral home. As we walked into the funeral home, I noticed that Raphael had been cremated and his urn and a picture of him were on a pedestal near the front. However, I also *saw* Raphael and a person who identified himself as either a cousin or younger brother of Raphael's who had passed many years previously. I began rapidly writing down what I was *seeing, hearing*, etc. on the funeral announcement.

Raphael and his "friend" were wearing green and white soccer uniforms, which I had never seen Raphael wear before, and were holding up a green and white soccer ball as if that were really important. I then *heard* Raphael say that he was really looking forward to doing some fishing in the mountain streams. He *told* me that he had done that in his native country, Peru, and was looking forward to doing it again. Raphael then showed me an old (1942-1945) pickup truck and said his uncle Tio or something like that, had taught him how to fix automobiles on that truck. The hood was up and I could *see* that his uncle was a rather tall man with bushy white hair and looked very much like pictures I have seen of Mark Twain, but a lot gruffer looking. I had heard that Raphael was an excellent auto mechanic in real life.

When it came time for Raphael's wife, Luz, and their daughters to speak, Raphael stood on the left side of one daughter with his hand on her shoulder. When the other daughter got up to speak, he moved to the other side of that daughter. With the older daughter he poked her in the ribs like he was trying to cheer her up and make her smile. He *told* me to tell them that everything would be OK. When it came my turn to speak, I remember saying something about what a nice neighbor he was and that I was sorry I had not spent more time with him. I remember him standing off to the side just noting what I was saying and being aware of who was present at his funeral. Then he seemed to focus on Luz, lovingly trying to help her find a sense of peace.

As we left the funeral home he *told* me that he wanted me to tell his wife everything that I had *seen* and *heard*. As we got in the car to go home, I *heard* Raphael say, "Tell Luz that she can throw away the holey socks in the bottom drawer." As we drove home, he kept repeating this phrase to me over and over again, and finally I mentioned it to Dotti and Terri. It made no sense to me at all but it was obviously important to him. Although Terri is quite sensitive herself, she gets "weirded out" by psychic stuff and said, "Lowell, you're just weird!" and then laughed. I said, "I know, but he keeps saying it over and over again."

When we got home we were invited to Raphael's family home for refreshments and to "share," a traditional after-funeral ritual. Although I was not aware of Raphael's presence when I first arrived, I knew I needed to find a way to share what I *got* at the funeral home with his wife and two daughters. At one point I found them all gathered in the kitchen together so it was a perfect opportunity to talk to them away from the other guests. I told his wife Luz, "I'm not sure whether you know it, but I am *psychically sensitive* and I need to share with you some information that I picked up from Raphael at the funeral home." They cautiously listened.

I told them about the green and white soccer ball that Raphael kept showing me and the dead brother or cousin or someone with him. They laughed and explained that green and white was the color of Raphael's Peruvian soccer team, and that Raphael and his late cousin played soccer a lot together. I then shared that Raphael had *told* me that he was looking forward to mountain stream fishing again and they again laughed and told me that he loved to fish in the mountain streams near their home in South America. I then mentioned the guy with the white hair and the truck, and told them that I knew that "Tio" meant uncle in Spanish but that he insisted that his name was Tio and that he was Raphael's uncle. They replied that Raphael's uncle's name was Zeo and he had indeed taught Raphael to fix automobiles with a 1940's truck. They said that he was tall and had bushy white hair.

I then cautiously asked the daughters whether their father approached one of them on the right side and approached the other one on the left side, and whether he poked either one of them in the ribs to cheer them up. They hugged each other while laughing tears and said "Yes, that was so our dad." They also said that whenever either one of them would "get down" he would poke them in the ribs with his finger and say something in Spanish to cheer them up.

By this point Luz and her two daughters were all crying and laughing and had a look of amazement on their faces. Raphael had given me enough information to let them know that I had indeed communicated with him. I then said to Luz, "I know that you will probably think I am totally crazy, but as we were driving home from the funeral home, Raphael kept telling me to tell you that, "You can now throw out his holey socks from the bottom drawer." "Does that mean anything to you?" Both Luz and her two daughters again began laughing through their tears and she said, "Yes." She stated that indeed Raphael kept several pairs of worn holey socks in the bottom drawer of their dresser that he always wore to church and that he would never let her throw them away. It was then very clear to me that Raphael truly wanted his family to know he was still very much present. At that point I became aware of Raphael's presence in the kitchen and he was grinning from ear to ear as he embraced his wife. She apparently sensed him because she smiled and said she could *feel* his presence. They all thanked me and as I left, I heard Raphael say "Gracias amigo, you are a true friend."

Over the next several weeks, Raphael's children and his wife came over and spent several sessions with me as I tuned into what I could pick up to help them come to grips with Raphael's death and their very untimely loss. A few months after Raphael's death, they sold their house, moved out of the neighborhood, and I lost contact with them.

Flying with Corey

In 1999, I decided to get my Private Pilots License and began flying with AV ED Flight School in Leesburg, Virginia. I had wanted to fly all of my life and as the reader may recall when Suzanne asked me what I wanted to be, I said either an Airline Pilot or an Engineer. I became an Engineer rather than an Airline Pilot, but the passion to fly never left me.

Shortly after I started my flying lessons, John Kennedy, Jr. had his fatal plane crash, and Dotti was more than trepidatious about my flying, but I was determined. Then within a few weeks after John Kennedy's plane went down, Dotti's niece, Barbie suffered the heartbreaking loss of her eldest son, Corey, in a plane crash. He was a wonderful young pilot whom I had met a couple of years previously. Corey began flying when he was just sixteen and he loved to fly. The day of the accident he decided to "buzz'" his Grandfather's farm (Dotti's brother Darvin). As he dove low over his

Granddad's and uncle's heads, he tipped his wings. However, he failed to notice that the ground rose up faster than his little aerobatic airplane could climb. He hit the top of a tree next to the house, taking about 12 feet off the top of the tree. His Grandfather and uncle Mike watched in horror as they saw him hit the tree and cartwheel into a nearby cornfield. They were in complete shock as they ran into the cornfield to try to find the airplane, fearing that it might catch on fire. When his Granddad found the plane, there was no fire but Corey was slumped in his seat with a bruise on his forehead. As his mother, Barbie, tells the story, as she heard the ambulance roar past her farm on its way to the crash site, she felt Corey touch her shoulder. She knew the ambulance was for him. She felt his presence, she felt his love, and she knew he was gone. He was just 21.

When I learned of Corey's accident my heart ached for the family's loss. He was a good pilot and he didn't deserve to die so young. One night a few days after we heard about the accident, I had been reading my large flying textbook and had set it securely on the bathroom vanity. In the middle of the night Dotti and I were awakened from a deep sleep with a loud crash. We both got up and I trepidatiously ran around the house to see if someone had broken in. Everything seemed fine. However, as I went past my bathroom I noticed that my big textbook had fallen to the floor. I immediately *knew* that Corey was trying to get my attention. As I picked up the book and placed it back on the vanity, I *heard* him tearfully say, "I broke the 500 foot barrier! I broke the 500 foot barrier!" referring to an FAA rule. I told Dotti what I heard and then blessed him and told him that he needed to let go and send comfort and peace to his whole family – his mom, his dad, his siblings and his grandparents, because I knew they were all devastated. Over the next several days I kept *hearing* Corey lament, "I broke the 500 foot barrier! I broke the 500 ft barrier!" I felt the great sadness and sorrow that he was feeling for his mom. Yes, Spirits express "feelings or emotions" of regret and anger. Dotti told her niece, Barbie, and her husband, Doug, about my experience and about my continuing to tune into and *talk* to Corey, which seemed to comfort them.

I continued to *see* and *hear* Corey over the next couple of years. I would *see* him on the ramp at the airport, walking in between the planes. Sometimes he would sit in the right seat while I was doing practice maneuvers, and one time I had an instructor in the right seat but when I looked over at him Corey was there as well. It startled me, and my instructor asked me what was going on. I felt a chuckle from Corey. I do believe he was with me, enjoying some flight hours from the other side. I got my Private Pilots License on Christmas Eve 1999, five days before my sixtieth birthday. I have since gotten my Instrument Rating and I absolutely love to fly.

A couple of years after the accident, we visited the Iowa farm where Corey had his accident, and I saw exactly where he crashed. It appeared that he was lower than 200 feet on his pass and I noticed that there was a 70-foot or so tree on a hill next to the house. I also noted that the hill itself raised another 50 feet or more from the low point where he passed over his granddad. You could still see where the top of the tree had been taken off. As I stood there, I said to Corey, you sure did break the 500-foot barrier, and I *heard* him say with a sad chuckle, "Yeah I know."

Sandy's Dad

Shortly after my divorce from Suzanne in 1979, I met Rick and Sandy at the Unity Church. Although we were not really close, we shared common friends from the church and a number of Unity weekend retreats at Capon Springs in West Virginia. I always saw Sandy as a very energetic lady who seemed very interested in Metaphysics, while her husband Rick seemed to question almost everything through his intellect. In spite of all the Unity truths and principles he was exposed to at church and retreats, Rick just didn't seem to *get* or *take on* what were considered to be the most basic Metaphysical principles. He was very smart, good at his profession and a good father, and I respected him for those things.

In June 2003 at a Unity Church Social gathering at our Minister's home, I "bumped into" Sandy. Earlier that day I had presented a *Spiritual & Psychic Development Workshop* at the Unity Church, and as we talked, Sandy asked how the workshop had gone. I told her it was great and shared some interesting mini-readings I had done in the class. As we were standing there talking, Sandy commented, "I wonder what [my] Dad is doing?" not really expecting an answer but merely being inquisitive. I stopped, tuned in and said, "Painting seascapes." I had *heard* those words in my head, and *saw* her dad at an easel painting a seascape scene. Sandy said, "You sure have connected to my father's energy," because, as she proceeded to tell me, her father was an artist, and a seascape he had painted forever graced their family's home. She stated that her father loved the water and his dream was to live at the water's edge, and was driven to make that dream a reality. Thus my statement served as a perfect sign that I had indeed tapped into Sandy's dad's energy and it really peeked her interest. Sandy asked more questions as she delved into many Metaphysical realms, all of which I was able to answer. I had truly captured her interest and a few days later she invited me to a session with some of her fellow spiritual explorers. As she often tells her friends, my responses to their questions reinforced her belief in my authenticity in accessing information, as well as in my accuracy.

Since then, Sandy has been one of my strongest Marketing and PR advocates. As she has so often stated, there is hardly a place that she goes that my name doesn't come up in her conversation and she is constantly sending clients to me for readings, for which I am eternally grateful.

Reading For Sandy's Siblings

In the winter of 2003 Sandy invited me over to talk to her brother Art and sister Connie who were visiting for the Christmas holidays. When I arrived she stated that her brother was interested in a reading. As we sat around talking, they told me that their aunt had died several years previously and that their cousin, who had lived with their aunt, had recently died from a heart attack as one of those Santa Ana wind California fires got closer and closer to her home. As the executor of their cousin's estate, Art was having to go through their "stuff" and they wanted to know how their aunt and cousin were and was there anything special they needed to know.

As I sat there talking to them, I began *seeing* all of these images and *hearing* their aunt and cousin talk to me. I said that they seemed like "old maid seamstresses" and that there were a lot of weird looking clothes, at which point everyone laughed. I also told them that I *saw* stacks of old what I thought were Look magazines and that some of them contained important documents, and old money or certificates of some kind in them that were quite valuable. As I write this I remember saying that either they were Look Magazines or that they were to look in the magazines, I wasn't sure which.

I also told them that their cousin and aunt were serious pack rats causing Art, Sandy and Connie to all burst out laughing again, and they began telling me stories about their aunt and cousin being seamstresses who made weird colored clothes and that they indeed were serious pack rats. When the laughter calmed down, Art asked what they should get rid of and I *heard* in my head and responded, "the clothes" at which they burst out laughing again.

When I talked to Sandy about this get together in preparation of writing this story, she reminded me that their mother was also visiting for Christmas. She said that when we were talking, their mother walked into the room then turned around and walked out, and that as she did I laughed and told them that all of their Auras seemed to collapse when their mom walked in. Sandy reminded me that when I mentioned this to them, they very shyly acknowledged that they were feeling a kind of admonition, and they again all laughed uproariously.

Channeling For Rick

In the winter of 2003, Sandy's husband, Rick, became aware that he was beginning to forget things and was not thinking clearly. This was very unusual since Rick was regarded as a very clear thinking, intellectual type of person. His legal consulting business relied on that ability.

Sandy suggested that Rick contact me to see if I could tell what was going on. When Rick called me, he stated that he was having some mental difficulties, without specifying exactly what they were. He sounded somewhat confused and quite vague. I was not too suspicious because Rick could often be vague when he talked to me. However, something inside told me that he was having a spiritual "mid-life crisis," meaning that Spirit was pushing him to begin to pay attention and begin to recall the Metaphysical information he had been exposed to throughout his life. I knew that this was going to be a struggle for Rick because it would cause him to have to "get out of his head and into his heart."

When I would see him at church or social gatherings, it seemed that he was becoming increasingly more vague. Each time I would remind him that he needed to begin to apply the Metaphysical principles he had been exposed to over the more than twenty years I had known him. What I *sensed* was that he seemed to be lapsing into the early stages of Alzheimer's or dementia. Little did I know how accurate that *sense* was.

In March of 2004 Rick's problems reached crisis proportions. He developed severe tremors, behavioral issues, a bloody rash, among a host of other symptoms, and became increasingly confused. He was hospitalized but as Sandy told me, "the doctors weren't sure what was wrong with him." She asked me to do a Medical Intuitive reading for him in May. Because I was not comfortable doing a conscious Medical Intuitive reading with that much riding on my pronouncement I chose to do a channeled reading.

The channeled reading indicated that Rick was suffering from extreme exposure to toxins, and that these toxins were the cause of his increased mental "fogginess." The reading mentioned that he had grown up and played in his dad's tanning factory (something that I did not know), which caused him to be exposed to toxic material such as xylene, naphthalene, phosphoric acid and tannic acid, and other toxins used in the tanning process, for an extended period of time. The channel further stated that years of additional exposure to these and similar toxins had seriously affected his pancreas, liver, and brain. Sandy later told me that he had grown up in a turn-of-the century house with lead paint and lead pipes as well. The channel stated that the toxins had reached a level that his body could no longer purge or get rid of them, which is known in medical circles as "body burden."

The reading stated that these toxins were in fact spread throughout the lining of the brain and distributed within the lining of his liver. It stated that it would take some serious detoxing to begin to remove the toxins and gave the name of a chelation therapy doctor in the area. The reading also indicated that a normal test would not find these toxins because, "the chemistry that they use to test same does not allow for a discrimination along the wall of the lining of [the] liver." It also indicated that, "…it cannot be seen in what would be termed a CAT scan or MRI."

The reading recommended chelation as well as acupuncture for a period of six to nine months. When I came out of the channeling session and later read the transcript, I questioned the chelation recommendation because that is a process normally only used for heavy metal toxicity removal, and the reading did not indicate that Rick had heavy metal toxins. However, Sandy took Rick to several holistic doctors who all confirmed through several heavy metals tests that his body was in fact carrying high levels of lead, mercury, aluminum, and manganese, all of which would have a significant neurotoxic impact upon his body. Rick had a total of ten chelation therapy sessions and several acupuncture treatments but they did not seem to help or have any measurable impact upon the heavy metals "burden" confirmed through follow-up testing, and so treatments were discontinued.

Several subsequent readings by myself and another psychic specified that although these physical factors were seriously stressing Rick's physical body and mental faculties, the greater challenge was his soul's need to take on, accept and begin working with the spiritual principles he had been exposed to throughout his life. The readings were essentially telling him that he needed to work on his spiritual development and that the physical healing would follow.

In her long search for answers, Sandy took Rick to many specialists and discovered a doctor on the Eastern Shore of Maryland who was focused on biotoxin research, working with chronically ill patients who manifested a wide range of symptoms without answers. His research found that their illnesses were linked to the body's inability to remove toxins from mold, Lyme disease, and other toxic agents. His research team had discovered a series of markers (as seen in blood tests) that indicate biotoxin exposure, including certain genotypes[47] that are especially susceptible and compromise the body's ability to process out or eliminate biotoxins. They estimated that this occurs in 1 in 4 people in the United States.

Sandy told me that testing of Rick's blood revealed that indeed he had the "dreaded genotype." In fact, the doctor noted that many of Rick's markers indicating toxic exposure were "off the charts" including one measuring inflammation, and was likely at the root of his horrendous pain. Rick was diagnosed as having toxic encephalopathy, consistent with what the Channeling session had said about the toxic impact to his brain. The doctor indicated that treatment for those with toxically compromised systems similar to Rick usually didn't have a sustained favorable outcome.

However, Sandy soon discovered that much of the medical community was unfamiliar with this research and/or unwilling to consider it. Although the reading was revealing, in that it helped identify what the problem was, current medical testing is insufficient as well as procedures for detoxing, not widely understood or embraced by the medical community.

As a result, Sandy has since become an avid advocate,[48] educating and helping people understand how environmental issues significantly affect our health today, including what we inhale, and what we ingest and absorb into our bodies. Ironically, prior to his own illness, Rick had a career helping chronically ill or injured clients with legal settlements related to vaccines, sick building syndrome, and other environmental agents. Through their journey, she believes Rick "took the bullet" to bring awareness of these increasing 21st century realities. Although many things were tried over several years, Rick got progressively worse and the care consultant recommended placement in a dementia facility, where he currently resides, slowly deteriorating.

---

[47] The genetic constitution of a cell, an organism, or an individual (i.e. the specific allele makeup of the individual) usually with reference to a specific character under consideration. For instance, the human albino gene has two allele forms, dominant A and recessive a, and there are three possible genotypes -- AA (homozygous dominant), Aa (heterozygous), and aa (homozygous recessive). See: http://en.wikipedia.org/wiki/Genotypes

[48] See Sandy's web site; http://www.GutsGraceAndGusto.com

Alison's Ghost and The Lewinsville Hanging Tree

One day at work, a colleague named Alison, who sat in the cubicle next to me, came into the office quite upset and confidentially told me that she believed their newly purchased house was "haunted." She said that she was experiencing a *feeling* of someone watching her in various parts of her house, especially in the kitchen, on a regular basis, and although she wasn't really frightened, she was concerned for her two young children.

As Alison talked, I *saw* her house in my "mind's eye" and *saw* a young black woman in her mid-20's in a muslin rough pinkish brown fabric dress. The young woman *told* me that she had been a slave who was hung from a nearby tree because she had refused her master's sexual advances. She said she had been whipped and that her body was left to hang for three days as an example to others. I later learned that her "husband" and two children were made to watch, which pained her greatly. I shared what I saw with Alison and told her that she was in fact being "watched" by this young woman. I assured Alison that she did not need to be frightened because this young slave was not a disruptive ghost; she just wanted her story to be heard. I explained that ghosts (discarnate entities) can tell who is psychically sensitive, as Alison is, and when they want to be heard they often make their presence known by moving objects or catching the attention of a person via their peripheral vision.

I suggested to Alison that she use the Unity Prayer of Protection[49] and the Robe of Light Protection Prayer.[50] I gave her a copy to read and told her to memorize it and that it was important that she not deny this presence, but rather talk to the young woman and send her loving light. I also told Alison that it would be helpful if she would tell this ghost that she must not scare her children or otherwise upset the household. I explained that as Free Will spiritual beings, we (the living) have the right to request that discarnate entities not interfere with our lives, and they must obey. It is a Metaphysical

---

[49] Unity Prayer of Protection – "The Light of God surrounds me, The Love of God enfolds me, The Power of God protects me, and The Presence of God watches over me, Wherever I am, God is and all is well."

[50] The Robe of Light Protection Prayer – "I surround myself with a Robe of Light, consisting of the love and power and wisdom of God, not only for my own protection, but so that all who see it or come in contact with it will be dawn back to God and healed."

law. However, I also explained that like a two-year-old child, they may not initially understand and we must continue to insist until they get the message.

Over the next couple of weeks Alison explained that she had been using the Robe of Light affirmation and was sending loving light to the entity, and that she was no longer experiencing the entity's presence. One evening as Alison was leaving the office, the slave lady appeared to me and told me her name was Sarah and that she wanted to thank Alison for the light she had been sending her. As Alison was saying goodnight, I yelled to her "Oh by the way, the slave's name is Sarah and she thanks you for sending her light." That got Alison's attention and now that Alison's "new friend'" had a name, it was easier to focus and send loving light to her.

The next day I shared several additional details with Alison that I learned from this young black slave. She *told* me that she had been hung in the mid-1850's from a very large double trunk tree near Alison's house that had been used as a hanging tree for many years. Even though I had never been in Alison's house, and Alison had not told me about her house, I described the area where Alison's house was and where the "felled tree" was relative to her house. As I continued to tune in, more details about the tree, the landscape, and area around Alison's house began filling in for me. I stated that the tree was about a quarter mile from her house, out the back and to the right, and that I *felt* the tree had very recently been cut down. That evening Alison asked her young daughter, Hallie, who I had identified as an *Indigo* with slight *Crystal* characteristics, if a very large tree had recently been cut down in the neighborhood. At that, her daughter became very excited and explained that yes indeed there was a very large tree that had recently fallen and was being (or had been) cut down in approximately the same area I had described. She stated that, in fact, it was a very famous tree that Arborists from around the country came to study. When Hallie asked her mother why all the interest in this tree, Alison explained a little about Sarah's story and Hallie said, "Oh my God, that is cool" and ran off with a friend to take a look at the tree.

When the teenage girls got to the felled tree, a man named Jeff was working on his lawn adjacent to where the tree had fallen. Hallie, being the talkative little girl that she is, told him all about Sarah and the "hanging tree" and Jeff told her that a lot of strange things had happened in his house. He explained that it had gotten so bad that they had to have a Catholic Priest come to the house and do an exorcism. He explained that his wife, Paulette, was putting their toddler to bed one evening and a bottle magically transported itself from across the room to the baby's crib. He said that his wife was also frightened because their older daughter was *seeing* people who were not there. In one incident their older daughter said, "What is that man doing in the back yard, mommy?" Without looking, Paulette said "Oh it's probably Mr. Johnson," thinking it was the next-door neighbor. But then her daughter said, "But Mr. Johnson does not have dark skin, mommy." Paulette then asked her daughter what the man had on, and she said that he was wearing old coveralls and didn't have any shoes on. When her mom came to the window, there was no one there.

When Alison's daughter returned and shared these stories, Alison called Jeff. At first he thought she was going to "chew him out" for frightening her daughter, but Alison assured him she was not angry, only interested in what he knew and had experienced. She explained that she had this "psychic friend" at work and told him everything I had said about the hanging tree and the ghosts. He asked if I would please talk with him and his wife. Things were happening in and around their house and his wife was very frightened. Alison assured him that she would pass on the message and have me contact them.

Connecting With Paulette and Her Family

A couple of days after Allison talked to Jeff, his wife, Paulette, called me at work. She explained that she was a scientist and was not sure she believed in "this stuff" but she knew what she and her daughters were experiencing, and it frightened her. She reaffirmed the story about the baby and the bottle, her daughter's seeing the man in the backyard, and then told me about lights being turned on and off throughout the house. She also told me, "Sometimes it sounds like someone is walking up and down the stairs." She explained that although she had a Catholic Priest come to the house and perform an exorcism, it apparently did not work. As I was talking to her I *saw* the man her daughter had seen outside and I *heard* that his name was Benjamin, and I *knew* that he was the father of Sarah's children. I was *told* in my mind that as slaves, they were not allowed to marry back then. He explained to me that Sarah had been hung (as I had picked up) and expressed how hurt and angry he was that their two children were made to watch and that Sarah was left hanging for three days and each day the "master" would bring him and the children out past the tree to make sure they saw her hanging there. I explained to Paulette that Benjamin was not an evil energy and would not harm her children; he just wanted to be heard.

I then "tuned in" to Paulette's house to gain a sense of what the noises in her house were about. I was *shown* a young white servant girl, probably about fourteen in a dress similar to Sarah's. It was explained to me that she was the servant who looked after the children back then. She said she was the one who gave the baby the bottle, but it was someone else who had been turning the lights on and off. I then *picked up* that it was Sarah's former master who had been turning the lights on and off. I tuned into these ghosts energies and emphatically told them to leave Paulette and Jeff's children alone, to stop turning the lights on and off, and that they needed to go to the light. I told Paulette to write down and memorize the Robe of Light Protection Prayer, and explained that she could tell the ghosts to simply leave. I agreed to meet with her, her husband Jeff and their children to see what additional information I could "pick up." This was getting very interesting for me!

Dotti and I met Paulette at Alison's house and I explained again what I *saw* and understood and tried to explain to Alison and Paulette a little about how "this psychic stuff" worked for me. Paulette felt more assured when she learned that I was a real scientist even though I was psychic. As we walked out of Alison's back door I explained again where I *saw* the hanging tree, which Paulette and Alison confirmed. I told them what I *picked up* as we walked the quarter mile or so to Paulette's house. As we walked I described the terrain as it was during the time period these events took place, and *picked up* information about an old Native American campground that was very near Alison's house. I stated that the current path we were taking was a "trail of tears" for the Native Americans. I told them that this same path was used during the Civil War to transport the injured and dead soldiers to the river – the nearby Swains creek and the Potomac River, and then to the Lewinsville military headquarters.

As we got to the felled tree I was aware of, and somewhat overwhelmed by, the many "souls" that had been unjustly hung there and felt great sadness yet gratitude that the tree was finally cut down, never to be used for hanging again. As we stood there, I told Alison and Paulette that I was being *shown* that three properties had occupied this area back then. I stated that the name "Macall" or something like that with a weird spelling was the "master" who owned this particular place. As we walked through Paulette's backyard and onto her back patio, I saw through the large window into the playroom where Paulette's two little girls were. I identified the older girl as an *Indigo* and the younger one as an *Indigo* with a lot of *Crystal* characteristics. They were looking toward the fireplace mantel and I *saw* the young white servant girl standing next to the mantel, where Paulette's children seemed to be looking. I explained what I was *seeing* and told Paulette that this "entity" was the same one I *saw* in my mind when she and I had talked on the phone.

As we went into the house, Paulette explained that her youngest daughter, Cara, often looked beyond her and sometimes waved at something or someone and smiled. She said that once in awhile she would seem frightened but most of the time she simply waved and laughed. Paulette said it was disconcerting to her because she did not know what her daughter was responding to or *seeing*. I explained that in my opinion, all young children are sensitive and can often *see* Spirits (dead people) and other energy forms and that most of them simply "grow out of it" or become less sensitive because it becomes less important. Paulette introduced me to her daughters and they both seemed to look around me rather than at me, which is what I often observe when kids are sensitive to energies (Auras).

Notice this behavior when you are around children. This usually indicates that they are looking at the Aura pattern around people, not how the person looks. This actually happened to me recently at a California Pizza kitchen. There was a lady with two boys—one about four years old and one about six years old who were being rambunctious as young kids typically are. As I looked at the two boys, the six year old stopped what he was doing and just stood looking at me. My friend Sandy said that she actually saw his shift as he looked at my Aura. I told his mother that he was seeing my Aura, gave her my card, and explained a little about what was going on psychically. He continued to stare at me, but as I talked to him and told him that I saw 'lights' too, he went back to playing with his brother. That happens to me a lot! Sometimes I can 'hear' them asking or wondering what is different about my Aura. My Aura reflects that I am psychic, and they don't quite understand what it is they are seeing; just that it is different from other people.

After meeting and talking with Paulette's husband Jeff, Paulette took her older daughter, Kelly, and me upstairs to her daughter's bedroom, while Dotti and Alison stayed and talked to Jeff and their younger daughter Cara. As we entered Kelly's bedroom, I told Paulette that the young white servant girl was there, and I verbally told the young servant that she needed to leave and that she was not to further disturb Paulette's children. I then invoked the power of the children's Guardian Angel,[51] and told Kelly, who had been very quiet up to that point, that she did not need to be afraid at night any more.

---

[51] The Children's Guardian Angel prayer I use is: "I call upon the children's Guardian Angel to surround and protect (the child's name – Kelly) from all harm and to touch her heart and mind so that she always knows that you are there and that she can call upon you."

The room seemed to immediately light up and the young white servant left. As I did this, Kelly became very talkative and began showing me her toys.

Paulette, Kelly and I went back down to the main level to join Jeff, Dotti, Allison and Cara. As we talked, Paulette told me about a room downstairs where she and Jeff *felt* and *saw* strange things and where her children refused to go. As I *sensed* their basement, I described a workbench and told Jeff that I could see him at the bench and that out of the corner of his eye he would see things. Jeff said he did not experience that but perhaps the previous owner had, because the previous owner did indeed have a workbench in that room and apparently did a lot of work there. Paulette then led me downstairs, and as I approached the basement area, I could feel a real "chill." As Paulette opened the door to the room where no one wanted to go, I felt a very angry presence exit the room past me as we entered. I was compelled to look up at the ceiling and although there was simply a normal light, in my mind's eye it appeared as if I was looking up at the bottom of a wagon. I realized that the ground above where we were (we were below ground level) was the place where the bodies from the hanging tree were loaded onto a horse drawn wagon. I *sensed* that one body (the Spirit that exited the room as we entered) had actually been buried here and that although his skeletal remains had long ago been removed, his energy was still present. I told Paulette what I *saw* and experienced and she immediately "crossed herself." I tuned into the entity and told him to go to the light. I blessed the room and suggested that whenever Paulette or Jeff entered the room they needed to say a prayer for the entity who had been buried there, and to tell the entity to go to the light until they no longer felt his energy present.

We went back upstairs and Paulette, Kelly and I then went into the children's playroom. I told Kelly that I also *saw* her playmate (the young white servant girl) and that she was holding either a basket or a doll. Kelly quietly corrected me saying it was a basket with a doll in it. So she knew I was able to see what she was seeing. Paulette asked that I tell her daughter's playmate to leave and to "make it OK" with Kelly. I explained to Kelly that the man she had seen in the back yard was very sad because his wife had died and that he would not disturb her again. I told her that if she saw him to simply say, "Hi" and send him on his way. She seemed to accept that explanation and said that she *knew* he was sad. Paulette and I then talked to Kelly and told her that she needed to send her playmate "on her way" and that she needed to play with her sister Cara instead. At first she didn't want to give up her "friend" but she finally agreed to do so.

I told Jeff and Paulette that I was available via phone at any time and that they needed to continue the Prayer of Protection Affirmation. In our conversation, I discovered that Jeff was very familiar with what I was talking about because his family was connected to Unity School of Christianity.

Shortly after I met with Paulette and her family, my co-worker Alison did some internet research and discovered that a General named William MacKall (the unusual spelling) did indeed live in that area and in fact was buried in the nearby Lewinsville Presbyterian Cemetery.

Remembering Past Lives

In addition to providing stories of psychic experiences, I felt it necessary and desirable to include information and stories of how Past Life Recall experiences and the Regression Therapy process can and has been very helpful to many people.

Whether or not you believe in Past Lives, Regression Therapy can be very helpful to clients who have suppressed memories, whether from this lifetime or a previous lifetime. Regression Therapy involves a trained Hypnotherapist talking a client through a relaxation process that allows them to get in touch with or access their subconscious mind. In this hypnagogic state they are able to recall memories or childhood experiences long since forgotten. This can include "in utero" experiences as a fetus, as well as memories of experiences in a previous lifetime. Such suppressed memories, once uncovered, can completely alter one's life in a very positive manner as revealed in the following paragraphs.

Many Lives, Many Masters

The most well known example of Past Life Regression Therapy being used to heal a patient from a current life problem is documented in Dr. Brian Weiss' book *Many Lives, Many Masters*.[52] Dr. Weiss was a traditional psychotherapist who graduated from Yale Medical School and was treating a young patient, Catherine, who sought his help for some serious phobias. He had seen her for quite a while and she seemed stuck, not making any progress using all the "normal" psychiatric modalities. After over a year, Dr. Weiss decided to give hypnotism a try and hypnotized Catherine. When he asked her to, "Go back to when and where these problems began," much to his surprise, Catherine regressed to a previous life. In this beautifully written book, Dr. Weiss shares with the reader, the process of Catherine's healing

---

[52] *Many Lives, Many Masters* by Brian Weiss, MD, Copyright © 1985, A Fireside Book published by Simon and Schuster, Inc.

sessions, and Dr. Weiss's education into past lives, as she discovers the many lives she had lived and how those lives significantly affected her current life. Using classic hypnotherapy techniques, Dr. Weiss was able to help Catherine begin to recover and eventually become completely well. In the process Dr. Weiss's eyes and mind were opened to a whole new field of psychotherapies – Past Life Regression Therapy.

A Real Example of a Friends Healing

Maureen, my friend from our Unity Church – the lady whose granddaughter Mae is able to see Nature Spirits – had a profound experience during a group training exercise with Dr. Weiss. She documents her experience in her book, *Pulled by God for Conversations with Spirit Guides.*[53]

Early in our friendship, I learned that Maureen had been diagnosed with severe sleep apnea at a well-known sleep clinic and had been suffering from this debilitating condition since she was thirty-seven years old. She found that she could not use the C-PAT machine that helps people with this disorder to breathe during the night. Maureen, who was retired after many years as a psychotherapist, attended Dr. Weiss' Past Life Regression seminar to learn more about past life regression. During one of the group PLR exercises, while in trance, she remembered a lifetime in Greece where she was in a fire. She saw herself running from the fire but could not escape the smoke and died from smoke inhalation. Maureen understood that she was thirty-seven years old when she died. Dr. Weiss instructed each participant to rise above his or her death and to look down on it from above, which removes the possibility of living through the pain again. When Maureen came out of her trance, she felt perfectly fine and that night for the first time in years, her apnea was gone. It has not reappeared since that day. In this case Past Life Regression effectively eliminated the debilitating condition Maureen had suffered for over thirty years. It clearly changed the quality of her current life.

Similar experiences have occurred with clients that I have read for in which I revealed a past life trauma that was still affecting them in their current life. Once they know about it, it allows their subconscious mind to accept it and they no longer feel the need to continue to hold onto that

---

[53] See *Pulled by God for Conversations with Spirit Guides* by Maureen Malloy-Clifford, LPC, CSAC, 2009.

experience. They can then be "healed" from that debilitating memory – albeit a subconscious one, literally overnight.

Healing A Child's Fears

One example is a reading I did for a young 12-year-old girl, Lyndsay, who was fascinated with libraries but was also frightened when she was in one. She had repeated dreams of burning and choking in a fire. When I read for her, the "records" indicated that she had been a librarian in the Alexandria, Egypt library when it was burned. The records reflected that she had died trying to save irreplaceable historical artifacts. When that lifetime was revealed with all of the explanations about that experience, her fear of fire and libraries went away and she has been able to pursue her passion of working in a library. As her mother's testimonial on my web site says, "Thank you, I now have a changed daughter. Everything that seemed so unsettling to her is now so clear. You have really been a miracuous addition to our lives! Thanks again for everything. You truly have changed our lives."

Personal Past Life Recall Experiences

For me, recalling past lives is something that has happened on a regular basis. These recalls usually happen spontaneously while I am doing something else, although occasionally I have dreams that reveal a past life or meditation experiences that reveal past life information. Earlier in Chapter 2 I outlined a couple of Past Life Recalls I had as a Catholic Priest. The following additional experiences will hopefully help the reader better understand how past life information is revealed and how to learn from this information. I also include information about how to heal and release even the most difficult or embarrassing past life recall experiences, as well as how to forgive yourself and others.

> *Past life recall can be as simple as a déjà vu 'feeling' experience or as elaborate as a full motion video you see with your inner eye. DO NOT discount those images or feelings, but work with them to figure out what they are trying to tell you. They can be spontaneous or induced as several of the following were for me.*

On The Great Wall of China

In the spring of 1994 I spent two months in Beijing, China working as part of a proposal team. I was the Network Architect on the IBM design team, writing a proposal to create a telecommunications network to tie all of the banks in China together electronically. On one of the few breaks we took, we went to the Great Wall of China at Badaling and I "jogged" on the wall passing lots of other tourists. After having jogged about twenty minutes, I stopped to catch my breath and was immediately transported back in time. All of the people around me disappeared and I found myself standing there in the middle of the wall. I was a soldier and my commandant was yelling at me in Chinese. There were lots of other soldiers all lined up on either side of the wall, with several horses. As I *saw* this scene, I *knew* that I had been a sentry on the wall, and the previous night I had fallen asleep at my post. As a result, the wall had been overrun. Although injured, I was not killed but many others were and I was being "publicly reprimanded." As I stood there listening to the ranting of my commandant, he suddenly lunged forward pushing his sword through my heart. As he did, I *felt* the pain and immediately came back to the present time. I found myself gasping and grabbing my chest as other tourists looked at me strangely. I had been killed and I thought, "I deserved that" and simply smiled. I was back in the present feeling fine. It was a very confirming experience because I had *sensed* that I had been there before and I had to laugh at how much information was conveyed in such a short period of time. The entire flashback experience probably only lasted a little more than 30 sec but it sure was exciting and interesting. Owning your role and accepting responsibility goes a long way to releasing Karmic ties or debts.

A Peasant Priest In Japan

While attending an A.R.E. conference on Meditation in the early 1970's, I experienced a past life recall where I was a peasant Priest or Monk in Japan in the employ of a very mean Shogun Warlord around the 1250 CE time frame.

I had taken a break to meditate in the Meditation Room in the A.R.E. library building. As I began my meditation I asked to be shown a lifetime I might have had in Japan because in our morning session I felt powerfully drawn to some images of Ancient Japanese relics and symbols. As I quieted myself, I began *seeing* images of myself as a peasant Priest or Monk and it became clear to me that I was both the spiritual leader for the people and warriors, as well as the teacher of marshal arts. The images I became aware of included the specific armor patterns that the warriors wore as well as the pieces of cloth – sashes worn on the right shoulder to indicate each warrior's specific rank or position. I was aware of the gardens and the housing, which was slightly elevated, two to three feet off the ground. I *saw* specific individuals whom I interacted with, including the Shogun Warlord himself, who was yelling at me and actually swung a sword at me, which I dodged. When he did that I *knew* that eventually he would have me killed, because he knew he could not do it himself. I was aware that the warrior the Shogun would choose to kill me was a sergeant who had a grudge against me in this lifetime when I was in the service in France. Too bad I did not recognize it back then.

I was then taken forward to the end of that lifetime and saw myself in the garden area tending to a bonsai tree. I *saw* myself crouched by the tree and then became aware of being pierced in the back with a spear that came through my chest. I was aware of the piercing pain and looked down to see the spear sticking out of my chest. I looked around and saw the warrior who threw the spear and it was indeed the sergeant who was my assistant shop supervisor (in this lifetime) when I was in France. The scene changed and I realized where I was – in the A.R.E. Meditation room. I had apparently made some sounds because a couple of people there were holding their fingers to their lips indicating that I needed to be quiet. I left and tried to write everything down that I had remembered.

Several years later in 1995 when I was in Japan, I went to Kamakura and was absolutely in awe of the Giant Buddha there. As I stood in front of and walked around this inspiring statue, I had a déjà vu flashback of having been there as a Priest or Monk and connected that experience to the lifetime I had recalled several years previously at the A.R.E. Meditation conference.

A High Priest Of Egypt

When I first heard about Ancient Egypt and the White Brotherhood in the Edgar Cayce readings and at an A.R.E. conference, I felt a strong affinity for and a tremendous curiosity about both. I was told by many spiritually aware people I respected at the A.R.E. and other organizations, that many of us interested in the Edgar Cayce readings most likely had lifetimes in Atlantis and ancient Egypt. Several readings I had from *Lama Sing* confirmed this. A few of the Cayce readings suggested that those who had been a member of the White Brotherhood in the past would most assuredly be a highly evolved being in the current lifetime. This really drew my attention and curiosity because I was having dreams and being told in my meditations that I had been a Priest in the White Brotherhood in the past. Thus, when I had the following past life recall of being a High Priest in Egypt I simply acknowledged it and documented what I was told and what I *saw* and *sensed*.

The recall of my lifetime as a High Priest in Ancient Egypt was one of the most vivid, powerful and humbling past life experiences I ever experienced. It occurred following a particularly powerful meditation in the late 1970's. I had been asking my guides for information that would help me understand my past lives and their influence on my current life. I had asked specifically about any past lives in Ancient Egypt because I previously had several imaginative glimpses of being in Ancient Egypt in the past but had attributed them to fanciful imaginations.

Following a short but powerful meditation, I was guided to play a CD of Paul Horn playing his flute in the Great Pyramid.[54] As I again quieted my mind and listened to the music, I began to "imagine" or create a picture of the Great Pyramid in my mind, then the scene suddenly changed. I *saw* myself standing on a platform of an elevated multi-columned stone building and *knew* that I was the high priest of Egypt responsible for the Spiritual well-being of all the people. There was a tremendous sense of great pride, great humbleness and an almost paralyzing sense of responsibility. As I *saw* myself standing there, I *saw* that there were thousands of people gathered to hear Spiritual guidance regarding Ra (God). As I completed my speaking and provided a blessing to the crowd, I had this awareness of a great peacefulness regarding how I was able to "connect to the people." I *sensed* that I had achieved balance in judicial power and mercy. The feeling was not an egotistical one but a feeling of tremendous responsibility and humility. I *saw* several other scenes about that lifetime in which I was interacting with everyday people and with the Royal Family and other Priests of the Temple. I *saw* myself in a white robe with a hood carrying a long "shepherds staff" with some sort of magical powers and I *knew* that I was a Priest of the White Brotherhood.

White Brotherhood Initiation

Several months after my past life recall experience as the High Priest of Egypt, I was talking to my friend Mack from our SFG Study Group about my experience and listening to him tell me about his recall of being a "Priest of the Temple" in Ancient Egypt as well. We both then recognized that we had shared that past life together and began discussing what we recalled about that lifetime. That evening as I went to bed, I asked for additional information regarding that lifetime and had the following very powerful dream:

In the dream, I saw myself in some sort of initiation ceremony associated with the Great Pyramid. It was just prior to sunrise and I was in a white robe with a hood walking toward the Great Pyramid carrying a long 'shepherds staff' that had some sort of 'magical' powers. It was the same kind of staff I had seen in my previous

---

[54] Paul Horn's Inside the Great Pyramid CD, 1977

Ancient Egyptian High Priest past life recall, and I knew that I was seeing an earlier experience in that same lifetime. There were several other High Priests and Initiates following behind me carrying torches and their own 'staffs.' We were all chanting as we ceremoniously walked toward the Great Pyramid. I saw myself climb up a couple levels of blocks and then enter the Great Pyramid (alone) and intuitively knew that I was going to the initiation chamber – what we know today as the King's chamber. I somehow knew that I entered without a torch to light my way but was still able to find my way. It was not revealed to me exactly what I did there but somehow I knew that I lay down in the open Sarcophagus and performed some sort of centering or meditation process – I was aware that I had continued the chanting from when I entered the pyramid, both as a protective mechanism, and a centering process. I then saw myself outside the Pyramid and the High Priests and other Initiates were standing there chanting and holding torches. I intuitively knew that I had 'passed' the first stage of my initiation into the White Brotherhood

In another scene, I saw myself wrapped in a gold thread laced grayish robe with red on the inside of the neck area. I was wearing my white robe underneath the outer robe. I then saw myself within a large enclosed hall with what I believe were oil lamps on the walls. I saw myself walking down a ramp into an area about 10 ft x 20 ft filled with water or some other liquid and I knew there were some sort of poisonous snakes or other creatures in this pool. The deepest part was about chest deep and I continued chanting and walking up a ramp out of the water. Beyond this area was an area of fire that I had to walk through and knew that I could somehow walk through the fire and not be burned but that I had to concentrate and surround myself with some sort of energetic protection. As I emerged from the fiery area into another large enclosed building area, I became aware that I was met by the High Priests all holding their 'magical' staffs which they lowered toward me and verbalized some sort of incantation blessing. They were all wearing multi-colored robes, and I again became aware that I had 'passed' the severest and final test, and had become a Priest of the White Brotherhood. However, I also knew in my mind that they referred to it as a 'Priest of the Temple.'

When I awoke, I wrote this experience down and the next time I saw Mack we spent a great deal of time discussing it. This dream was very re-affirming because I had been told in my meditations, in other dreams, and in a previous *Lama Sing* reading that I had been a member of the White

Brotherhood in the past. Although in the past I was not sure I could believe it, this dream experience was very convincing and reaffirming.

I recalled this dream experience as I went though my ordination as a Priest of the Order of Melchizedek in this lifetime and was extremely grateful that this lifetime's initiation process was not nearly as demanding.

In The Time Of The Master

In another past life recall experience I remembered being an Essene Priest in the time of the Master Jesus. I have known all my life that I must have known or seen and interacted with the Master Jesus in a past lifetime. A figure that I have identified as Jesus has appeared to me many times throughout this lifetime and I feel a strong affinity with him and his message.

As mentioned in Chapter 4 while at the Unity Christmas Conference in 1973, I dreamed that I had walked on the beach with Jesus. I subsequently had a reading by Al Miner, and *Lama Sing* confirmed that both Al and I had indeed been with the Master Jesus. Several years later, while teaching a class about the Essenes, I had the experience of seeing myself as an Essene Priest from the Mt. Carmel community. In that lifetime, I had gone to the Essene community at Qumran and was leaving that community when I met the Master Jesus. In my past life recall, I recognized Him as a Master Rabbi, but not as "the Messiah." We talked and I remember Him telling me to be more gentle and patient with others for they did not understand the things I did. I have experienced repeated recalls of that lifetime and that scene several times over the years. I have had glimpses of recognizing (in that lifetime) the Messianic Consciousness that Jesus was only after he was crucified. I also have "memories" of regretting that I had not recognized that "truth" prior to His death. I later became a disciple and supporter of Jesus brother James.

When I visited Israel in 1977 I had many past life recall experiences, one of which was at the site of Qumran. There I had a flashback to what the community looked like when I was there, and I recalled a particular argument I had with one of the community leaders. I had another recall experience when we visited Galilee, one at Mt. Carmel in Haifa, and another at Caesarea. All were powerful experiences that helped me connect with those places and those lifetimes.

Significant Lifetimes of Clients

I have done readings for many clients in which information is revealed about significant events in that individual's lifetime that continues to have a major impact on that client's current lifetime. When this information is revealed, it confirms their own "suspicions" or feelings and often heals a "problem" or fear they have been holding on to. The following are a few of those profound experiences.

Keppler's Assistant

About two years ago as I began to read for one client, I saw him looking though a telescope. There were several parchments with hand drawn images of elliptical orbits with a sun figure drawn at the center. There were also several incomplete hand drawn images of our solar system on a table a few feet away from where this person was sitting. I knew that he was Keppler's assistant. In that lifetime, he was a very smart young man with a very high forehead indicating that he was losing his hair from the front, but his hair was long and stringy in the back. The reading indicated that in his "early career" he was instrumental in coming up with the correct elliptical calculations and drawings for the planets orbits. The reading also indicated that he came up with the calculations and drawings of the orbits of several of the moons of Jupiter later in his life.

In his current lifetime this individual is an engineer and is fascinated with both Astronomy and Astrology. He stated that he has always had a fascination with Keppler, but without any basis for thinking it, he somehow felt that Keppler had not done all of the work that he is credited for. The reading confirmed this. It stated that Keppler took credit for several of this man's findings and theories. Interestingly, in this lifetime this person is quite secretive in his work and somewhat fearful of people stealing his ideas. The client in fact confirmed this and stated that when he was very new as an engineer he was almost fired because he would not share his ideas with one of his co-workers until he had written it down and tested it. The "Records" indicated that this was a Karmic test for him in this lifetime and that he needed to learn to forgive Keppler for stealing his work and claiming it for his own. As the client was leaving, he stated that although this information was not what he came to me to ask, he was delighted with the revelation. He said that it made a great deal of sense to him and helped explain his otherwise unexplainable "paranoia" about someone stealing his ideas in this lifetime.

Assistant To One of The Wise Men

In one of my recent readings, I read a past lifetime for a client named Jonathan. As I tapped into his past lives, he appeared as a young student of and assistant to a "Wise Man/Astrologer" from the area of what is now eastern Iraq in the time of the birth of Jesus of Nazareth. The Akashic Records indicated that Jonathan was studying Astrology and Religions at the time and was working with his master and other prominent Astrologers and

"Wise Men." They were trying to understand the meaning of what later became known as The Star of Bethlehem. The reading indicated that in the spring of what would now be considered 4 BCE he accompanied his master and other Wise Men[55] who had gathered in his city (along with their entourage) on their way to Bethlehem, following the light of "the star." The records indicated that his master was "The One Who Brought The Myrrh."[56] It further indicated that when they arrived at the location where the baby Jesus lay, Jonathan was left to tend to the camels while his master and the other Wise Men went "to honor the Christ Child." The reading stated that although he did not *see* or *interact* with the Christ Child, he was intensely aware of the tremendous *light or Aura* of the Christ Child, and that it made a life long impression upon him.

The reading stated that the energy or *light* of the Christ Child seemed to accompany the group as a protective shield and guiding energy as they returned to their homeland. It further stated that Jonathan relived and talked about that experience for many years as he became a teacher and shared these experiences with his students. The reading stated that as the years passed, Jonathan heard about a wonderful young Rabbi who was teaching in the area of what is now Israel. It indicated that Jonathan was also aware of a young Rabbi who passed through their area on his way to the East (India), meeting with several Clergy and Wise Men of that day. The reading stated that Jonathan later heard some of those Wise Men who had met with Him, speak of this very wise, yet very young Master being. The reading indicated that Jonathan knew it was the same energy he had encountered at the Manger Scene those many years previously, and was humbled and grateful for the awareness of the presence of this Master being.

The reading stated that this lifetime was revealed to Jonathan to help him understand why he had such a strong feeling of being present when the Christ Child was born. The reading stated that he felt he had somehow *known* Jesus. When I asked Jonathan about this, he confirmed that ever since he was a very small boy he somehow knew that he had been in the presence of the baby

---

[55] The reading did not indicate the number of Wise Men, but simply said "other Wise Men"

[56] Matthew 2 is the only reference to Magi (or Wise Men) from the East in the Bible. Matthew 2:11 states that they brought "gifts of gold and of incense and of myrrh" but does not name the Wise Men. The accepted names appear to be Gaspar, Balthazar, and Melchoir.

Jesus. He had told his parents and his pastor but was reprimanded for having such grandiose ideas of exaggerated importance. He stated that although he knew it internally, he could never be quite sure because he did not see an image of the baby Jesus when he had that feeling, only a powerful feeling that he could *sense* the loving energy of the Christ Child. Of course the reading of the Akashic records confirmed this. This revelation significantly helped this client understand the basis of his childhood feelings and awareness and helped him come to terms with this lost memory. As he left he thanked me for helping him reconnect to a long lost memory. He said, "and that is not even the reason I came to see you, but you answered that question as well. Thanks."

Creating An Indigos & Sensitives Support Group

During the summer of 2005, following an *Indigo & Crystal Children* workshop that I gave at the Unity of Fairfax Church, I was urged to create a support group specifically for *New Age Kids and Young Adults* and their parents, teachers, and counselors. An energy worker friend, Stacie, who had attended my *Indigo & Crystal Children* workshop and a *Spiritual & Psychic Development* workshop, asked me to create a Support Group for these *New Age Kids.* She had two *Indigo* children herself, and felt it would help them as well as several other *Indigos* and parents she knew. We set up a weekly open discussion support group that we named *Indigos & Psychically Sensitive Teens and Adults Support Group.* This group has allowed me to share my psychic gifts and mentor others as they explore and develop their psychic sensitivities as well. It has been a genuine laboratory where everyone is encouraged to share their experiences and explore their sensitivities.

In these meetings, group members share their dreams, their psychic experiences, ask questions about what their experiences mean and how to learn to control them, etc. We also discuss how to protect one's self from unwanted or negative energies, which many have experienced. In the group meetings, I often do mini-readings for members or help those members who have had psychic experiences learn how to put their experiences in perspective. It is amazing to watch group members open up and realize that their experiences are not weird but actually understandable and often shared by others. To watch the expression on group members' faces as others share an experience similar to or the same as an experience they have had is very gratifying.

New Age Kids
Indigos, Crystals, and Star Children

"New Age Kids" Aura Pattern

As I indicated previously in Chapter 4, my awareness of and interest in *New Age Kids* began shortly after I moved to the Washington, DC area in 1972 when I met Tabatha, the new born baby of Mack and Tanya – a couple in our SFG Study Group. Tabatha was a very happy, delightful and beautiful baby girl with large penetrating dark brown eyes. However, almost immediately after she was born, I recognized that her Aura pattern was fundamentally different from any Aura pattern that I had seen before. I began recognizing that her Aura indicated that she was a highly spiritually aware and a very psychically sensitive "old soul." It also indicated that she was very intelligent and came in knowing a lot of information, and that she had a very strong "Warrior Spirit" energy, meaning that she was a very purposeful and determined little girl, with very little patience.

When I asked my Spirit Guides about what I was *seeing* with Tabatha's Aura and what it meant, I was told that her Aura pattern signaled the coming of a new generation of highly spiritually aware entities that were beginning to appear all over the world. They said that these entities could potentially change (raise) the consciousness level of humankind. I began referring to Tabatha's Aura pattern as the *New Age Kids* Aura pattern. My Spirit Guides had told me that I needed to continue to watch for this "different" Aura pattern because more and more new souls would be expressing it. They also said that it (the Aura pattern) would also be changing over time.

Sure enough, shortly after Tabatha was born, I began noticing this unique Aura pattern around several other young children. Over the next several years, as I continued my own Spiritual and psychic development, I continued to observe more and more children being born with this *New Age Kids* Aura pattern. However, much to my surprise, I began seeing babies with this unique Aura pattern being born to friends who I knew were "not spiritually aware" nor interested in Spiritual development. I also noticed that several friends and people who I knew in my Spiritual development circles were having children that did not express this unique Aura pattern. I concluded and began to believe that Tabatha, and these other kids with this *unique* Aura pattern were part of a special group of entities who were here for a specific purpose, just as my Spirit Guides had told me. It was not just because their parents were spiritual seekers.

Examples of Early New Age Kids

Throughout the 1970's I had a number of synchronistic encounters and discussions with kids who expressed the unique *New Age Kids* Aura pattern. These encounters simply confirmed my understanding that these kids represented "a new consciousness" that was coming into the earth plane, although I did not use that terminology back then. The following are a few examples of encounters I had with kids who expressed the *New Age Kids* Aura pattern during my initial awakening to this "phenomena."

Emily's Past Life Recall

Emily, the young daughter of one of the many SFG Study Groups in our Northern Virginia Council, was an exceptionally bright young girl with the *New Age Kids* Aura pattern who I would see periodically at Council events. She was very outgoing and almost as soon as she began speaking, she would periodically speak words that I could not understand. Initially I just thought she was speaking some form of baby talk or "made up language." Her Aura pattern indicated to me that she was a very wise Ancient Egyptian Spirit who had been responsible for "chiseling" many hieroglyphic messages. When I told her parents what I was seeing, her mother said that made sense because Emily was fascinated with a picture book of *Tutankhamen* they had on their living room coffee table. Her mom said that when Emily was just old enough to begin walking she would stand by the coffee table and look and point at that book. Emily loved to look at those pictures and would attempt to mouth words they (her parents) could not understand.

One day when Emily was little more than three years old, her mother reported that she began speaking to her in a different language. When she asked her what she was saying, Emily said "I'm talking to you in the language we used to use," and then ran off to play. Later her mother inquired further and Emily said, "I was just playing with you mommy," but her mother knew it was more than just made-up play words. Emily's mother phonetically repeated what her daughter had said to her SFG Study Group and asked if anyone knew what language it was. One of the group members, who was of Egyptian heritage and worked as a translator, said it sounded like an old Egyptian or African tongue but that she would have to check with someone in her office. It turned out to be a form of an early Egyptian language or dialect used with Hieroglyphics.

Emily's parents encouraged her fascination with languages, and by the time she was of school age, she was able to speak three languages quite well.

East Indian Kid in K-Mart

In the early-1970's, I encountered a young Indian boy who displayed the *New Age Kid* Aura pattern in the Fairfax, Virginia K-Mart. I was simply shopping when I heard "someone" say to me in my head, "I remember you, but you probably do not remember me." I looked around to see who was "talking to me" and noticed a four or five-year-old East Indian child in a shopping cart looking very intensely at me. I heard him *say* telepathically that he had been a neighbor and student of mine in a past life in the late 1800's in southern India where I was an English teacher. He said that I was "taken with the land and the culture" implying that although I was a foreigner in his land, that I had acclimated to and embraced the culture. His mother, who was in a Sari with a rose dot on her forehead, *heard* him say his initial statement and knew (probably from experience, and possibly from her own sensitivities) that he was "speaking to me mentally." She apologized to me, but I simply bowed and said *Namaste* and said that it was OK because I understood. She then told me that he was always saying things like that to people and that he remembered quite a few details about different past lives. She said she was not sure all of it was "real" but was obviously not opposed to entertaining such things. I thanked her and then thanked him for reminding me of our past life tie. As I again bowed and said *Namaste* to both him and his mother I *heard* him say in my mind that he was grateful to see me again. This young boy was obviously a very "wise old soul" and I have thought of him often, and wondered what ever happened to him.

Children At A.R.E. Conferences

At the A.R.E. Conferences I attended throughout the 1980's and 1990's I met many Spiritually aware people including quite a few young kids who expressed the *New Age Kids* Aura pattern. At these events, I was especially aware of the difference between the Aura patterns of older spiritually aware individuals and the Aura patterns of these *New Age Kids.*

One particular boy, Nathan, who was about ten years old when I first met him, had a very powerful *New Age Kids* Aura pattern and I talked to his parents about what I *saw* with him. They told me that I was one of the few adults he would spend time talking to. He expressed a very defiant attitude with most adults but was much more tolerant of me. Over the years Nathan and I had several conversations – mostly what was going on at the conference and what was going on with him. A couple of years after I first met him, he told me that we had been brothers in Greece – in ancient times – and that I had taught him to swim, and had in fact saved his life. Initially I did not remember any of what he told me, but then I began having dreams about that lifetime and confirmed with him and his parents, many of the things I picked up.

The important part of my experiences with Nathan and other *New Age Kids* that I saw at these conferences and elsewhere was that I began recognizing that their defiance behavior paradigm was different than the defiance behavior paradigm of many other non-*New Age Kids*. Primarily it was their impatience with growing up. Having to be in a child's body while knowing all of the things they knew, and yet not having the knowledge or experience of what it meant. I recognized that was a common challenge that all these *New Age Kids* shared. I discovered that they also felt a tremendous drive and frustration knowing that they had a purpose (their soul's purpose), but not knowing what that purpose was. Unlike Spiritual seekers I met who were interested in their soul's purpose, these non-*New Age Kids* seemed to just be curious about their soul's purpose, where as the kids that expressed the *New Age Kids* Aura pattern seemed much more driven about finding their purpose. As I encountered and interacted with more and more of these pre-teens, teens and young adult *New Age Kids*, I discovered that understanding their soul's purpose was an important and common frustration they all shared. When I was able to work with them and help them figure this out, their sensitivities and understanding increased significantly, and their frustration and impatience levels were greatly reduced.

Discovering The Term "Indigos"

When Dotti's first granddaughter, Payton, was born in April 1998, we received the call and immediately rushed to the hospital, which was just a mile or so away. As we walked into the room, I became aware of an extremely bright Aura around her new granddaughter – it literally filled the room.   Although I was aware of her extremely bright *light*, what overwhelmed me most was my awareness of the absolute presence of God in this tiny baby. When I finally held her in my arms, this awareness brought tears to my eyes, and I *said* in my mind, "Help me remember. You were just with Him. Help me remember." It was for me an overwhelmingly powerful experience that still brings tears to my eyes as I remember that energy. It reminded me of the story of the three-year-old child asking his newborn sister what it was like to have just been with Jesus.

Shortly after Payton was born, I noticed that she displayed the *New Age Kids* Aura pattern I had been seeing for so many years and told Dotti what I was *seeing*. Payton's pattern indicated that she was very bright, very psychically sensitive, and quite spiritually aware. When she was very young I would talk to her about her Aura and have her *feel* the energy around plants, her parents' dog and other animals we would see. I was very aware that she was quite sensitive to them and I wanted to encourage those sensitivities. When she began walking, she would walk around our house and look at and feel the energy of the plants, and mouth words at them, which gave me the opportunity to talk to her about what she was *seeing* and *sensing*.

A little over a year after Payton's birth, Dotti picked up a copy of Lee Carroll and Jan Tober's newly published book entitled *The Indigo Children – The New Kids Have Arrived*[57] and we began reading it. As we read it, I realized that the kids Carroll and Tober were describing in their book fit the same behavior and Aura pattern that I had been referring to as *New Age Kids* since my first encounter with them in the early 1970's.

In their book, Carroll and Tober state that the "term" *Indigo Children* was coined by Nancy Ann Tappe and they tell the story of how Nancy Ann came up with that term. As Nancy Ann was developing her own *Life Colors System* in the early 1970's, she began seeing a new color, *Indigo Blue,* around young children. Since in her experience this was a new color in her Life Colors System, she began "looking for" this particular color. She subsequently published her own book entitled *Understanding Your Life Through Color* in 1982.[58]

Carroll and Tober state that the appearance of *Indigo Children* indicates, ". . . a new generation of higher consciousness beings are being born." They also state that *Indigos* are not an American phenomenon, but in fact they (and others) have seen it on several continents. That is consistent with what my Spirit Guides had told me so many years previously. They further state that the *Indigo Children* "phenomena" seems to go far beyond cultural barriers and encompasses multiple languages. They continued, "This phenomena has escaped mainstream attention due to the fact that it is just too 'weird' to consider in the paradigm of 'normal' accepted human psychology."

In my own experience I would agree that it is definitely a worldwide phenomena. Because I live in the Washington, DC area I have met and done readings for people from countries around the globe. In preparing this manuscript, I went through the list of people I did a reading for and had identified as either an *Indigo* or *Crystal*. It includes people from: Ireland,

---

[57] *The Indigo Children – The New Kids Have Arrived* by Lee Carroll and Jan Tober, Hay House, Inc, Copyright 1999.

[58] *Understanding Your Life Through Color* by Nancy Ann Tappe, Starling Publishers, 1982.

England, France, China, Japan, Ethiopia, Russia, Turkey, Germany, Argentina, Venezuela, Brazil, Mexico, Canada, the Middle East, Thailand, Cambodia, Viet Nam, and Australia. So clearly my own experience reflects that this is indeed a worldwide phenomena, which my Spirit Guides had told me so many years previously.

Carroll and Tober state that the "phenomenon" is increasing. That is, more reports continue to surface and that many professionals are beginning to observe and acknowledge it. They state that there are some emerging answers to the challenges associated with teaching and otherwise working with these spiritually advanced children.

Following the publication of Carroll and Tober's book, the term *Indigos* has become the accepted term throughout the literature for what I had been calling *New Age Kids* and I have adopted that term as well. Although I continue to periodically refer to them as *New Age Kids*.

Indigos Characteristics

Although I identify *Indigos* via their Aura pattern, I realize that not everyone can see the Aura. Therefore, to try to help those who cannot *see* or *sense* the Aura, I have put together the following list of general characteristics that I observe in the Aura pattern of *Indigos*.

- They are highly spiritually oriented – very connected to the source of their being.

- They have a great intuitive knowledge but usually have no cognitive basis for that knowledge. This goes beyond just being psychic – knowing things psychically.

- Most have an intense impatience with the life process of "growing up." Unlike people of my generation who wanted to be older because we saw it as a means of being more independent and less controlled, with *Indigos*, it is as if they do not want to have to go through the growing up process itself.

- Many are highly psychically sensitive to energies (Auras). Some can *see* them; others are simply very sensitive to them and can readily pick up on what people are really all about. These kids can readily tell when someone is being dishonest or has "dirty lights," especially up until they are pre-teens or teenagers.

- Most remember bits and pieces of their past lives, and when they receive confirmation on what they *see* or *sense* they get really excited. When these kids learn that an adult (like myself) can *see, sense* and *pick up on* the same things that they do, and can help them understand this "gift," they feel validated.

- Many have a very difficult time "fitting in." They often feel different and out of place, even with their own siblings. This is especially true if their siblings do not acknowledge or have turned off their own psychic sensitivities. If these kids (and their parents) allow and support this "out of place" feeling to continue, they can become morose or depressed about life.

- Many come into this life with a sense of royalty and often expect to be treated that way. Even if they don't exhibit the "treat me like royalty" behavior, many of them have a strong sense of self-worth and a feeling of deserving to be here. This is true even if they can't figure out what it is that they are here to "do."

NOTE: As I have indicated previously, a very big frustration for ALL *Indigos* that I have encountered, is knowing that they are here for a purpose and not being able to figure out what that purpose is! For many of them this is a "crazy making" experience! However, once someone is able to help them discover this for themselves, it opens them up to being even more sensitive and aware. It also creates a great sense of oneness within themselves.

Other characteristics that I observe include:

- Many are very uncomfortable in their bodies – more so than the typical teenage "I don't like how I look or how I am built."

- Most seem unwilling to take any advice or correction from their parents and are often very stubborn and arrogant. They do not like absolute authority. They also dislike ritual-oriented systems, especially systems with rules that do not require creative thinking or do not make sense. They take great pleasure in defying Systems with rules or tasks that do not have a real creative purpose. They often deliberately refuse to do those tasks or follow the rules. It is what I call the *Indigo* defiance paradigm, which I talked about earlier.

- Many will either refuse to wait in a queue or have very little patience in doing so. Often times they will think nothing of cutting in line, or trying to. Like their sense of royalty, it is as if they feel that they should not have to wait.

- ALL *Indigos* exhibit what I term a *Warrior Spirit* energy. The way this shows up is whatever they set out to do that they feel passionate about, they attack like a warrior. I have observed that most parents like this about their children.

- Many exhibit a hyperactive energy (commonly diagnosed as ADD or ADHD) that often prevents them from sitting still for very long. They also bore easily. Since I have been a rather energetic person all my life, I have never thought of this "behavior" as a possible "disorder." But I recognize that it can be if left unchecked in a classroom setting. The exception to this behavior is that if there is a topic they are really interested in, they can become very immersed and can sit still, totally captivated for hours.

- They typically operate from a Win-Win Cooperation paradigm as opposed to the classic I Win, You Lose Competitive paradigm.

- Several whom I have met and interacted with were exceptionally bright in specific areas. Perhaps this "characteristic" is simply a child tapping into and exhibiting past life talents and capabilities.

"Softer New Age Kids" Aura Pattern

In the mid-1980's I had my first encounter with a child who had a new and different Aura pattern than any I had seen up until that time. It was a much softer *New Age Kids* Aura pattern and I began referring to it as such. Natie was the three-year-old son of a lady I was dating. Natie's mom, Millie, was newly divorced and had two boys: Natie and Sam a 5-year-old whom I identified as a *New Age Kid.* When I first met Natie, I noticed that his Aura pattern was much softer than his brother's and different from any other Aura pattern I had seen up to that point. Natie's Aura pattern indicated that he was a very Spiritually advanced Spirit who was very bright and very loving. His Aura pattern indicated that he was much more aware than any of the *New Age Kids* I had been seeing up to that point. When I asked my Spirit Guides about this different Aura pattern, they confirmed that it was a new and more loving energy pattern. They reminded me that they had told me that I would be seeing this change. They reiterated that I needed to pay attention because there would be a lot more entities with this softer Aura pattern entering the earth plane.

One day after Millie and I had been dating about two months, we were in her kitchen waiting for her ex-husband to return their two children. As the two boys came into the kitchen, Sam gave his mom a hug, asked for a glass of milk, and then ran to his room to play. However, young Natie ran up to his mom and gave her a big hug and said he missed her. Then he told her that his dad was upset but not at her. He said that his dad's *lights* (a term he picked up from me) were very red and he was very mad with his new girl friend. His mom just laughed. He turned to me and said that my *lights* were a lot nicer (than his dad's), then turned and ran off to play. I just smiled. Later that day when Natie came to me to ask for a glass of milk, he told me that he could tell what his mom and dad were thinking and that he liked my energy (his words).

During the approximate eight months that Millie and I dated, Natie and I (and sometimes his mom) had a number of conversations about Auras. He was curious about what I *saw* and asked me to explain what certain things he *saw* meant. He would often talk to me about God, heaven, and Jesus. This surprised his mom because although she took her kids to a Methodist Sunday School, she was not religious. For me, these conversations were always such a delight because he would talk to me, ask questions, listen to my answers and then simply say "Thanks," give me a hug, and run off to play. He was indeed a loving gift and a delightful experience in my life.

When Millie and I quit seeing each other, I missed Natie tremendously because he taught me so much about myself, about life, and about this new *Softer New Age Kids* Aura pattern. After that experience, I began noticing this *unique softer* Aura Pattern around other very young children. As I became more sensitive and more aware, I began seeing more and more very small children with this same or similar Aura pattern, just as my Spirit Guides had told me I would.

Discovering The Term "Crystal Children"

In February 2001 Dotti's second grandchild, Jaden was born and almost immediately I noticed that his Aura pattern was very different from his older sister. He expressed the *Softer New Age Kids* Aura pattern I had been seeing since the mid-1980's, and sure enough as he grew, his behavior reflected a much more naturally loving and softer energy than his older *Indigo* sister. As he grew he was also much more interested in "playing with" plant energies, as well as the Aura around the family dog. Whenever he saw an animal in our neighborhood he would try to pet it. But what I found interesting was that he would sometimes just "pet" their energy rather than their physical body. As he grew, I noticed that he loved life and was very comfortable in his body, which is typical of the *Softer New Age Kids* I had been observing.

A couple of years after Jaden was born, we picked up a copy of Dr. Doreen Virtue's little book entitled *The Crystal Children.*[59] As I read her

---

[59] *The Crystal Children – A Guide to the Newest Generation of Psychic and Sensitive Children*, by Doreen Virtue, Ph.D., Hay House, Inc., 2003

book, I recognized that the *Crystal Children* described in Dr. Virtue's book fit the behavior and Aura pattern that I was seeing in Dotti's grandson and other kids I identified as having the *Softer New Age Kids* Aura Pattern. However, I noticed that in Dr. Virtue's book, she states that these "kids" didn't start coming into the earth plane until the 1990's. However, that does not match my experience because I began seeing them in the early to mid-1980's. Other than that, her description of *Crystal Children* very closely matches the energy and behavior that I have observed with children I have identified as having the *Softer New Age Kids* Aura pattern.

The term *Crystal Children* has become the accepted term throughout the literature for what I term *Softer New Age Kids,* and I have since adopted that term as well. Several other books have been written on *Crystal Children* since Doreen Virtue's book (see the book list in Appendix B) but I consider her book to be one of the best in describing the difference between *Indigos* and *Crystals*. A more recent (2007) and excellent book on *Indigo, Crystal and Star children* is *"The Children of Now"* by Meg Blackburn Losey.[60]

Crystals Characteristics

As with the *Indigos,* I determine whether a kid is a *Crystal* via their Aura pattern. However, to try to help those who cannot *see* or *sense* the Aura, I have put together the following list of general characteristics that I observe in *Crystals.*

- They are much more spiritually aware than even the *Indigos*. They don't believe in God, they KNOW God.

  When Dotti asked her grandson Jaden where God was, wondering if he would say "Heaven;" he responded, "God is everywhere. He is in the trees, the sky, the flowers and He is in my heart." Jaden is a true *Crystal*. He gets it!

- They are very naturally loving, and are very vulnerable as well.

- Their presence "feels" much softer than an *Indigo* or non-*Indigo* energy person, even to those who do not *see* or *sense* Auras.

- They have deep penetrating eyes – they share this commonality with *Star Children,* which I will talk about later.

- They love being alive and love to play.

---

[60] *The Children of Now*, by Meg Blackburn Losey, Msc.D., Ph.D., Copyright 2007

- They are very smart and physically and mentally active and typically have a great sense of direction.

  When Jayden was about four, Dotti was driving him and his sister to the lake but was lost. Jaden was sitting in his little car seat in the back and said, "If you turn left, and then left again you will get to the lake." When Dotti asked him how he knew that, he replied, "Grandma Dotti, I have a map in my head." Of course he was right.

- Like the *Indigos*, they come in with great intuitive knowledge but usually have no cognitive basis for that knowledge. This goes beyond just being psychic – knowing things psychically. However, *Crystals* are more relaxed about this than their *Indigos* counterparts

- *Crystals* use telepathic communication and can become very frustrated if the adults around them do not respond. Watch how two baby *Crystals* look at each other as they mentally communicate.

  When Jayden was about four or five, Dotti and he were at a museum and a mother with a small baby in a stroller stopped next to Jaden. Dotti said that Jaden and the baby locked eyes and simply stared at each other for several minutes. The lady with the stroller then moved on. When Dotti asked Jaden if he was talking to that baby, he said, "Yes" as if that was obvious.

- They tend to be even tempered, and easy going as long as you don't get in their way of wanting to do something. They can be extremely purposeful and determined.

- They are fascinated with crystals and special shaped stones. They are also fascinated with rainbows and water.

- They love animals and nature. It is not uncommon for a *Crystal* to openly talk with animals. Sometimes they will also *see* and interact with Nature Spirits, like I used to.

Combination Auras

Over the past few years I have become much more sensitive to and aware of the subtle differences between the energy patterns or Auras of *Indigos* and *Crystals*. I have also become much more sensitive to the differences of the energy patterns or Auras within the *Indigos* and *Crystals* groupings. As a result, I have determined that there are rarely pure *Indigos* or pure *Crystals*. From my experience most children and young adults have, or express, a combination of these energy patterns or Auras.

For example, I have noticed that the *Indigos* without any *Crystal* characteristics have a much "harsher" Aura. Also, they are usually significantly less patient or tolerant than those who have some *Crystal* energy in their Aura pattern. They seem to be a lot less open to spiritual things as well. However, I have also noticed that *Indigos* with at least some *Crystal* energy in their Aura pattern tend to be more open to their sensitivities. They are also much more in touch with their spirituality and more open to expressing it. Their energy pattern is also a lot "softer."

On the other hand, *Crystals* without the *Indigo* Warrior Spirit energy tend to be much more laid back, yet not shy. They tend to be seekers trying to understand what their soul's purpose is. These children or young adults love being alive and having the opportunity to make a difference in the world. However, *Crystals* with the *Indigo* Warrior Spirit energy in their Aura tend to be more forceful in their approach to life. These entities can be very self-determined and tend to be more focused than their "*Indigos* with *Crystal* characteristics" counterparts. One trait that I see in all *Crystals* is that they are usually very comfortable in their body. They generally have an excitement for life and it shows.

I see a big difference between *Crystals* with *Indigo* characteristics and *Indigos* with *Crystal* characteristics. *Crystals* with *Indigo* characteristics tend to want to change things by manipulating the existing rules or paradigms and create change in that manner. However, *Indigos* with *Crystal* characteristics tend to want to break up the existing rules or paradigms and figure out how to change things after the fact. I have also noticed that children (and young adults) who express a strong *Indigo* Aura pattern are much more prone to being morose about being in a human form. As a consequence parents need to be aware of this because these individuals can become disconnected or depressed, whereas that is not as common in children (or young adults) who express strong *Crystal* characteristics.

I have noticed that many *Indigos* have turned off their sensitivities, or do not want to be *Indigos*. I refer to these as Reluctant *Indigos* or Repressed *Indigos*. Although there is a slight difference between these two energy patterns, it is very hard to put into words, but it clearly shows up in the Aura pattern that I see. I have not seen this Reluctant or Repressed energy form in children (or young adults) who express the *Crystal* energy pattern – even a little. What I have found is that when I am able to talk to Repressed or Reluctant *Indigos* about their sensitivities and about being an *Indigo*, I am usually able to help them understand that their sensitivities and "differentness" is not something to shy away from but embrace as a strength and uniqueness. It is a delight to see their energy change when I am able to help them understand their sensitivities and purpose.

Crystals usually do not turn their sensitivities off. They may not talk about them, but if they meet someone who is sensitive that talks about "psychic stuff" they can become quite animated. When I am able to talk to these kids, it is not uncommon for a *Crystal* child or young adult to open up to me and tell me all kinds of things that they have *seen* or been sensitive to that they have never shared with another. They are always delighted to learn that an adult has similar sensitivities and is able to explain things to them. I assure them that their sensitivities are normal and can be useful.

Labels or Labeling

To those who are concerned about "labels" I offer the following clarification. The terms *Indigos, Crystals, Star Child*, etc. are simply names that those of us who are sensitive to the Aura pattern use to try to "characterize" what it is we *see* and *sense* in an Aura. It is not used to "label" a person anymore than saying someone is a Blonde or Capricorn.

As I have become more sensitive to the subtle differences of the energy patterns (Auras) of all of these *New Age Kids* or as I have recently been calling them, *Children of The New Consciousness*, I am much more likely to tell someone that they are an *Indigo* with *Crystal* characteristics or vice versa than I am to say they are an *Indigo* or *Crystal*. However, a person's Aura does reflect a predominance of colors and a pattern that I characterize as reflective of an *Indigo*, or *Crystal* energy "being."

Other Aura Patterns – Rainbow and Star Children

My interest in and awareness of *Rainbow Children*[61] and *Star* or *Starseed Children* is much more recent than my experience with *Indigos* and *Crystals*. Although I have yet to encounter an entity that expresses what I would consider to be a *Rainbow Child* Aura pattern, I am open to the possibility that they exist. I know that Dr. Doreen Virtue talks about them, and I believe she is a credible psychic. However, until I am able to have someone point to a *Rainbow Child*, and I am able to see their Aura pattern and determine the subtle difference, I don't know how to talk about them. So I will simply say that some people apparently *see* an energy around certain children that they call a *Rainbow Child.* Although Doreen Virtue's "Angel Therapy" web site

---

[61] See Doreen Virtue, Ph.D.'s book *Angel Medicine* (Hay House, updated edition, September, 2004) and her Angel Therapy web site: http://www.angeltherapy.com/article1.php

talks about them, her discussion is not sufficient for me to make that distinction. So how the *Rainbow Child* energy pattern or Aura differs from an *Indigo Child* or *Crystal Child* or even a *Star Child* energy pattern, I cannot say.

The most recent energy pattern that I have encountered is what I would term a *Star Child* energy pattern. I am still in the process of trying to distinguish and understand the subtle differences in the Aura patterns of *Crystal Children* and *Star Children*, because to me they are very close. For me, there is an "other world" *sense* or *feel* to the *Star Children's* Aura pattern that I am very much aware of. Even my partner Dotti, who does not see Auras, senses this.

However, in addition, I have a *knowing* that these kids are from a specific different Star System. Sometimes I *hear* a message from them telling me which Star System they are from, while in other cases, I just have an *awareness*. The *Star Children* I have encountered so far have told me (in my mind) that they are from: Sirius, Alpha Centauri, Arcturus, a star called Cygnus Alpha, someplace called Omega One, Omega 9 (somewhere near the 2nd star in the Big Dipper handle), and someplace called Romulus. One toddler, about two years old, told me he came from "the I." In my mind's eye I saw the Eye of God nebula [The Helix Nebula; NGC 7293] when he said this.

The oldest of these children that I have encountered was probably about three, so this is a very new phenomena for me. These entities are highly Spiritually aware, have an intensely bright Aura, and have penetrating eyes that look straight through to the core of your being when they look at you. There is no hiding anything from these little ones. They will tell you who they are, not the other way around and you will know that what they say is true. With them there is no sense of a separateness from God, simply an awareness that you are in the very presence of the God source.

As fate would have it, Dotti's third grandchild, Taylor, born July 2007 has the Aura pattern that I believe is a *Star Child*. When she came into this earth plane she was wide-eyed and immediately looked directly into her father's eyes. So intense was her stare that the doctor even commented on it. When I saw the first pictures of her, I *picked up* that she was a *Star Child* and that her dad Shannon had been her father in a previous life, which I shared with him and Dotti's daughter, Kris. I had previously identified Shannon as a Reluctant *Indigo*, and I believe his *Star Child* daughter is about to provide him a powerful awakening. We will just have to wait and see how this plays out.

When Taylor was about five months old I was holding her and I asked her (in my mind) where (what Star System) she was from. She immediately turned her head toward me, looked at me with those penetrating clear blue eyes, and told me (mentally of course) that she was "From Arcturus – the same as you grandpa." She then gave me a great big smile. About two months later when I was playing with her, I heard her say to me (again in my head), "Do you remember, do you remember?" As I thought about what I was *hearing*, I had a vision in which I saw her as a young graduate student of mine from England. I was her professor and we were on a river in South Africa doing some sort of botanical research. As I tuned into this scene, she began to laugh and excitedly jump up and down on my lap. I *knew* that she had shown me a past life connection with her and I just internally smiled. I look forward to what the future will bring for her and what she is to teach her parents, her grandmother, and me.

Star Children Characteristics

As I indicated above, the *Star Child* energy pattern or Aura is one that I am still in the process of trying to sort out. However, in an attempt to be complete I have included the following characteristics that I believe will help the reader determine whether a child is a *Star Child* or not.

- The first clue is their extremely deep penetrating eyes. When a *Star Child* looks at you, you feel as though they have looked at your very soul. This can be very disarming, especially if you are someone who is trying to hide something. You cannot hide anything from them.
- Like the *Crystal Children*, *Star Children* don't believe in God, they KNOW God.
- Like the *Crystal Children*, *Star Children* are very naturally loving, and are very vulnerable as a result, but not as vulnerable as *Crystal* Children. These kids know that they are from the stars whether you do or not. I believe they will be fascinated with the night sky as they grow up, just as I have been all of my life.
- They love being in a body but may not be able to make it work the way they want it to. This can be expressed as wanting to go someplace and not being able to make their body work to get them there. This could be quite difficult for them (and you) until they can tell you what they want. This might be expressed as a temper tantrum. Coordination could potentially be a problem.
- *Star Children* are not limited in their thinking to our present understanding of physical laws. After all they come from different Star Systems, where things don't necessarily operate the way they do

in this dimension. I believe this holds great possibilities for humankind in the future.

- Like the *Indigos* and *Crystals* they come in with great knowledge (and in many cases wisdom). However, unlike the *Indigos* and *Crystals*, I do not believe they will feel frustrated about this. I believe they will simply accept that they have this knowledge and not be concerned about where it came from.

Since *Star Children* are a new energy pattern and are not old enough to provide validity to my understanding of what I *see* in their Auras and what it all means, I look forward to being able to add to this list of characteristics as I get the opportunity to interact with more and more of these delightful *Star Children* or latest *Children of the New Consciousness*.

Their Purpose and My Hope For Their Future

I believe that the entities expressing the *Indigos, Crystals, and Star Children* Aura patterns have a special Soul's Purpose as a group, which some of them realize, but unfortunately most of them do not. One of their Primary Life Purposes – AS A SOUL GROUP – is to change mankind's thinking from a focus on COMPETITION (I Win – You Lose) to a focus on COOPERATION (I Win – You Win). They intuitively know this is how "the game" is meant to be played, and they have it within their Aura pattern to implement it in all areas of their lives. However, many of them simply need to be reminded of it. A second purpose is to express their Oneness Consciousness, which is the underlying principle of all "true" religions: Hinduism, Buddhism, Jewish Mysticism, true Christianity (not fundamentalism), and true Islam (not Jihadism), rather than Separateness Consciousness. Unfortunately, separateness is what most of the current religious orthodoxies teach.

If these *New Age Kids* can be taught Meditation and learn the Spiritual truths of Oneness, I believe they will embrace the Cooperation paradigm and eschew the Competition paradigm, and will cause a significant change in the consciousness of human kind regarding the *Have's and the Have Not's*. This shift will result in a more equitable distribution of wealth and responsibility throughout the world. Those who "have" will understand that they have a responsibility to reach out to and assist those who are less fortunate, and will willingly and graciously do so. Also, those who do not have will understand that they have a personal responsibility to put forth the effort to achieve what they want, not simply expect it to (or let it) be given to them. That is the balancing energy of the Cooperation vs. Competition paradigm that these *New Age Kids* or *Children of the New Consciousness* are here to teach and implement, and that will be their true gift to the world. If and when they do this, they will become at peace with their purpose, and the world will be a significantly better place for everyone. It is my hope and prayer that humanity draws on these "kids" higher purpose and gives them opportunities and challenges to express their Divine essence rather than seduce their lower purpose with excesses and greed.

Every time I have the opportunity to interact with these *New Age Kids* or *Children of the New Consciousness* – be they *Indigos*, *Crystals*, or *Star Children* or a combination of those energies, I make it a point to remind them who they really are, "A Spiritual Being who is expressing in a physical form." I also remind them of their responsibility to reject the Competition and Separateness paradigm and embrace and begin to implement the Cooperation and Oneness paradigm.

Indigo and Crystal Children Workshops

In the spring of 2004, about four years after Carroll and Tober's *Indigo Children* book came out and a year after Dr. Doreen Virtue's book on *Crystal Children* came out, the movie *Indigo*[62] was released. There was a lot of interest in *Indigo & Crystal Children* within the Metaphysical community and I was asked to give a workshop on these "kids and young adults" for the Northern Virginia A.R.E. Council. I was delighted to share my experiences and to help those *Indigos* and *Crystals* who might be present, as well as their parents, grandparents, teachers, therapists and counselors to understand this "phenomena." There were about sixty-five people present.

As part of the workshop I "read" Auras for several of the participants and identified several young adults who were present as *Indigos* and/or *Crystals*. What I found particularly exciting was that when I came to an *Indigo* or *Crystal* child or young adult and read their Aura and told them what I *saw* and what I thought it meant, they all confirmed that they were sensitive to the Aura as well. They also shared that they felt out of place with their *gift*, and were delighted that an adult had similar experiences as theirs. After the workshop, several of them told me that they could at times tell what I was going to say to a person and wanted confirmation of their own psychic sensitivities, which I of course gladly shared with them. The change in their

---

[62] *Indigo* (the movie) is a film staring Neale Donald Walsch, Sarah Rutan, Gregory Linington, and Meghan McCandless. It was directed and produced by Stephen Simon and was released in 2003

Aura pattern when they got that confirmation was astounding and quite delightful.

I was asked to conduct that workshop for several other groups throughout the Northern Virginia region and the Virginia Beach Eastern Shore area, which I did over the next three years.

A "Chance" Meeting With Nancy Anne Tappe

Carmen, a personal friend of Nancy Ann Tappe – the lady who coined the phrase *Indigo Children*, attended my first workshop on *Indigo Children*. About a week prior to my workshop she called me and asked if I knew Nancy Ann Tappe and how long I had been aware of *Indigo Children*. I told her I did not know Nancy Ann, but that I had read about her in Carroll and Tober's book on *Indigo Children*. I explained that I became aware of *Indigos*, or what I termed *New Age Kids* since the early 1970's, and explained a little about my initial discovery. Carmen stated that Nancy Ann also first identified the *Indigo* Aura or energy pattern in the early 1970's time frame. She said that Nancy Ann was coming to town to stay with her shortly after the workshop and she invited me to participate in "an evening with Nancy Ann Tappe." I of course was delighted to accept her invitation thinking that this would be fun.

A couple of weeks after the workshop I went to Carmen's home and met Mrs. Tappe. When she greeted me, Nancy Ann commented that she had heard great things about my workshop on *Indigos*. She then told me that in her Aura color scheme, I was a "Tan," and that she was very aware that I saw Auras too. Nancy Ann then explained that she has a condition called synesthesia (see explanation below) and that the *lights* or Aura that she sees with her psychic "sight," is slightly different from what she sees with her synesthetic sight. That to me was fascinating because I had never heard that term previously, nor met anyone with that "condition."

Synesthesia[63] /syn·es·the·sia/ (sin?es-the´zhah)

- a secondary sensation accompanying an actual perception.
- a dysesthesia in which a stimulus of one sense is perceived as sensation of a different sense, as when a sound produces a sensation of color.

---

[63] From the on-line medical dictionary site "http://medical-dictionary.thefreedictionary.com/Synisthesia"

- a dysesthesia in which a stimulus to one part of the body is experienced as being at a different location.

In a private conversation with Mrs. Tappe, I told her that although I also saw a lot of indigo Blue in the *Indigo* children's Auras, it was the "pattern" of their Aura that I responded to and "judged" more than the indigo blue color in their Aura. She said that she understood, but that in her experience, no two psychics *see* exactly the same colors or patterns with these kids anyway. In her experience the patterns and Aura colors of these kids (as well as everyone else) vary in hue, intensity, color combinations, etc. much like IQ scores do for a population. I responded that I agreed with her assessment, but that I felt that unless these kids could begin to understand their Soul's Purpose, they could become and remain very frustrated. Nancy Ann agreed.

The evening event proceeded and Nancy Ann Tappe talked about her Aura color scheme. She went on to describe her experience with *Indigos*, which mirrored my experiences very closely. However, much to my surprise, when a question was asked about *Crystal Children*, Nancy Ann said that she had never seen a *Crystal Child*, so she could not talk about them. That truly surprised me because of my own experiences. It turned out to be a very enjoyable and informative evening.

Indigos & Sensitives Support Group

As indicated in the last chapter, in early 2005, at the urging of many parents, counselors, therapists and *Indigos* and *Crystal* young adults who had attended my workshops, I started a weekly Support Group called *Indigos and Psychically Sensitive Teens and Adults Support Group*. The group meets weekly at the Unity of Fairfax Church in Oakton, Virginia. Initially the group consisted of four *Indigo* teens and young adults, the mother of two of the teenage *Indigos*, and several mothers of *Indigos and Crystals* who later joined the group. A number of adults and young adults who were psychically sensitive and wanted to learn more about their sensitivities also joined. The group grew to about 25 people and has since dropped to about 12-15 people who have been meeting every Wednesday evening for the past four plus years. It is run as an Open Discussion Format and is open to anyone interested in exploring and discussing his or her Spiritual and Psychic experiences and sensitivities.

To help my *Indigos & Sensitives Group* members understand the depth and breadth of their sensitivities, I occasionally take the group to *haunted* places such as houses, graveyards or other historical places to explore what they can pick up and get validated. These trips have proven very helpful to all group members. The following are a few examples of places we have visited and some of the experiences that various members have had.

A Visit To Weston House

In the summer of 2006 I arranged to take my *Indigos & Sensitives Group* to the historic Weston House in Casanova, Virginia. According to the website for the Weston House,[64] "The property goes back to Robert 'King' Carter's land grant, while the 7,5000 square foot farmhouse, originally a two-story log cabin, was built by the Fitzhugh family sometime around 1817." According to the Historical Society tour guide (docent) who accompanied us on our tour, it had been used throughout the Post Revolutionary War period, the Civil War period, and, "as a weekend get-a-way for soldiers from the nearby Vint Hill Station." It was also used as a summer camp for girls. I knew nothing about the place prior to our visit and I told the group members *not* to investigate any information about the place prior to our visit.

I had done a reading for Betsy, whose family was the resident caretakers, and she had invited the group to visit to see what we might pick up. We arranged a carpool to the location on a Saturday with 17 adults and children, including a highly sensitive seven-year-old *Crystal* child named Colten. His highly sensitive *Indigo/Crystal* mother, Kat, and his spiritually-minded military father, Kevin also accompanied our group. It proved to be a very enjoyable and highly enlightening outing.

We met Betsy and the Historical Society docent, Jeanne who was a friend of Betsy and was very knowledgeable about the history of the house. She said that she had been giving tours for over fifteen years. Betsy and Jeanne briefed us on which rooms and out buildings we could "explore" and I then instructed the group to explore each room, each out building, and the grounds around the house, sensing into or "picking up" whatever they could. They were to write down or otherwise document what they *saw, sensed, felt, heard* or *knew* as well as document any tastes or smells (Clairgustance) they experienced. I gave them (and myself) one hour to walk around and explore, and then we all met back on the front porch to review what each of us *got*. Some people explored the inside of the house while others went to the out buildings and the grounds.

---

[64] See the Weston Farmstead web site: http://www.HistoricWeston.org for additional information.

It turned out to be a very haunted location with many ghosts from many different time periods. This made it somewhat puzzling and difficult for several group members to interpret because of the overlapping "energies of time." After the hour or so of exploring, we all gathered back on the porch, including Betsy and Jeanne. When everyone was gathered, I told everyone that I was going to mention each room in the main house, then each of the out buildings, and then the grounds. I said that as I did so I would ask everyone to describe what they *got* in each area. The process took the better part of two hours, because everyone wanted to talk and we all got a lot of information and had a lot of questions. As I began, one of my young adult students, Kyla, who had been in our group for about a year but had not expressed a great amount of sensitivity up until that time, felt chills as she shared that she actually *saw* a little girl ghost in one of the bedrooms, which really freaked her out. As Kyla described what she saw, several others chimed in with their own experiences of *seeing* or *sensing* this little girl, including young Colten and his parents. Betsy and the tour guide both confirmed that they had heard similar stories about people *seeing* this little girl as well, which was very validating but freaked Kyla out even more. Kyla also reported *seeing* a lady looking out the upstairs window, which was confirmed by several other members of our group including myself. Several of them picked up that there had been a fire there, which Jeanne confirmed.

When we talked about the earthen basement, young Colten became very excited and talked about *seeing* a dead soldier with a full uniform in that area. He said that while he was down there he was having trouble breathing and his dad brought him out. Kevin said that he thought there might be mold or something of that nature down there. Several group members refused to go into the basement because they could feel bad energy ghosts there. I reported that when I went down the steps, I *picked up* that it had been used to hide slaves during the Civil War period and that several of them had died down there. I said that I too *sensed* and *saw* the presence of a soldier. I stated that I was *told* that the soldier had been placed there and was thought to have been dead. However, he *told* me that his body had been placed under several other bodies, and that he ended up suffocating. I was made to understand he was troubled and therefore haunting that space. I told Colten's parents that I thought that was why their son was having trouble breathing not because of a mold problem, although it did have a "musty" smell. When I did so, little Colten said, "See, I told you Daddy." Betsy and Jeanne both reported that several people had reported similar experiences of *seeing* a soldier in that area and of having trouble breathing when they go down there. Betsy confirmed that members of her family have either *sensed* or *seen* that soldier and she reported that many people refuse to go down to the earthen basement area.

I reported that when I went into a dining room area on the first floor I found myself in the midst of a meeting with General Robert E. Lee, a two-star general (Maurice or McClure, I was not sure of the name), who I somehow *knew* was his "first in command aide" and several other two-star and one-star generals which I only recently realized were really Confederate Army Lt. Colonels, and Majors.[65] There were also a few "many-striped" Calvary sergeants present. The meeting was a rather heated briefing of a recent battle. What was puzzling to me was that while I *saw* this meeting of the Confederate forces going on, as I looked through the window out onto the front lawn I also *saw* an encampment of Union soldiers. Initially that did not make sense to me until I realized that I was seeing multiple time periods. When it was later explained that indeed General Robert E. Lee had met in that very room several times, but that Union soldiers also used the house during the war, then I understood. The Historical Society docent stated that Union Soldiers had indeed camped on what is now the front lawn. I was seeing scenes from two different time periods simultaneously. I refer to those energies as "energies of time." The Spirits aren't actually "hanging around" but the energy of the people and events that have taken place there are what we pick up on.

Many other stories were told about "events and happenings" as well as ghosts who were picked up that day. For several weeks following that visit, many group members commented on how surprised they were about how accurate their information was. It was a very confirming experience for everyone. Kyla seemed to be the most affected by the experience because following that experience, her sensitivities increased significantly and she has since become a very open and psychically sensitive young lady. A year later, my young assistant Justina took several group members back to the Weston House one weekend when I was not available. Many individuals who had gone previously picked up additional information and several new members excitedly shared what they got as well. Weston House is a fascinating place to visit if you are interested in exploring your psychic sensitivities.

---

[65]See: http://en.wikipedia.org/wiki/Confederate_Army and
http://members.cox.net/polincorr1/csa7.htm for rank insignias worn on
Confederate Army Uniforms.

A Visit To Flint Hill Cemetery

Another "experimental outing" that I took my *Indigos & Sensitives Group* members on was a visit to the Flint Hill Cemetery in Oakton, Virginia just as the sun was setting. As the reader may recall, many years previously I had taken several SFG Study Groups to this cemetery on a similar psychic exploration experience. As with my previous group tours to this cemetery, I instructed them to walk around and see if they could *see* or communicate with any ghosts and see if they could tell what the people died from, etc. Several group members reported *seeing* a rather stocky, but not obese, elderly lady, probably in her late 50's. They said that she had white hair and a sort of flat dark colored hat, dressed in a 1930's-1940's pinkish dress with dark flowers or irregularly shaped dark colored poke-a-dots. They reported that she was wearing long black gloves and carried a black handbag. She seems to be someone who constantly *haunts* that cemetery, because I have seen her almost every time I have been there. I also *saw* an older former "grave digger" on the road that runs on the periphery of the graveyard. I sensed that he had died in the 1990's. Several others reported that they also *saw* or *sensed* him.

After about an hour, I gathered the group together and told them I was going to try an experiment. I pointed to an area of gravestones and asked the group what they *sensed* about the dead people buried there. I had each person describe what he or she picked up about the graves in that area. We then walked over to that gravesite or area and read what the grave marker(s) said and tried to see what else we picked up. In many cases when we did this, one or more students got a first or last name, sometimes a family relationship – husband and wife buried together, or a family grouping, etc. This initially "freaked out" several group members but as we did this several times with several different areas, they became more open to and interested in the experience. In many cases we could not prove that what we picked up was "valid" – such as reason for death, etc. but many times we picked up the sex and age of the person or persons, the names, etc. It was a fun experiment that I have carried out many times in many different cemeteries.

So as to not freak anyone out, we left before it got too dark, but several people noted in our discussion after the "outing" that they felt an increased sensitivity to ghost energies the darker it became. I explained that although I do not completely understand it, that indeed seems to be true. Even I don't "enjoy" going to a cemetery when it is really dark.

At the following Support Group meeting, one student who is very intelligent and sensitive but overly analyzes almost everything, reported that she felt that she might have "picked up a Spirit" from the cemetery. She explained that throughout the week she experienced several strange pains in her neck and head and had other "weird" experiences. I told her and the other group members that I *saw* a dead person standing behind her "wondering" why she was not *seeing* him. I told her that her *lights* indicated to him (the ghost) that she was sensitive and he did not understand why she was not responding so he was "doing things" to try to get her attention. I *talked to* the ghost and explained that although Gail's *lights* indicated that she was sensitive, she was not as open to her sensitivities as her *lights* indicated. I told him that she did not want him around her, and that he needed to leave. He seemed to acknowledge my message because he immediately left, although with a puzzled look on his face. Gail reported that she felt an immediate relief and that she felt him go away. At the next meeting she reported that she was no longer aware of his presence.

> *When you go to a place that you suspect might be haunted you need to 'talk to' the Spirits and tell them that although you may not 'see' them, that you acknowledge their presence and that you do not want them to bother or otherwise frighten you. You can always ask them [the Spirits -- if you are open to doing this] to show themselves in a way that you can 'see' or experience their presence, and they will usually find a way of making themselves known to you. If you are frightened, you can always use the Robe of Light Protection Prayer and send them to the light.*

A Visit To Harper's Ferry

In July 2008, I took my group on a *ghost tour outing* to Harper's Ferry, West Virginia.[66] I wanted them to see if they could pick up on what the tour guide said, as well as see if any of us could pick up additional information the guide might not know. I had pre-arranged to meet the tour guide at 7:00 pm at a particular location. However, when we arrived it was raining quite steadily. While we were waiting for the rain to stop and for our tour guide to show up, I noticed or *saw* several soldiers with rifles (they seemed to be sentries) and a couple of tents on the ridge between the railroad tracks and the road. I also saw a woman (who seemed to be somewhat deranged) running on the ridge and on the railroad track. Her clothes were on fire and as she ran, she was hit by a train. This scene repeated itself several times in my mind. I also saw a scene where she was just standing there with a charred body. I told several group members what I was *seeing* and had them try to

---

[66] Contact Ghost Tours of Harpers Ferry 304-725-8019 for tour information or
   http://www.HarpersFerryGhost.20m.com

tune into that entity and that scene. Only two members could *see* her, but several others *sensed* her presence. Finally the rain let up and our guide, Anne arrived.

I explained to Anne who I was and what our group was about and stated that we were interested in picking up on things before she talked about them, if that was OK with her. She said, "Yes, absolutely! I would love to know what any of you pick up." She said that she had been doing this tour for about fifteen years and usually received additional information from sensitive people or groups in the past. She was open to documenting any additional information we picked up and had a digital recording device to record our observations. As a result, as she came to a place she was going to talk about, she would pause and ask what any of us got about the place before she "gave her spiel." As we came to the first street corner, I stated that I *saw* and *sensed* the presence of a black man and some sort of mob. I said that the scene changed to a much later time frame and I *saw* a scene involving an auto accident at the same corner involving several people. She stated that a black man was killed by a mob at this corner. I noted to the group that I did not *get* that he was killed. She could not verify the auto accident incident.

When she took us to the stone stairway leading up the hill to the St. Peter's Catholic Church, she again asked if any of us *got* anything. None of us did but I said, "Not here but there is a lot of energy at the top where the church is." She just laughed, then talked about the history of the building next to the stairs and other facts. We then ascended the stone stairway. When we got to the top we discovered that the Church was locked. She then asked if any of us got anything "here." Several of us *sensed* that a "lady in a red dress" was killed, pushed off or over a wall. She confirmed that a lady in red was killed or committed suicide. Several members of the group said, "It wasn't suicide, she was pushed!" I told her that I also picked up on a young priest hanging himself just inside the church. However, since the church door was locked I could not show her where I saw the priest hanging. She said that she was unaware of that incident. She then told us a story about many people seeing an older priest walking down the hill and turning and entering the side of the church where there is no entrance. When she took us along side the church, I *sensed* into and located where the priest went through the wall. Several group members as well as Anne reported it being much colder where the "non" entrance was.

She then led us to another two-story building with a balcony, and with a covered up well about twenty feet from the building. As we approached the house she asked what we were *getting*. I told her I could see several prostitutes on the second story balcony (some black and some white). As we got closer to the area where the covered up well was, I said that I felt like I was a woman and that my insides were being torn out of me. It was so painful that I was bending over in pain. I told her that young children had been locked down there for long periods of time as punishment, and that aborted and stillborn babies had been placed in that well and had died. She confirmed my story. She said a lot of people pick up really bad energy at that well, and that there are stories of children being put in the well as punishment. She was not sure about dead babies.

She then took us to another building close by and as we approached I asked, "Who is that man with the lantern in the top window?" and I pointed at a dormer window on the third or fourth story of that building. Several other members in our group sensed his presence as well. She said that man is often seen by others. She then told other stories about that "tavern and rooming house" and concluded the tour. As we headed back to where our cars were parked, she entertained us with many other stories. As we approached the ridge with the soldiers near the railroad track I asked her about the deranged lady on fire that I saw. Anne shared a story about that lady and said that a lot of sensitive people report seeing her. We thanked her and several members said that they were looking forward to coming back for another Ghost Tour.

Continuing to Learn

Our *Indigos & Sensitives Group* continues to explore other *haunted* places and continues to explore their sensitivities both in our group discussion and in their every day lives. I am grateful for the opportunity to help them understand that what they are experiencing is not crazy, although they report that it often feels like it is. As I tell my students, they simply need to understand and begin to put the things they *see, sense, feel, hear* and *know* in a perspective that allows them to understand what they (their experiences) mean. As I often tell them, life is nothing but a series of opportunities to learn and our experiences are our process for learning the things we came here to teach and to learn.

For those readers who might have a further interest in this group, please check out the **Ongoing and Upcoming Events** tab on the author's web site,[67] listed at the bottom of this page, for meeting times and location. The author is interested in creating similar groups throughout the world, but believes that

---

[67] http://www.ReflectionsInLight.org

it requires a psychically sensitive individual who is willing to be both a teacher and a student to facilitate the group. Two members of the author's Fairfax group have moved to Ireland and are available to create a group there if there is interest. I welcome your interest in starting your own *Indigos and Psychically Sensitive Teens and Adults Support Group.* Simply send an email to the author at "Lowell@ReflectionsInLight.org" for further information.

What The Literature Says

I have tried to coalesce what I consider to be the most important characteristics of *Indigo Children, Crystal Children* and *Star Children* contained in the literature that I am familiar with as of this writing.

Indigo Children Characteristics

In their book entitled The Indigo Children – The New Kids Have Arrived,[68] **Carroll and Tober** list the following 10 Common Traits of Indigos.[69]

- They come into the world with a feeling of royalty (and often act like it).
- They have a feeling of "deserving to be here," and are surprised when others don't share that.
- Self-worth is not a big issue [with most of them]. They often tell the parents "who they are." [That is many children talk to their parents about a past life they remember about being a merchant, cowboy, slave, soldier, etc.]
- They have difficulty with absolute authority (authority without explanation or choice) [which makes terrible 2's have a whole new meaning].
- They simply will not do certain things; for example, waiting in line is difficult for them. [They are literally operating from a different life model paradigm.]
- They get frustrated with systems that are ritual-oriented and [systems that] don't require creative thought.
- They often see better ways of doing things, both at home and in school, which makes them seem like "system busters" (nonconforming to any system).
- They seem antisocial unless they are with their own kind. If there are no others of like consciousness around them, they often turn inward, feeling like no other human understands them. School is often extremely difficult for them socially.

---

[68] *The Indigo Children – The New Kids Have Arrived* by Lee Carroll and Jan Tober, Hay House, Inc, Copyright 1999.
[69] Bracketed comment and emphasis added.

- They will not respond to "guilt" discipline ("Wait till your father gets home and finds out what you did").
- They are not shy in letting you know what they need.

In addition, Carroll and Tober list the following characteristics that **Dr. Doreen Virtue,** a gifted sensitive and teacher that they interviewed, believes will help one identify "gifted" (*Indigo*) children:

- They have high sensitivity.
- They have excessive amount of energy.
- They bore easily – they may appear to have a short attention span.
- They require emotionally stable and secure adults around him/her.
- They will resist authority if it's not democratically oriented.
- They have preferred ways of learning, particularly in reading and math.
- They may become easily frustrated because they have big ideas but lack the resources or people to assist them in carrying these tasks to fruition.
- They learn from an exploratory level, resisting rote memory or just being a listener.
- They cannot sit still unless absorbed in something of their own interest
- They are very compassionate; and have many fears such as death and loss of loved ones.
- If they experience failure ealy, [they] may give up and develop permanent learning blocks.

In Carroll and Tober's interview with Dr. Doreen Virtue, she states that high IQ and frozen creativity is a clue that you have an *Indigo* child that is trying to conform, or has somehow shut down to fit in.

Another person that Carroll and Tober interviewed in their book was **Debra Hegerle**, a teacher's aide who has identified and works with *Indigos* in California. Debra lists the following key characteristics she believes are indicative of *Indigo* children:

- *Indigos* process their emotions differently than non-*Indigos* because they have high self-esteem and strong integrity.
- They can read others "like a book."
- They can see your hidden agenda even if you can't! They will often use the hidden agenda against you – they know how to push your buttons.
- They have inherently strong determination to work things through for themselves and only want outside guidance if it's presented to them with respect and within a format of true choice.

- They come in with their intentions and gifts easily identifiable from birth.
- They suck up knowledge like a sponge, especially if they like or are drawn to a subject.
- Experiencing life helps them learn best, so they create the experiences they need to help them with their current problem or area where they need to grow.
- They respond best when treated like a respected adult.
- If you are constantly getting resistance from [an] *Indigo*, "check yourself" first – are you operating with a subtle hidden agenda?
- *Indigos* have innate healing abilities – but they may not realize it.
- They vacillate between needing each other and wanting to be alone.

Carol and Tober's book goes on to say that "Indigos are born masters – each and every one! They expect you to do what they are doing naturally and if we don't, they keep pushing our buttons until we get it right – that is until we become masters of our own lives."

As indicated previously, in Carol and Tober's book they interviewed *Nancy Anne Tappe* as well and she states the following about *Indigos*:

- *Indigos* do not respect people based on their having gray hair or wrinkles. You have to earn your respect from the *Indigos*.
- To deal with *Indigos* you have to be willing to give up your authority. You cannot "talk down" to these kids. Even though they are much younger and perhaps not as "wise" or have the experience that we have, you MUST reason with them and earn their respect for your "wisdom."

Nancy Ann states "What I find that works is to simply say "what I have found that works for me, is ___ " and then let them argue why that would not work for them if that is what they choose to do and let that be OK." She says that you cannot (should not) attempt to convince them by words…you need to "prove yourself" by your actions! She further states that *Indigos* are fearless – that is, they believe in themselves. For example:

> "If you try to tell an Indigo that they are doing something wrong, when they believe in themselves, they know that you don't know what you're talking about."

So what Nancy Tappe suggests to parents is that they set up boundaries where they don't tell their children not to do something. Instead, say,

"Now, why don't you explain to me why you want to do that. Let's sit down and talk about it. What do you think will happen? Just play it out with me. What do you think would happen if you did that?"

When the child tells you what they think would happen to them, simply ask, "Okay, how would you handle that?" Then they'll tell you how they would handle it. As Nancy Ann is suggesting here, you need to include them in the conversation and help them see that there are consequences to what they do.

Crystal Children Characteristics

In her book on *Crystal Children,*[70] **Doreen Virtue** states that *Indigo Children* share some characteristics with the *Crystal Children* in that both generations are highly sensitive and psychic and they have important life purposes – to *"mash down old approaches that no longer serve us; quash governmental, educational and legal systems that lack integrity."* Dr. Virtue then lists the following Characteristics of *Crystal Children.*

- Usually born in 1995 or later [my experience is since mid-1980's]
- Possess large eyes with an intense stare
- Have magnetic personalities
- Highly affectionate
- Start talking late in childhood
- Are very musically oriented, and may sing before talking
- Use telepathy and self-invented sign language to communicate
- May be diagnosed with Autism or Asperger's syndrome
- Are even-tempered, sweet, and loving
- Are forgiving of others
- Highly sensitive and empathetic
- Very much connected too nature and animals
- Exhibit healing abilities
- Quite interested in crystals and rocks
- Often discuss angels, Spirit Guides, and past –life memories
- Extremely artistic and creative
- Prefer vegetarian meals and juices to "regular food"
- Fearless explorers and climbers, with an amazing sense of balance.

---

[70] *The Crystal Children – A Guide to the Newest Generation of Psychic and Sensitive Children* by Doreen Virtue, Ph.D., Hay House, Inc., 2003

- Like the *Indigos*, *Crystals* have a great ability to sniff out dishonesty – they know when they are being lied to.
- Also, like the *Indigos*, *Crystals* are unable to conform to dysfunctional situations at home, work or school.

Dr. Virtue states that the main differences between *Crystals* and *Indigos* is that *Indigos* have a "warrior Spirit" whereas *Crystals* are blissful and even-tempered and that *Crystals* are the generation who benefit from the *Indigos'* trail-blazing. Dr. Virtue states, "*Crystal Children* have beautiful, multicolored, opalescent (opal – milky iridescence) auras in pastel hues like a quartz crystal's prism effect."

Channeled Instructions and Predictions

Since the late 1970's I have been channeling the Archangel Gabriel[71] and during of these channeled sessions, people have asked questions from a wide range of topics. In the most recent Channeling Sessions, questions have been asked about such topics as: Earth Changes, Social and Economic changes, the war in Iraq and the conflict with the Muslim world, terrorist attacks, the 2008 Presidential election, and many others. These questions have often required a "predictive" response. Additionally, a lot of questions on such topics as: Death and dying, Heaven, Angels and Archangels, Meditation and Chanting, Karma, the purpose and causes of Disease, the souls of Animals, Christmas and the birth of Jesus, and many others, were also asked in these sessions. These questions often required a directive or instructive type of response, which has often been quite profound, interesting and helpful.

Although I was initially reluctant to include the material from these sessions, especially the "predictions," in this book, my students and many of my friends convinced me that I needed to in order to capture the depth and scope of the kinds of information that comes through these channeled sessions. The questions and responses I have chosen to include here are taken from four Channeling sessions that I conducted in April 2006, June 2006, December 2007 and December 2008 for members of my *Indigos & Sensitives Support Group* and *A.R.E. SFG Study Group*. I have also included questions from a recent channeled session in January 2009 that I carried out for several people who were interested in obtaining information regarding the world economic markets and the use of Sacred Geometry to understand world economic dynamics. There were also questions about upcoming sociological changes, earth changes, and other metaphysical topics.

I believe the reader will find the questions that elicited an instructional response to be both interesting and useful, and I hope and trust that the reader will personally question the responses that provided a predictive response with an open mind. It is recommended that the reader respond from your heart center, then do what your own Spirit guides you to do. I have cut down and/or changed the wording of some of the questions and responses in an attempt to clarify the meaning and eliminate redundancy. However, the exact

---

[71] See the answer to question 2 on page 241 regarding the Archangelic Hierarchy

wording can be heard on the recorded sessions on the CDs, which can be obtained on my web site.[72]

Earth Changes[73]

Q1)   Siobhan: Many psychic readers have made predictions of massive Earth Changes and there seems to be a consensus belief among many people in spiritual oriented groups (including these groups) that massive Earth Changes will happen in the very near future. Please comment on such Earth Change predictions, giving the reasons for the "false" or incorrect predictions.

A1)   Gabriel: The false or incorrect predictions as it were, are more in terms of the entities being in accord with the alignment of the energies as understood at the time [the predictions were] made. Predictive information is simply information brought forward but [it] is not "set in stone." In fact, the energies of groups [such as these groups] can alter such possible outcomes. For example, it is understood that the breaking up of the western portion of the United States as predicted by Mr. Cayce was in fact deterred, alleviated or softened in some form by many, many groups meditating and bringing forth planet healing energies and therefore the breaking up has not occurred as originally predicted. Does that make sense?

Siobhan: Yes, thank you.

Q2)   Siobhan: Are there to be Earth Changes that will significantly affect many people throughout the world and/or here in the United States such as the Tsunami in South East Asia [Dec 2004], or the massive mud slide in South America [Guatemala, Oct 2005], and if so please give details as to the type or nature of such Earth Changes and the specific causes?

A2)   Gabriel: As previously stated, predictions are based upon the energy of information that is brought forth at the time of the reading. *As we currently see things, there clearly are massive geological changes in process, which will cause major geographic changes in the near future. Some of these changes will in fact be very destructive to the earth and people as it were.*

---

[72] http://www.ReflectionsInLight.org
[73] Excerpted from the April 2006, June 2006 and January 2009 channeling sessions

However, it must be understood that when such occurrences do happen, there are massive amounts of souls and massive amounts of guides on the inner planes awaiting the souls transitioning. For example, when the Tsunami occurred in Southeast Asia [Dec 2004] there was a massive tear within the fabric of shall we say humankind. Yet there was a massive surge of souls coming through that caused a large number of souls that had been trapped and stuck in various planes to join the transitioning souls seeking the light. So all was not lost for even though people died, in their massive transition, they in fact brought forth much light to those that were trapped on the inner planes. Does that make sense?

Siobhan: Yes, thank you.

Q3)   **Siobhan:** Have there been signs of weather manipulation, and will there be Earth Changes or distortions that will affect the East Coast of America, specifically Northern Virginia?

A3)   **Gabriel:** [Yes] there have in fact been multiple processes of attempting to manipulate the weather over an extended period of time. The [weather] process is not well understood by mankind, and mankind's attempt to manipulate has in fact caused significant ripples within the weather patterns. Those ripples are in fact causing significant difficulties and will continue to cause significant difficulties for quite some time.

There is an attempt on the part of mankind, because of mankind's limited understanding of what death means, to do everything it can not to allow that process to continue in its normal gathering shall we say. Such manipulations of weather are part of that process but part of that process is also oriented toward the greed and massive [gross] misunderstanding of individuals, specific individuals who have much and do not give or give very little. Is that understood?

Siobhan: Yes, thank you.

Q4)   **Siobhan:** Assuming that significant Earth Changes or disruptions are to occur somewhere in the world, please comment on the time frame (or time frames) of such changes, and if appropriate please identify what geographical regions will be most affected and which will be "safe zones."

A4)   **Gabriel:** We answer this with a sense of humor for there are entities within this room who were in fact a part of the disruptions of Atlantis in the later times and have some fears or trepidation's thereof of such occurrences happening again. *You can be assured that there will be massive earth disruptions throughout the world including the United States over the next 3 to 5 years.*

There is a process within nature where a cycle is completing within itself and that cycle will be completed within 3 beginning and ending in 5 years from this current time frame. That process includes massive or geographical changes along both the coastlines of the continental United States *as well as coastlines of the Southern America* as well. Thou will also find *disruptions within the Pacific region* that is islands and the disruption of volcanic activity. *At the same time or near proximity thereof, you will have disruptions* in what would be considered the *Vesuvius* [near Naples, Italy] and *Pelée* [on the island of Martinique in the Caribbean] areas. Does that make sense?

Siobhan: Yes, thank you.

Q5) **Siobhan:** Will the East Coast of America, specifically Northern Virginia, be affected?

A5) **Gabriel:** The East coast of Virginia as you term, the area known as *Virginia Beach* and those areas in that proximity are what is termed a *safe zone or a geologically safe area.* It is not to say that there will not be energy shifts and changes both from a physical perspective as well as a land mass perspective, but in general terms is safe. Does that make sense?

Siobhan: Yes, thank you.

Q6) **Siobhan:** What will be the signs that Earth Changes are approaching, are in progress or are about to happen? Are there specific signs that one can observe or become sensitized so that will alert us to such pending Earth Changes? Are there any in this group who are or could become sensitive to these changes. What steps should be taken to enhance their sensitivity?

A6) **Gabriel:** As regards the question of, "Are there entities within this group who have specific sensitivities to earth changes?" The answer is yes. There are 3 individuals with such sensitivities. As regards the question of, "What are the signs?" The signs are you see them as we speak, and the mere fact that you are asking the question is [another] one of the signs. But the signs of the weather changes throughout the United States as well as throughout the world are in fact some of the early signs. However, many of the signs are on what we would term the inner planes, [which] individuals tap into [via] sensitivity to the

Mother Earth energy. That sensitivity can be had and can be understood. Is that clear?

Siobhan: Thank you, yes.

Q7) **Siobhan:** What attitude should be held by group members regarding such Earth Changes, and is there something specific that the groups represented here should be doing on a regular basis that can help balance the energies behind the Earth Change forces, so as to alleviate the negative impact of these disruptions and reduce or alleviate the great suffering that such Earth Changes or disruptions would surely create?

A7) **Gabriel:** As previously stated, the attitude that the group should or must hold is attunement with that of the higher self. There are processes such as meditation and attunements whereby the group can gather and direct its energy of healing toward the alleviance or the minimization of the impact of such earth changes. It's not that the earth changes are to be stopped, but merely understood and minimize the loss thereof. The loss is the loss of human life for that is still a valuable quantity. However, the loss of human life does not mean the end of existence, it simply means a change in form. When it is well understood that that is the process that occurs, then the process of the loss of life, although it may be a sad occasion, is simply the process of the loss of life, it does not mean the loss of an entity. Therefore by tuning into the alignments with these higher energy forms, the group can in fact bring about a healing process that can work in conjunction with the processes that are currently happening with Mother Earth, and in that manner cause the alleviance or the reduction of the significant impact of same. Does that make sense?

Siobhan: Yes, thank you.

Q8) **Sandy:** As regards earth changes and associated possible cataclysmic events, is there some way our two groups should be preparing for these changes other than spiritually trying to do whatever we can to minimize those effects? If indeed our purpose is to bring forth these Ideals into the world, how can we protect ourselves so that we can carry on?

A8) **Gabriel:** Although the question is asked with an energy of a real attempt to understand, there seems to be a misunderstanding of what the channel previously stated about potential earth changes, and we would address the question as follows: Although the potentiality of significant geological earth changes, and sociological and economic upheaval processes do exist in the world, they are as a potentiality not a certainty.

When we say these terms, we are expressing the fact that all those potentialities do exist, but the important thing for one to do is to simply work at increasing the loving, healing, and connecting energy, and not worry about protecting ones self from these forces but simply keep your consciousness focused on continually being a channel of blessing to those you meet day by day. That is the most important aspect that needs to be understood. The actual working out, the actual implementation, the actual processes that occur [earth changes, sociological and economic changes, etc.] are not as important as your response to those processes. By holding an understanding, and holding an attitude of being "at one" with whatever the God force would have you be with, then you are "attuned" and regardless of what happens around you, that's simply the material aspect. So we would not fear, we would simply surround our self with the energy that we know is positive and allow the energy that is negative to simply be dissipated or to be reflected back in the form in which it was sent. Is that made clear?

Sandy: Yes.

Q9)   **Sandy:** My question relates to, "What will arise from the predicted destructions?" and "What is the purpose for these destructions?" "What will they bring forth?"

A9)   **Gabriel:** The Phoenix ashes. Let me elaborate. The entity grouping known as *Indigo*, and the entity grouping known as *Crystals* are in fact groupings that have made a commitment to the creator to come in and create, shall we say, an atmosphere and environment in contradiction to the negative and greedy aspects that have been, shall we say, attempting to separate and tear apart that which was known as humanity. That being said, their task is very formidable. For it requires a massive change in consciousness, and that massive change in consciousness must occur in people who do not want to change their consciousness. Therefore, the way it is happening, and the way it will continue to happen is one individual at a time. But when that one individual makes that commitment of being in attunement with their highest ideal in carrying out the purpose for which they came, that one individual will counteract perhaps 100 other individuals who are at odds with that attunement. We see enlightenment not destruction, although destruction may be seen by some. Do you understood?

Sandy: Yes.

Q10) Doug: Lowell mentioned that Yellowstone was going to erupt in the near future. How will this happen and what will take place around that and when?

A10) Gabriel: The entity the channel that you refer to as Lowell, indeed has tapped into and has foreseen the significant disruptive volcanic and steam energy building in the Yellowstone area. The great geyser that is often looked at within Yellowstone by many people is but a spit of what will occur when the eruption does occur. *The exact timing is not known to the channel but the eruptive activity can be thought to occur within the next five years of earth time as we see it.* A significant area will in fact be changed as in the twinkling of an eye. Many people will be significantly affected as will the immediate environment of that area and there will be significant after-shocks causing trepidation and fear among many, not only within that region but within other regions within the United States. *For there is an energetic connection that will cause other activities similar in magnitude to occur along the eastern portion of the United States as well.* Is that understood?

Doug: Yes.

Q11) Sandy: As a follow up to that. Is the Washington DC area a safe area, whether from natural disaster or from outside forces?

A11) Gabriel: Within the lifetime of the entity that is seeking an answer to this question, there will be significant geological disruptive energies within the region you refer to as Washington. But more significantly north thereof in what is now known as New York City and that local area. Will be significantly affected as well, *within a period of ten years or less following the Yellowstone event.* Is that understood?

Sandy: Yes.

Q12) Doug: What areas would be physically safe areas?

A12) Gabriel: We would caution thee that it would be much better for you to be concerned about the safety of your soul development than the safety of your physical body. For your physical body can be significantly affected in a negative way but if your consciousness is such that your soul is not negatively affected, that is the more important factor for the entity. Although this may seem trivial to thee or a trivial answer to thee, it is not trivial. For the importance of one's soul is the most important thing that one must consider but we will attempt to answer your question because the entity does have a concern about geographical locations that are [or will be] less susceptible to geological changes.

The mountainous regions in the northwest portion of Georgia and the southwestern portion of South Carolina would be locations of safety. Not that there will not be disruptions, but that the disruptions will not be catastrophic in nature. There are also portions in the northwestern portion of the United States, and as we would say, although the ground will shake it will not break. Similarly in the region known as Oregon, there too, the ground will shake but will not break. Those are but a few of the locations. Portions of Arizona would also be areas of safety. But again, we would emphasize, safety of physical body although understood to be of concern consciously, must be secondary to the safety of the soul. Is that understood?

Doug: Yes.

Social and Economic Conflicts[74]

Siobhan: It appears that in the United States as well as throughout the world today, there are many different groups with many different leaders with many different purposes, which appear to be at the root cause of the Social and Economic conflicts here in the United States as well as throughout the world.

Q1) **Siobhan:** Please comment on the Social and Economic conflicts that we are observing and experiencing throughout the world. Please help us to understand the Karmic patterns that are being played out and how we can avoid repeating past mistakes or becoming caught up in manipulation. What attitude should be held by group members regarding such Social and Economic conflicts throughout the world as well as within the United States, and what steps can we take (individually and as a group) to play a positive role in bringing peace and attunement?

A1) **Gabriel:** The conflicts, Social, Economic, and terrorist as you refer, are indeed a working out of Karmic patterns. The Social and Economic conflicts that are observed by human kind throughout the world are but a small portion of the energy disturbances that are in

---

[74] Excerpted from the April 2006 channeling session

place and in effect around the planet, and around the Social and Economic framework that you call society.

The Social conflict is more in terms of advanced Egocentric energies that are restrictive and exclusive [in nature] rather than inclusive and supportive. Those energies are quite dire to the survival of mankind. That being said, there are many individuals that have come into this earth plane to experience the Karmic retribution of things that have been sown in the past. So there is much conflict, death, and destruction etc. that is in fact [a] retribution or repayment of that which has already been created, not necessarily the result of what is being created. This is simply the opportunity for souls to experience harsh environments, both Socially and Economically as a result of [their] past choices and mis-steps.

However, there is a positive light that can be attributed to such conflicts. If one were to create within themselves an environment [understanding] whereby the conflict no longer is perceived as a conflict but merely as an opportunity to create goodness and create togetherness, and create an atmosphere of connectedness, then those individuals would not perceive the conflicts as conflicts. However, the conflicts themselves would [still] exist, for the entities desiring to create that atmosphere would be in conflict with the energies that are trying to prevent that atmosphere from being created.

[This is expressed as] a conflict of interest between the have's, or those with much, and the have-not's, or those with little. The attitude which must be held and which must be thought of when considering these conflicts is more in terms of observation and awareness of the Karmic ties behind them rather than a judgment of positive or negative energies as it were.

It is not that thou are to look upon the devastation and the starvation and the poverty, etc. that you observe within what you call your news media throughout the world and be hardened to it or taken in by it, but more in terms of observing, sending light and love out as an empathetic energy to those entities who find themselves entrapped in their own creations. Is that made clear?

Siobhan: Yes, thank you.

Q2) **Siobhan:** Is there anything that the group can do specifically to hold a good attitude?

A2)   Gabriel: A good exercise would be for the group as a group, as well as individuals individually, to hold in their mind the thought of those in lack being provided more self sustaining energy, at the same time, holding them responsible for their own creations, for they in fact are creating that which they are experiencing, or at least have done so in the past and therefore are reaping that which they have sown. Such could be done via a meditation process either as a group and/or individually in which you send light and love to those in need and those in suffering. Is that clear?

Siobhan: Yes, thank you.

Q3)   Siobhan: Is there something specific that the groups represented here should be doing on a regular basis that can help balance the energies behind these Social and Economic conflicts, so as to alleviate the negative impact of these conflicts and reduce or alleviate the great suffering created by these conflicts?

A3)   Gabriel: As just stated, the group and individuals of the group need to hold within themselves the concept that there can be a balancing energy between the conflicting energies of those who have and those who have not. Additionally, the group and individuals need to send light to those who have so that there will be a softening of their heart and their purse strings. This would be a great forward advancement for such groups. Is that understood?

Siobhan: Yes, thank you.

Q4)   Judy: Will there be economic change in the United States before the next year?

A4)   Gabriel: You can be assured that there will be a significant economic down turn in some respect prior to the next presidential process [2008 election]. However, that down turn will in fact affect the higher level [the more economically affluent] individuals, than the lower [less economically affluent] individuals. You ask, "How can that be with the current process that we have. If there is a down turn does it not equally affect all individuals?" All we know is from the determination that we are shown, there appears to be a shrinking at the top and an expansion at the bottom. Does that make sense?

Judy: Yes.

Muslim and Western World Conflict[75]

Q1) **Siobhan:** Can the channel please comment on the apparent conflict between Muslims throughout the world and the western world that we are seeing being manifested around the globe?

A1) **Gabriel:** The conflict as you term it that you observe between what is termed the Islamic or Muslim culture or religious groupings, and what you term the Christian-Judaic culture or religious groupings, is due in great part to a conflict between groupings vying for egocentrical control, one over the other. One needs to understand that although the entity Mohammad who wrote the Koran, brought forth much "truth," much of what he wrote has been distorted in a manner that would allow those individuals who are egocentrically and power oriented to enforce their own egocentric perspective on Muslim people in the name of Islam, when in fact their actions are the antithesis of what Mohammad taught.

It can be said that those individuals – the Jihadists – that use [the] Islam [religion] for their own egocentric purposes are in fact an expression of the Anti-Christ energy that is referred to in the biblical passages. The Christ energy is about "at-onement," about creating an environment among peoples that is supportive and loving and caring toward all individuals, where as the Anti-Christ energy is about creating a divisive or oppositional energy that is designed to tear apart, separate, and to make that which is good and harmonious, as wrong. That is the basis of the Islamic Jihadist, who do not represent the principles taught by Mohammad and his followers, but in fact represent the opposite of what Mohammad and Jesus taught.

Indeed, there are cultural differences between the Muslim world and the Christian-Judaic or Western world, but the differences are much more about sociological and/or cultural differences, rather than religious differences.

The warring or terrorist groupings – the Jihadists – have simply distorted those sociological and/or cultural differences to create a divisive rather than unifying energy. So we would say, that if one were to understand that the divisive energy or as you refer to it as the

---

[75] Excerpted from the June 2006 and December 2007 channeling sessions

Muslim terrorists, is an Anti-Christ energy, and if it can be looked upon as that, then you can utilize those expressions of prayer, those expressions of love that will allow you to negate, or dissipate that negative and divisive energy so that it does not have the negative impact it desires to have. Is that understood?

Siobhan: Yes.

Q2)   Siobhan: Are you saying Gabriel that the Anti-Christ could come from the Islamic culture?

A2)   Gabriel: We are saying that [the] Islamic culture as expressed by the extreme Jihadist energy forms, is in fact the Anti-Christ in manifestation.

Q3)   Siobhan: Is there something that these groups or individuals should or could be doing to diffuse the negative terrorist energy?

A3)   Gabriel: As already expressed, the channel and the group members in both the *SFG Study Group* as well as the *Indigos & Sensitives Support Group* are already creating a healing energy form as a result of their chanting process. That energy form can be used to counter or dissipate or dissolve the energy of the Anti-Christ, if a mere change in the wording and the idea associated with it can be implemented. What we are saying is that the grouping as it exists, is already in the process of creating the necessary energy to counter, that which is the Anti-Christ energy that is being expressed in the radical Islamic Jihadist grouping continues to create. Is that made clear?

Siobhan: Yes, thank you.

Q4)   Sandy: Prior to this meeting tonight [12/12/07], Kevin Colyer, one of our group members who is currently in South Korea sent a question, unfortunately I cannot remember his question. I just saw that it came in [via email] and that it was related to the balance between the Muslim and the western world. . . .

A4)   Gabriel: [interrupting] We have the information you are seeking. The question that Col. Colyer requested information on was; "Was there something that individuals and groupings should be doing to increase the compatibility or understanding of the Western Consciousness with the Muslim Consciousness." We would rephrase the question in terms of, "Is there something that can be done between the Western Consciousness and the Consciousness of the Jihadist world." Let us simply say that the Jihadist forces are disruptive and destructive to the oneness aspect, which can be identified as or associated with the Anti-Christ energy as has been previously communicated.

In order to bring about an understanding of the Western consciousness or culture by the Muslim world, and an understanding of the Muslim consciousness or culture by the Western world, there needs to be an acknowledgement of and acceptance of the cultural differences by both sides. The leaders in the Western world and the Jihadist leaders of the Muslim world are both trying to impose their own cultural and consciousness views on what each other do. If there is to be a coming together, both must understand that they cannot impose their will, and their way of thinking upon the others.

There needs to be a recognition [that] the Divine Being God is not a Christian, is not a Jew, and is not [a] Muslim, and that no one religious ideology is the correct one, yet all have aspects that speak to the essence of what God is. That is what truly needs to be understood and embraced if conflict is to be avoided. Is that understood?

Sandy: Yes.

Q5) **Sandy:** How long do you anticipate the war going on in the middle east?

A5) **Gabriel:** The conflict that you refer to as war is understood to be the conflict in the country known as Iraq. That conflict is a continual conflict within the governmental bodies themselves, and the factions thereof of peoples. It will not be stabilized for some time. However, there will be political, and shall we say, international pressures upon the Iraqi governmental body to resolve their conflicts. The United States will simply be one of those, not the primary one. *We see a positive extraction of military forces from the country known as Iraq. However, the country known as Afghanistan and even Pakistan will in fact be increased in a significant way and will be, shall we say, much more intense than even the most intense battles that have been experienced within the Iraqi campaign.* For the geography of that region wherein the cells of self-interest are abiding, make it very difficult to physically combat those kinds of energies. The greatest effort needs to be put in terms of creating an atmosphere for the peoples – the everyday peoples – giving them hope and understanding, that they can create a different future than the experience of their past. It is a cultural change that is needed to be, shall we say, enhanced. Has already begun but it needs to be enhanced.

So the war as you ask will continue but in a different campaign in a different set of countries and there will be a stabilization relative to the United States government's perspective within the country we know as Iraq, within the first 6 to 9 months of the current, or shall we say, the incoming administration. Is that made clear?

Sandy: Yes.

Terrorist Attacks[76]

Q1)   **Siobhan:** Please comment on the Terrorist Attacks that we are observing and experiencing throughout the world as well as here in the United States. What attitude should be held by group members regarding such Terrorist Attacks throughout the world as well as within the United States?

A1)   **Gabriel:** The Terrorist attacks, as you term them are merely expressions of egocentric behavior by people who do not fully understand the impact of their actions, and do not fully understand the Karmic retribution that they are setting in place. The attitude that one must take or should take as regards terrorist attacks and the effects of the terrorist's actions, must be one of in terms of enlightenment for them that they might see that which they are impacting. And also a sense of opening their eyes that they might see that which they have limited vision of.

Terrorism is a way of causing conflict and/or difficulty within a grouping that one individual or groups of individuals do not agree with the ideal that is held by another grouping. When it is understood that such actions cause significant Karmic retributions, then it can be understood that terrorism can in fact be defeated, but the defeat comes not in overcoming or destroying the terrorists, their actions or their desired cause, but more in terms of allowing them to understand that the actions that they take have Karmic responsibilities that must be paid, perhaps even in the lifetime that they are existing in.

There needs to be a greater understanding between peoples in general, and that process is in fact happening but it is happening at what you would considered to be a v-e-r-y slow pace. Therefore we would have you hold within your mind the concept that God's justice must be

---

[76] Excerpted from the April 2006 channeling session

carried out and that the carrying out must be done in a manner that would allow Love and the energy associated with same to be the predominant energy. When you can do that, both as a group and as a society then what you will find is that the terrorist activity diminishes if not completely goes away, for the need for them to be terrorists disappears. Does that make sense?

Siobhan: Yes, thank you.

Q2) **Siobhan:** Can we expect a Terrorist Attack in the United States (and/or other parts of the world) comparable to September 11, 2001 attacks in New York City and Washington, DC? If so, please comment on when and where these attacks might occur, and what form they might take?

A2) **Gabriel:** The question in terms of "Will there be Terrorist attacks of the magnitude as you term the September 11, 2001 attacks upon the World Trade Centers and the Pentagon?" *Yes those attacks and similar are in planning stages as we speak.* That being said, there are also forces of positive energy in counter position attempting to nullify or ameliorate the energies that would [support] the successful carrying out of such attacks. As to form, and as to location, and as to timing. The form is multiple. There are plans in the process of what would be considered a nuclear kind of process or a nuclear attempt *in this country. There is also that same process going on in three other countries as well.* That being said, as far as the timing it is not set by the planetary alignments as to when such attacks will occur, but we would definitely feel that *before the springtime of next year [2007], at least one such attack will either have been carried out or have been stopped just short of being carried out.*

Siobhan: Thank you.

Q3) **Siobhan:** May we know the three other countries that they might be carried out in?

A3) **Gabriel:** The plans currently are for an attack to take place within what you would call the *United Kingdom,* again we would have cautionary aspects within the land that you call *France as well.* And there is still another one that is planned or in the process of in what would be considered *the middle east, or in terms of Jerusalem.*

Siobhan: Thank you.

Q4) **Siobhan:** Will anyone set off a dirty bomb or will there be a nuclear detonation in the USA? If so, when and where?

A4)   **Gabriel:** As previously stated *such attacks are being planned,* and we see the possibility of such happening within the world, not necessarily within the United States, but within the world, and *we would see that in the time frame before the next spring. [Spring 2007].*

Siobhan: Thank you.

Q5)   **Siobhan:** Assuming that Terrorists Attacks are to occur in the United States (and/or elsewhere), are such attacks predetermined or are there things that these groups and other groups can do to prevent them or otherwise prevent them from having their desired terrorism affect?

A5)   **Gabriel:** There are astrological alignments calling for deleterious and/or detrimental effects upon various groupings. However, that being said, those alignments are only potentialities; they do not constitute predetermination. As for this group and its ability to alter or to modify such occurrences? Yes indeed this group has that ability, as do many other groups, and there are many groups other than this group that are in the process of trying to calm and trying to bring alignment of better spiritual energies so that such attacks do not occur. Is that clear?

Siobhan: Thank you, yes.

Q6)   **Siobhan:** Is there something specific that this group should be doing on a regular basis that will help balance the energies behind these Terrorist Attacks, so as to alleviate the negative impact of these attacks and reduce or alleviate the great suffering created by them?

A6)   **Gabriel:** Would be in accord with this group's purpose to begin a process of what is termed verbal attunements [chantings]. Following the group chanting process, the group is to then ask that the harmonious energy created be exponentially magnified to create a loving and cooperative healing energy that can combat the divisive Terrorist energy. Such processes may also include drumming or other sounds and singing of form that will in fact align the group. Is that understood?

Siobhan: Yes thank you.

Attunement, Spiritual Progress, Religions, etc.[77]

Q1) **Diana:** What are the most powerful, helpful or healing energies and forces that are available to us at this time in our evolution? And how can we best recognize and utilize these energies both individually and collectively?

A1) **Gabriel:** The most helpful process that one may use to find "at onement" is the process of meditation. Although there are a number of forms of meditation, the deep meditative state wherein you attune yourself – individually or as a group – to the "oneness" energy within yourself is the most powerful. That attunement creates an emanating loving energy that goes out to all entities throughout the world as well as to all entities on the inner planes, and allows one to become sensitive to and experience that "God essence" and thus recognize that you are in accord with your soul's purpose.

Another process that can and should be used is after you meditate, or as part of the meditation process, learn to create affirmations and/or statements that affirm God's presence and power. However, as you do so, a question that you must ask of yourself is, "Am I expressing a desire to prevent that which I see as difficult or harmful, or is my desire in terms of, 'Let thy will be done,' let me simply understand?" For it is the later that is the more effective tool [process] in bringing about a restoration of the balance of those energies. Is that understood?

Diana: Yes, thank you.

Q2) **Kyla:** How do we know or what are the signs that we, as individuals and as a group, are spiritually and energetically progressing at the rate that we are suppose to be for the best purpose of myself and for the best purpose of the group?"

A2) **Gabriel:** Although this question is clearly one of sincerity and from the heart, and from one who is seeking to know that they are on the correct path, let me simply say that you are in fact on your correct path, and that this grouping is in fact on its correct path. However, it does not mean that there are not stumbling blocks and stones to be overcome in the process. To find out if you are on the right path,

---

[77] Excerpted from the April 2006 and January 2009 channeling sessions

simply ask yourself and know that the answer can be had – not from your mind, but from your Spirit. The answer is not a simple yes or no, it is an awareness that you are aware, that you are in attunement with the process, not that you are an A or B or C student but in fact that you are trying to be the best person you can be. You must keep in mind that every attempt that you make, from this perspective, is simply a learning process whereby the entity is allowed another opportunity to express their highest Ideal. You cannot fail, you can simply fail to achieve what you desire to achieve, but the success is measured in the attempt [not the result or outcome]. Does that make sense?

Kyla: Yes, thank you.

Q3) **Doug:** What is the soul's relationship with our physical existence and what is the likelihood of reincarnation?

A3) **Gabriel:** For the entity to ask the question is a little bit absurd, for the entity fully understands that reincarnation is in fact a reality and is simply wanting a confirmation. As for the relationship of the physical body to the spiritual body, as the entity the channel often teaches, "you are spiritual beings expressing in a physical form." Although you are governed by the physical format that you have chosen to express in this earth plane dimension, the essence of who you are is not limited except by the mental concepts that you hold. Is that clear?

Doug: Yes, thank you.

Q4) **Doug:** Others who claim to predict future events have cleaved to a notion of catastrophic events to come be it by man, nature or otherwise. What have you seen is to come?

A4) **Gabriel:** We will address the question in two terms. First of all, there are those entities within the earth plane including the channel himself who have the ability to tune into prophetic energies, which are indicators of potentialities to come. As the channel often states, events or outcomes cannot be certainly known until choices are made. For each of you within this earth plane are free will beings totally capable of altering the future by altering your choices and your perceptions of same.

As regarding the question of catastrophic upcoming events then. As has been predicted by both the channel, as well as those entities whom you refer, *there is the significant potential of catastrophic – both geological, economic and social catastrophes if you wish, that will in fact be expressed and/or experienced within the earth plane over the next 15 to 18 month time frame* as has been previously stated. There are other catastrophic potentialities that might also be experienced in the next three and the next five years time increments as well. So we would say prepare yourself to be able to understand and be of service to those in need that are significantly affected by catastrophic events. Be available to help them understand that they do not have to be affected in the way they seem to be affected if they will simply change their perspective and perception. Whether an entity survives such an event from a physical perspective is immaterial from a spiritual perspective. The survival is more in terms of, "Did one learn from that experience and did one reach out and touch others in a positive way during that experience?" Is that understood?

Doug: Yes, thank you.

Q5) **Sandy:** How do those of us here prepare for such potential catastrophic events? What are the recommendations so that we can be of service to help others?

A5) **Gabriel:** As has been stated previously by the channel, each of thee prepares by sending and creating within self an intention of being of service and then acting upon that intention by actively participating in assisting others in various forms be it financially, emotionally, or physically. Each form [of assistance] is important. Each has their realm of service but it is the intention [the Ideal] that the entity holds that is important. So as far as preparation, prepare by holding your consciousness in terms of intention to be of service without worrying about how that service must be specified or implemented. You will know at the time you are called upon. Keep in your heart the opportunity to serve as a fundamental principle by which you operate your life. That would be the best preparation. Is that understood?

Sandy: Yes.

Q6) **Doug:** There has been great debate and speculation on the age of the universe. The Bible talks about God creating the Universe approximately six to seven thousand years ago. However, science speculates in terms of billions upon billions of years. What is your opinion?

A6) **Gabriel:** We will not give an opinion here but we will simply give you factual information. The creation of the universe happened in a moment and that moment was significantly long ago in the way man measures time. The terminology of 6,000 years is simply a blink in the creation of [physical] reality. As the entity the channel has taught his students, the Creator created out of an examination of self, and as such time [and space] were created as concepts for man to begin to understand a physical reality, a limiting reality. But in the consciousness of God, and the serving Angels and Archangelic beings, there is no time or space. It could be said that time is simultaneous, and therefore the question although logically understandable [from your perspective], in this realm [it] is differently approached. For the creation, in this realm of understanding of time, happened multiple billions of years ago. The time that we see is a wrapped time if you wish, for the universe folds upon itself and that which was before becomes after and that which was after becomes before within the realm of Spirit. Is that understood?

Doug: Yes.

Q7) **Kyla:** Why does the world have so many religions, and why are they always in conflict and warring against each other?

A7) **Gabriel:** As the entity, the channel, has often said, the term Religion is more in terms of "Man's concept of God" and as such it is a limited consciousness, for it is an ego based consciousness. That is why the channel, continually expresses the fact that we must understand. That our groupings are more about understanding Spirituality. For example, in the understanding, in the expressing, and in the implementation of the Universal Laws that the group has been studying, those laws are more in terms of understanding Spirituality, and Spirituality as the channel has often expressed, is "God's understanding of man." So when individuals understand Spirituality, they begin to understand the expression of God within themselves, and they begin to understand how the expression of God within themselves is in fact in accord with the expression of God within other individuals, and therefore there's an "at-onement," an understanding that there is a commonality, not a division. That is the difference between Religion and Spirituality. And as far as, "why so many religions?" The so many religions is more in terms of ego expressions of their understanding of God and not looking at an understanding of God's expression of what man is all about. Does that make sense?

Kyla: Yes, thank you.

Q8) **Doug:** What can we gain from meditation and is there a preferred method?

A8)   **Gabriel:** The process known as meditation, as detailed by the channel in his teachings, as well as detailed by many others who have taught and talk about meditation, consists of quieting one's physical mind, to quiet one's conscious activation shall we say, and allow self to become attuned to the inner vibration of their own Spirit. The proper technique is really immaterial in terms of the effect. Some techniques work very well for some individuals. The same techniques might not work for thee. As the channel has often suggested we would begin by simply quieting oneself, listening to one's breath, for a period of ten to fifteen minutes every single day for a period of approximately one week to ten days. After this time period, the entity should notice a shifting, an increased understanding of the essence of who you are. As you continue this process of concentrating on your breath, we would have you begin to ask what the Father would have you understand, what the Father would have you know, what the Father would have you do to become more attuned to the essence of who you are. As you do this there should be a greater awareness of the essence of who you are, which will allow you to become attuned to the essence of others that you meet day by day. And the greatest work that one can do is to be in tune with the essence of who you are to such a degree that when you interact with others the essence of who they are begins to become activated so that you become the lighter that lights each of the candles that you meet day by day. Is this understood?

Doug: Yes.

Q9)   **Bart:** In regards to the gift [of insight regarding Sacred Geometry] that I have been given, can you please tell me what you want me to do with that gift? I'm still willing to keep looking, but I am very frustrated.

A9)   **Gabriel:** We would stretch the entity's imaginative forces to begin to understand the gift in the following manner. You do not ask your body to breathe for you. Your body simply breathes for you. For that is the function of the body. There is an agreement with your Spirit that's occupying your body that it will innervate and keep alive the physical form and that the physical form will utilize it's innate understanding as manifested as same. As regarding your understanding of Sacred Geometry and its application to understanding stock market forces, the models that you have come up with in a cognitive manner, influenced strongly by the intuitive understandings, are simply expressions of your Spirit. The use of these understandings to create a wealthy distribution for yourself and those you serve, is [in] accord with your soul's purpose, for you understand that your gift is to be used in a positive manner to help others as well as helping self.

Do not ask *why* you have that information. Ask in your contemplations and meditation *what you must do with that information.* It is your own internal understandings, your own connection with the Source of your being, and the purposefulness for which you are directing your life, that will really dictate how you think about and how you utilize the ideas and the information that you obtain either in your meditations or in your ponderings of those energies; those, shall we say, fragmented cords, those undulations of trends within markets, geographical markets or world markets we refer to here. As one understands, as you as a personality begin to understand your purposefulness, your role needs to be open to that information, document that information and utilize that information to create increased wealth that may be used in a supportive manner of [to] others as well as yourself. That would be the most appropriate use of that energy and that information that comes to you both in your mind, in your dreams and in your ponderings. That is your gift. Does this make sense to you?

Bart: Yes it does. Thank You.

Remembrance and Location of Heaven, Death, etc.[78]

Q1) **Agnes:** My 5-year-old daughter asked me a few nights ago where heaven is, and she wanted more than just "it's in the clouds" so I thought I would ask that question for her.

A1) **Gabriel:** Regarding your daughter's question, "Where is heaven?" We would have you answer it as such. If you were to have your daughter in front of you and you were to tap upon her heart and say to her that heaven is right there, and then have her tap upon your heart and have her say that heaven is right there. That would be a closer determination of where heaven is. For the mind of that little child understands far beyond your current understanding that heaven is a state of mind that she vaguely remembers. And by allowing her to understand that the heaven that she vaguely remembers is still within

---

[78] Excerpted from the April 2006 and January 2009 channeling sessions.

her, and that the heaven that you only "glimpsingly" remember is still within you, that in fact that will bring about the awareness that heaven is in fact not [some place] out there, but something within. Is that clear?

Agnes: Yes, very much, thank you.

Q2) **Agnes:** I have a huge interest in knowing when your loved ones or friends have passed over to the other side. Exactly what process occurs from the moment they, their soul leaves their body.

A2) **Gabriel:** The transition of an entity from the physical existence to that which you term death or that which I term release, is more in terms of an awareness that you no longer have the physical body that is weighting you down, or you no longer have the physical ailment that caused your precipitous process called death. There is basically an awakening on the other side as it were, although we do not like those terms.

It would be more accurate to say that death is more in terms of an awakening within yourself of who you really are. It's much like all of a sudden you look within and you find this beautifully bright flame that begins to expand and yet it does not consume, it simply enlightens you and makes you more aware. So the process that you call death is really an awakening awareness.

For those entities who transition and who are not aware, there are beings of light all around them who are sending light to them to bring that awareness about. When those entities who are not aware receive that light, they have the opportunity to either accept it or reject it, and when they accept it, they become aware of who they are and they can then fully express who they really are and make contact with those of us on this side.

The entity you refer to as the channel, has the ability to "walk in" or experience both sides of that veil and to communicate with those entities who are in darkness as well as those entities who are in darkness seeking light, as well as those entities who are in fact transitioned but still have the light. At that point, he can then communicate that information in a manner that makes those of the living understand information that is available to him from the Spirit domain. Is that clear?

Agnes: Yes, thank you.

Q3) **Agnes:** As regards homeless people. Is this something that's part of their Karma? Is there something we can do at large, or on a one-to-one basis to try to remedy the problem here in the United Sates when we have such abundance here?

A3) **Gabriel:** The matter of homeless people and/or those less fortunate who are in need, needs to be approached with great discernment. It must be understood and accepted that some individuals chose to live the way they live and be the way they be, and it is not for anyone to interfere with that process. As regards the question "when do I help and when do I not help?" When you can honestly say to yourself that you are trying to help out of a sense of your "at-onement" with yourself, and not out of a sense of having more than those individuals, then you can step forward and help them in a way that is most expressive of the help that they need. When you find the individuals who are seeking help, but the kind of help or assistance that they are seeking is not of the form that you are willing to or capable of giving, then you must simply bless them and let them go on their way, for they are choosing to do that which they are doing, and you must not allow yourself to be caught up in their self created limited expression. For to do so causes you to have a Karmic tie to that individual, which you may in fact not want to express. Does that make sense?

Agnes: Yes, thank you very much.

Q4) **Sandi:** In a previous question, you mentioned that some of us might only have partial remembrance of heaven. I would like to know what I might do to bring some of those memories more to the fore of my consciousness, so that I might overcome some of the problems and the struggles in my search. Thank you.

A4) **Gabriel:** Dear child, you need to understand that the presence of the creator is within you, and within every individual in this gathering. Your experience of fear or trepidation is simply you being afraid of being who you really are, rather than being afraid of anything outside of yourself. We have been shown that there have been times when you have in fact been shown that you are connected, but the light is so bright that you are fearful of it and turn away from it. Your question about memories of heaven we find rather humorous for you've been there many times, and many times you've been brought back with the remembrance of it, only to say it can't be that simple, it can't be that simple. Be assured, it is that simple. Do you understand?

Sandi: Yes, thank you so much.

Q5) **Bart:** My opportunity to be a Naval aviator and fly off aircraft carriers was a very special opportunity in this lifetime. On that note I gained a special bond with many of the people I flew with and one thing that is bothering multiple Naval aviators who are currently flying and did fly, is the status and the happening of Captain Scott Speicher, the entity named as Scott Speicher who was the first and only navy F-18 pilot to be shot down in the Iraqi war. Can you please give some closure to that for me, the entity, and for some of the people I will talk to about it afterwards? If you think that's appropriate. Please.

A5) **Gabriel:** Your question regarding the pilot who was shot down needs to be understood. The entity [Scott Speicher] is no longer in physical form. He made his willing transition rather than give into the forces that would have his information be used inappropriately. He exited his aircraft and he was in fact found after three days by opposing forces and extracted from the earth plane in a not very kind manner. However, through dignity he honored his country and he honored his family and himself, by simply allowing himself to be killed rather than dishonor himself and his country. The aviators of which you speak need to understand that at any moment in their life, at any moment when they are flying, they can call upon his Spirit and be aware of his Spirit as they continue their mission. For he wishes them well. Is that understood?[79]

Bart: Yes. Thank You.

Relationship To Animal Kingdom[80]

Q1) **Phillip:** I have a two-part question. First part is: What is our relation as human beings to the animal kingdom? And 2nd part, more in particular "What is our relation to companion animals such as dogs that share similar emotions to us?"

A1) **Gabriel:** As an energy form the animal kingdom has a spiritual awareness of its at-onement with what you call God, but not consciously as does mankind. In that regard, mankind can in fact

---

[79] The announcement that Scot Speicher's remains were found in Iraq in early August 2009 came as the author was preparing his manuscript. The author discussed the significance of this channeled information with Bart.

[80] Excerpted from the April 2006 channeling session

communicate both on the mental level as well as the spiritual level with those entities. As regards Karmic ties and Karmic relationships between mankind and the animal world, there is an idea or belief within the Hindu religion termed *transmigration* in which they believe that a person can come back or reincarnate and become an animal. Although that process did exist in the early expression of mankind, that process is no longer a viable process. Therefore, any interaction of humans with animals is in fact a human form interacting with an animal form. Is that understood?

Phillip: Yes.

Q2) **Gabriel:** Although the question, "What about terminating the life of an animal. What is the Karmic responsibility of the individuals who do that and what is the responsibility of the individuals who consume the meat thereof?" has not been asked, the entity as well as two other individuals in this group are in fact asking that question [in their mind] and so we will answer it.

A2) **Gabriel:** There is an agreement among [within] the animal kingdom, that some animals are brought into this earth plane to be food for other animals and food for the human form as well. That agreement allows that animals flesh to be consumed in a nutritive process, not in a taking of life process. On the other hand, when animals are extracted from their body in what would be considered a cruel and/or unusually painful process or manner, or for the purpose of satisfying someone's ego, there are indeed negative Karmic ties created. Also, if one knowingly then partakes in the eating of animals who have been killed in such manner, then there is in fact a Karmic tie for those individuals as well as those who took the life of that animal. Is that understood?

Phillip: Yes, thank you.

Deep Channeling Process and Angelic Hierarchy[81]

Q1) **Sandy:** [Please] explain the process that the channel uses to allow himself to become a channel for the entity **Gabriel** and **The Master** energy, and what happens to the consciousness of Lowell when he is in the channeling state?

---

[81] Excerpted from the December 2007 and December 2008 channeling sessions

A1) **Gabriel:** When the entity Lowell goes into the channeling state, he first raises his consciousness to a significantly high level and then his personality basically steps aside and he allows himself to be communicated through. As the energy of *Gabriel* expresses through this entity, his consciousness can communicate directly from this Archangelic level.

When *The Master* energy, the Christ consciousness energy, desires to express through Lowell, his consciousness is raised to an even higher state of awareness by the Archangelic beings that are all around him, to allow him to channel that higher energy level. When this is done, Lowell is physically healed in the process of allowing The Master energy to express though him. Is that understood?

Sandy: Yes.

Q2) **Sandy:** Are we to understand that this energy form [that is being channeled] is *Gabriel* the Archangel or simply a grouping identified with that name?

A2) **Gabriel:** Although we understand the consciousness that requires an answer to that question, it is best expressed in the following form. The *Archangel Gabriel* that you have identified us as, in terms of mankind, is more than simply an individuated expression, but a conglomeration of energies that are at such a high level that they have been identified over the years or over the eons as an Archangelic energy. The energy that the entity Lowell channels is sometimes directly from the Archangel Gabriel, and that is who is addressing you at the present time. And at this level we are aware very much of the energy forms of the entities present. For even though Lowell's consciousness is not present, the entities energies that we observe through this energy awareness that we are in contact with, is able to see the needs of each of thee. Some of thee require blessings at this time. Some of you are hurting physically. Some of you are hurting emotionally. Some have great questions. Some have a number of questions that are ego related. We are able to separate those out and see them clearly from this state. Is that understood?

Sandy: Yes.

Q3) **Steve:** Regarding the hierarchy of Angels. It seems that there's Archangels and Angels. Is there a difference in the hierarchy of Angels and how we should perceive them?

A3) Gabriel: The differentiation in the hierarchy as it is described, is simply a conceptual process for humanity to begin to understand the purposefulness for each of the Angels and/or Archangelic beings. As has been stated previously through this channel, this channel has at his command the entire council of Archangelic energies simply by calling upon them. But as has also has been previously stated, the Angelic energies that you identify as Michael, as Gabriel, as Azrael are simply nomenclatures or naming of an energetic form who is carrying out a particular purpose at a particular time in a particular form. Mankind simply needs to identify same, and as such has called them by a specific name. An Angelic being that is present with thee in a moment wherein you are in prayer, or a moment of need, or perhaps at your birth, is simply a Being that is capable of doing what is necessary to assist thee through the process you are seeking, or growing through at that time. It is not separate and apart from the Angelic energy hierarchy. It is simply doing a specific task, and that energy is a part of the whole. There is no differentiation from God's perspective, for all are simply energy forms that are carrying out their specific tasks. Does this make it clear?

Steve: Yes it does, thank you.

Q4) Steve: As we move forward with this evolving of humanity, we hear the term light workers and we use the term to talk about the energy of light in its many forms. As we are evolving, is there a change in the way we use light that corresponds to the awakening of mankind?

A4) Gabriel: We will answer you as thus. The term that many people in the metaphysical community use as light needs to be understood in terms of level of awareness of the individuals using that term. Some people use that term and they have a concept of a light similar to the stream of light from the sun, or from a light bulb. But the light that those more advanced entities understand is simply the presence, essence of an individual person's Being, and whether that person sees that light, or sees that essence, or is simply aware of that essence, they are "aware" of a light. The better term would be "I see the essence within you, rather than I see the light within you." For the essence may not express as a light, yet it is in fact what we would term "light" in the sense that it brings increased awareness and understanding of "connected to the source of thy Being."

Clearly there has been a movement and an increased understanding that many, many more people understand that there is a light within everyone, in the sense that there is an essence that is within everyone.

We call it a living essence, and that living essence has an experience for those observing it and those sensing it. It creates for them an awareness of that individual's connection to the source of their Being. Our job as light workers as you use the term, is to simply be so connected with the source of our own being that our light shines in a way, not that others might see the way, but in fact that others might see the essence within themselves and find their own way. So it is not to proselytize but simply to express the greatest understanding that you have, while understanding [being aware of] that your understanding must increase day-by-day as you go about your task of creating love in and around you, both for yourself and all those individuals that God sends your way. Is that made clear?

Q5) **Steve:** Yes but I want to talk or ask about the inflow of light and how that may be different.

A5) **Gabriel:** The inflow of light that you refer to is simply an awareness on your part that there are more energetic beings in and around the earth plane sending energy – light if you wish, but sending energy of understanding – an advanced or awakening kind of energy so that all who are able to or desirous of observing that or experiencing that, have the opportunity, a greater opportunity than would have been so had these light workers on the inner planes not been sent by God to help in this process. Is that made clear?

Steve: Yes.

Christmas and Jesus Birth[82]

Q1) **Sandy:** Does this Christmas hold special significance for us at this time?

A1) **Gabriel:** From the stand point of understanding of the oneness with the creative energy within same, and as those of the grouping are aware that there is a change about to occur, within the earth plane. Some are aware of it energetically. It will be a sociological as well as economical change, but it will be impactful to many who are present.

Q2) **Gail:** Have you any special message for us regarding the Christmas story? What year and month was Jesus born?

---

[82] Excerpted from the December 2007 channeling session

A2) **Gabriel:** The timing of the incoming Christ energy was not in accordance with that which is currently celebrated, but the date would be closer to what we would consider March 8, four years prior to the current existence.

Alzheimer's and Autism[83]

Q1) **Siobhan:** What is the purpose of losing mental faculties through disease such as Alzheimer's and to live for years not tuned in on many levels?

A1) **Gabriel:** We would bring some clarification to that statement. The process you call Alzheimer's and the process that you call other forms of, shall we say, mental deterioration, are in fact agreements that each entity has come into this earth plane with, to experience and to express and struggle with that Karmic challenge.

There are entities who come in with that Karmic challenge, who experience a deteriorated or detrimental state for the process of helping others learn how to be a better person, or how to interact with them in a better way. There are others who also come in and have taken upon themselves to take upon this, shall we say deleterious form of understanding and deleterious form of expressing in a mental way, in order to better understand that which they have lost. For some times it is better for an individual to lose something in the process to gain their understanding. The best way to interact with individuals who are expressing these mental difficulties is to begin to learn how to communicate with them in a manner other than simply through verbal processes. The mere fact that there is a significant increase in what you would call autism in today's society is greatly due in part to entities coming in desiring to communicate on a level other than what you would call physical communication. And it is our process or our learning opportunity, to be able to learn how to communicate with these entities in a way that is non-verbal. There are major strides happening in this process as we understand it today, and when we find someone who comes out of being an autistic child to one who becomes a verbal child, we take that as a progressive step and yet it may not be a progressive step for that individual. That in fact unless that understanding, unless that verbalization has come about through a

---

[83] Excerpted from the April 2006 channeling session

recognition that there is a different way to communicate other than verbally, then in fact that has been a failure. Does that make sense?

Siobhan: Thank you.

Q2) **Siobhan:** Just so I can be clear Gabriel, are you saying that when people lose their mental faculties on this plane, they are in fact tuned in on other planes?

A2) **Gabriel:** Absolutely!

Siobhan: Thank you.

Medical Healing vs. Natural Healing[84]

Q1 **Siobhan:** Can you comment on the utilization of energetic healing practices and tools, and natural healing remedies vs. traditional medicine healing methods, and how does one know or decide which healing method is the best healing course of action to take?

A1) **Gabriel:** The information in question is more in terms of alignment or attunement with bodily form. We would find that the natural remedies that have been discovered, and that have been known, and that are in the process of being rediscovering, are based on attuning or re-attuning the bodily form to its natural state. The effectiveness of healing, via medications, surgeries, laying on of hands, or via natural remedies, is greatly dependent upon the consciousness of the individual being healed as well as the consciousness of the person doing the healing. For example, if an individual seeking healing requires within its mind to have an educated doctor to carry out the medical diagnosis, and/or surgery, and requires the use of prescribed drugs, then other "natural" forms of healing including natural medication, will not be as effective, because the patient would set up an energy barrier that would not allow that healing process to occur in its natural way. Is that understood?

Q2) **Siobhan:** Um, could you say a bit more about that Gabriel? How does one decide which healing method is the best healing method or course to take?

A2) **Gabriel:** The best healing method for any individual, for any individual event, is more in terms of where is the consciousness of the

---

[84] Excerpted from the April 2006 channeling session

person seeking the healing? If the person's consciousness is such that he believes that he requires a pill or some other form of that nature, or a shot, or some inoculation, then in fact their mind set is such that other forms or processes of healing will not be as effective. So, it really depends more in terms of the mindset of the individual seeking the healing, and their basic belief systems. For clearly it is the MIND that determines the healing process. The mind sets up the process by which the body operates, and if the body is provided a medication that the mind does not believe in, that medication will not affect the result that it would normally affect if the person in fact had a mind set that would allow it to do the healing that is necessary. So therefore, what we are saying is that by the mere process of creating within your mind a mindset that allows you to create healing, whether it be from Aspirin or whether it be from some other form of medication, great healing can take place simply due to mental energy.

Siobhan: Thank you.

Q3)   **Siobhan:** What is the degree of impact of the factors of a) genetic predisposition, b) environmental toxins – disease factors, c) health maintaining practices such as diet and exercise, and d) one's mental/spiritual state and frequency of vibration on one's overall physical, mental, and spiritual health?

A3)   **Gabriel:** Although we have already answered this in the previous response, we will provide a little bit more clarity. As regards toxins and the body's ability to withstand toxins, there are multiple factors involved. One factor has to do with the Karmic responses that the entity has come in to choose to experience. The other factor is the current mental and spiritual state of the individual. Those two processes, those two expressions, shall we say, have a very significant factor in determining whether a toxin that is very toxic to one individual but not toxic to another can be effective. That is, when a person's mental and spiritual state allows them to understand that they have been exposed to a toxin, but they do not give in to the fact that the toxin has an ability to change their body form and/or their, shall we say, their spiritual mental processes, then that toxic, although may cause some, shall we say, deterioration or abnormality of the cell formation because of the biological processes involved, that biological processes can be slowed down and/or, shall we say, modified such that that toxin that could be, shall we say, terminal in some cases, not be effective in the cases where the entity has brought forth that energy which would allow it to, shall we say dissipate or change that factor.

As regards the mental state, as we [have] already stated, that is simply more in terms of the body's ability, the minds ability, to create an energy form around it that will allow it to withstand and/or to change its energy from exposure to such entities. And I say entities, more in terms of biological forms. For a biological form responds to mental processes in the same way it responds to the, shall we say, the biological structure of penicillin, or the biological structure of an antidote, or the biological structure of an antidepressant, or the biological structure of, shall we say, a narcotic process. All of these forms can be experienced and all of these forms can be expressed, merely through powerful mental processes, and there is medical evidence that is rampantly [rapidly], shall we say, arising that is both, has been there but has not been fully understood and it's beginning to be made more manifest. Is that made clear?

Siobhan: Yes, thank you.

Q4) **Siobhan:** Is there anything else regarding this topic that the channel needs to say at this time?

A4) **Gabriel:** There are a number of individuals in this grouping who have questions as to what did he really say? But it [must be made] clear and understood that the mental processes and the spiritual understandings have a far more significant effect upon the, bodily responses than do the biological processes that are involved. Is that understood?

Siobhan: Thank you.

The Year 2008[85]

Q1) **Sandy:** Are there any words of guidance or caution for anyone present regarding the coming New Year 2008?

A1) **Gabriel:** Hear ye, Hear ye all. ***The coming year is as a challenge to each of thee.*** For you are being called upon as part of this gathering to begin to express yourself. Express the Christ energy that you are aware of, and begin to advance yourself in your understanding in terms of becoming more of a channel, a blessing to every single one

---

[85] Excerpted from the December 2007 channeling session

you contact day-by-day. ***This is a year of reckoning,*** for those who are given the opportunity and take advantage of it will be significantly supported in their process. And for those who do not take advantage of that which they are given, much will be taken away. Is that understood?

Sandy: Yes.

Q2)   **Justina:** How can our group expand in vibration to assist in the upcoming earth changes?

A2)   **Gabriel:** As has been expressed previously, ***this next year is a year of testing.*** The format or the process that the entity asks about in terms of, "How can the grouping and the individuals within the grouping be of greater service to humankind?" The answer is, "To help the new energies [*Indigos, Crystals, and Star Children*] in their emotional, psychological, and spiritual expression in this world." Is that made clear?

Justina: Yes, thank you.

The Year 2009[86]

Q1)   **Sandy:** What can we expect in 2009 in reference to so many aspects of life; Earth changes, World disasters, Climate changes, Economic conditions?

A1)   **Gabriel:** Although we find this question somewhat humorous, we will attempt to answer the question without laughing. The energy of several individuals within this grouping and many individuals throughout the earth plane, are caught up in the process of fearfulness, wanting assurances that they will not be personally negatively impacted by any upcoming changes.

The difficulties; economic difficulties, that have occurred in this past year – in this past half year, have in fact been foretold by this channel previously, and the working out thereof, are different perhaps than he conceived of, or than was presented in the interpretation, the working out of those difficulties has been in accord with a pattern that was created many, many months before, by many individuals operating out of greed and self interest. That exposition – exposing that energy,

---

[86] Excerpted from the December 2008 channeling session

exposing that mind set, is in fact part of the exposing of those who would take and not give. That's why it was stated that the impact would affect those with more than those with less. *There is in fact an equalization that is beginning to express in the earth plane.* Not just within the United States, but within the earth plane itself. And the, shall we say, the difference between the very, very wealthy who are greedy, and those [who are] in great need will in fact be coming together in a very significant way over the next 6 to 9 months. *Within a 9-month period there will be a change in how the economic process within the United States operates.* Although this sounds very strange, *there will be some changes being made that will be much more restrictive in how things are operated at from a company perspective, and it will increase the access, shall we say, of peoples ideas, from all levels of life, to create a much more sociologically carrying and integrated pattern for this earth plane,* and for the United States itself. Does that answer the question?

Sandy: Yes.

President Elect Obama[87]

Q1) **Sandy:** Will Obama be safe in this administration?

A1) **Gabriel:** Many prayers have been stated and said for this entity. Many more must continue to be said, and surround that entity, the President Elect Obama with light and love and a level of protection. *Protection from those who are close to him as well as protection from those who would oppose him. For there are forces within his own administration that have their own agendas must be brought to the light in order for their own agendas to be made clear so that they might back off from doing what they are desirous of doing for their own egocentrical purposes.* The President Elect Obama has many challenges and these are one of those challenges. As has been recently expressed, and reported in the news, relative to his connection with political forces within the state from which he came. Those were non trivial and *he overestimated, or underestimated shall we say, the reality of the political egocentricalness of certain individuals who he trusted.* Is that made clear?

---

[87] Excerpted from the December 2008 and January 2009 channeling sessions

Sandy: Yes.

Q2)   **Doug:** It's been said that Obama has some type of link to Abraham Lincoln? What is the status of that? And also what is the likelihood of him being assassinated or removed from office in the next four years or eight years?

A2)   **Gabriel:** The entity Barack Obama, current president of the United States, is in fact the energetic reincarnation of the entity that expressed through the entity known as Abraham Lincoln.

The memory of the ending of Abraham Lincoln's life remains a memory within the consciousness of Barack Obama and there are many forces within the United States that are significantly oppositional to what Barack Obama is trying to do. Such energies and forces are in process of plotting for the removal of same. However, there are significant positive energy forces including the channel himself as well as other groupings associated with the channel, that are creating positive protective energies around the current president to protect him from the potentialities of that. Only time and choices will determine the final verdict or final outcome as it were. But much of what you say and much of what people tap into is related to the fact that Barack Obama himself, at least on a subconscious level, has a remembrance of having been assassinated in the past and is actively working to eliminate that potentiality in his current physicalness. Is that understood?

Doug: Yes.

World Markets and Currencies[88]

Q1)   **Sandy:** There's been talk about a Northern American Union with a new currency called the Amero. Has this trading block been agreed to?

A1)   **Gabriel:** There have been attempts by those within, shall we say, exclusive power control, to manipulate the systems of all three countries; the Canadian country, the United States, and the Mexican country, as well as other countries more southern than that as well, involving manipulations within the hierarchies – political thereof. However, those energies, and those operating peoples, will not

---

[88] Excerpted from the January 2009 channeling session

succeed in creating a system of interaction that would in fact be detrimental to the peoples and economies of all three countries. It would simply benefit some very exclusive entities and these are the entities that will be derailed by the loving energy that is infusing the earth plane by all of the high consciousness entities within the earth plane, as well as all the entities that have been sent from far and wide to create an environment to cause peace to eventually be created and maintained in a positive flowing manner within the earth plane. Is that understood?

Sandy: Yes.

Q2) **Doug:** The status of the economy in the United States has deteriorated significantly during the past year and subsequently eroded other world economics. What is the likelihood that our currency would be devalued and ultimately replaced, and if this is the case approximately when would this occur?

A2) **Gabriel:** The Question albeit may seem to be logical, has within it three realms of understanding. We will attempt to address each of these. The reality of the devaluation as you call it of the US currency, and the ripple effect upon the world economy is in fact a reality as you have experienced it. But that ripple effect has not, shall we say, met its end for it continues to vibrate and create additional ripples. The possibility of what you would refer to as a worldwide community currency is a possibility, and there are thoughts about same as being positive in nature. But the disruptive effect of the devaluation of the individual currencies that would contribute to that whole would be substantial and we find that the consciousness of most of humanity cannot conceive of same and therefore it will have to be impositional [imposed] rather than voluntary causing great disruptions within specific economies. There are forces at work in the positive realm to bring together humankind, but there are equally forces of negative vibrational energies that would create individuated pockets of increased wealth and increased, shall we say, sources. Those energies are being opposed by many of the entities who are in the light, such as the channel and his groupings, for it is understood that such a change would cause such a difficult process for humankind to process that it will have to be done in a very different manner than is currently being projected and or thought about by certain groupings shall we say. The question is rather complex. For the entity approaches the idea from the perspective of being a unifying function but does not take into account the fearfulness associated with the entities who would have their, shall we say, their currency, their principle of understanding of value, altered to such an extent that what they value would be valued in a different way by a different culture causing great disruptive energies. So although the principal at a very high level seems to be one of unification [it] is in fact when implemented divisive – diversive and divisive, rather than unifying. Is that understood?

Doug: Yes.

Q3) **Doug:** Yes. Will the stock market, as we know it with publicly traded stocks disappear? And if so when?

A3) **Gabriel:** The entity asks a question that is similar in nature to a question that was asked previously in a channeling session in which the entity the channel stated that there would be a major change in how the economic factors within the United States were implemented and perceived. The stock market as you refer is a vehicle in which people exchange value for value. Much of it has been manipulated for many years by subgroupings within that manipulation. Many of those groupings are being individually deteriorated, disrupted, torn apart as it were, and refused the opportunity from an energetic perspective of being able to manipulate that which they have freely manipulated for many many years. To state that the stock market of the United States or the stock market of other foreign countries other than the United States will not exist would be inappropriate. But the format in which they exist, and the value that they provide to the people who look to them, will in fact significantly alter and change in a way that is not understood completely by the entity, the channel. And we have somewhat of a difficulty in trying to articulate in a clear manner how that change may come about. For there are many entities and many choices and many energetic peoples as well as groupings that have a significant impact on what will come about. For as changes come about, the fear of entities involved cause other changes to occur so it is a highly dynamic situation. We regretfully say we cannot emphatically state that it will exist or it will not exist for there are too many individual determinations that contribute to the whole. Is that understood?

Doug: Yes.

Thoughts from Students and Clients

The following are thoughts and testimonials from some of my students and clients I have met, *read for* and helped in some manner. I have used their given names unless requested not to do so. I greatly appreciate their writing and allowing me to use their statements and testimonials. I hope and trust that the reader will read them and find comfort in the fact that real help can be provided when one gets themselves out of the way and simply lets "Spirit" convey what is needed by those who seek.

Betsy Anderson

I first met Lowell at a weekend workshop for *Indigo* children and their parents. I had never heard of *Indigo* children and my friend, Judith, who was hosting the event, said I should come. As a school librarian and former teacher of gifted children, I jumped at the chance.

The weekend was amazing. There were lectures regarding the student teacher relationship, healthy dietary choices and how parents could support their *Indigo* children. Of particular interest was a symposium of young adults who described what they 'saw' and experienced.

Lowell held his hand out and asked the participants to tell him what they saw. The children wrote their answers on a piece of paper, folded it, keeping their answers private. At first I saw nothing, but then I saw energy waves coming from his motionless hand. I had never seen that before. I thought of a ball, but put down something else, thinking that was silly. To my surprise, most of the *Indigos* thought it was a ball of light and Lowell confirmed their answers.

I met many delightful people who shared extraordinary spiritual gifts. I had never been with so many individuals who could see the "unseen." Many could see auras, some saw spiritual beings and "balls of light" or angels. I was introduced to a community of people who felt free to share and explore, with Lowell's guidance, their gifts of spiritual perception.

At the end of the weekend I had my first reading with Lowell. It was very emotional for me, as he seemed to know me inside out without me telling him anything but my name. He said he could see a lot from my aura. Without going into personal details, I came away from that first reading with the ability to be a stronger person and a better marriage partner. A message from my daughter, who died in 1995, was particularly valuable: Put up a fence.

Using the fence imagery has helped me mentally stand back and not take things personally.

My road to becoming a happier person started with my encounter with Lowell. I have had two other readings and in each one he has given me useful insights into my current behavior and thinking. My daughter came through again and thanked me for writing a book about her. Lowell had no knowledge of the book I had written several years earlier.

At another session with my twin he told us we had been together in many life times and told of a time when I had broken my left leg and communicated, telepathically, my cry for help to my twin. We do have a strong telepathic connection and I have a skin discoloration on my left leg, which he has never seen.

Lowell is an amazing person. I admire him for his abilities, but more for his humility and a willingness to help others. I have referred friends to him and they are very grateful for his advice and counsel. I have been to other psychics, but none are as personable and as "down to earth" as Lowell. He has been truly blessed and he is a blessing to me and countless others. The world, at least my world, is a better place with Lowell in it.

Thanks,
Betsy

Denise Fleissner

I initially had a reading with Lowell in April 2004 following an *Indigos* workshop he conducted. He helped me with some issues I was working through with my divorce and told me and my young son Luke that he had the ability to heal. A few days later I got to experience Luke healing me from a debilitating pain. I talked to my family members and friends about Lowell and how accurate and helpful his reading had been for me.

When my beloved sister Regina passed away in 2006 at the age of forty-five, leaving behind two teenage daughters and an abusive, emotionally toxic husband, our entire family was devastated. Regina's death was sudden and unexpected, and her departure left us all feeling emotionally paralyzed and scared for her daughters' safety. For months following Regina's death, she appeared to each of us in different ways. For three of us, it was in our dreams. For her twin, Yvonne, she came to her as the scent of her favorite perfume so Yvonne would know it was her. But for my parents, especially my mother, she presented herself in almost physical form, while Mom was awake.

As these encounters continued to surprise the family, I began sharing my experience with Lowell, and how he helped me through a painful divorce years earlier, and also how he helped my kids understand who they innately are based on experiences they had been having at school, at home and in their dreams.

My youngest sister, Kristen, a complete skeptic on anything non-scientific, asked if I thought Lowell could help her get through the many struggles she was having over Regina's death. I told her I knew he could. We all needed peace, but especially for Kristen, she needed forgiveness and healing that no one on this earth could give her. She needed to say goodbye. I arranged for Kristen and I to have a joint reading with Lowell.

When we arrived at Lowell's home, Kristen was scared, "What if I can't take what he says?" she said with a panic in her voice.

"Just go with what your heart feels," I told her.

"But what if I cry?"

"Then let it out"

"What kind of questions will he ask?"

"Your birth name and permission to access your *file*."

I didn't even get into that part with her because I knew he would explain, basically, he needed permission to access Kristen's file in a "heavenly library" to make sure he had the right information.

What I can tell you is that what Lowell was able to share, changed my family's life, forever. Within the first few minutes of being able to connect with our deceased sister Regina's energy, Regina told Kristen she was "sorry" for things she had done in our childhood, and now that she had this opportunity to communicate, she wanted to make it right. Kristen instantly burst into tears. As the reading continued, Lowell was able to articulate that Regina was showing him a hairbrush and telling Kristen she was sorry for pulling her hair when they were kids. Kristen cried harder. Then Regina told Kristen she was sorry she rambled on so much when she talked because she knew it was hard for Kristen, but that's just who she was. Kristen slouched forward and threw her face into her hands weeping, "It's me," she said. "It's me who is sorry Regina. I didn't listen to you and that's why I'm here to tell YOU that I AM sorry." Lowell waited patiently.

Kristen went on to explain to Lowell that she carried a tremendous amount of guilt for shutting Regina down over the years because Regina was an elaborate speaker and writer, and Kristen just stuck to the facts. They butted heads often over 'words' and Kristen simply had no tolerance for Regina's inability to leave her husband and make life better for her girls. Lowell listened, nodded his head and closed his eyes. Then he began again.

"Regina has two daughters," he said. We shook our heads yes. "And her husband, he's a 'small' man, in the mind I mean. He's controlling and hard to live with," and he was absolutely right! Kristen said, "Yes, he is. And we're worried about the girls. Regina, what do we do about the girls?" "We are trying to get custody of Julia, Regina, but we're not sure if that's the right thing to do. We're scared and we want to know if we're doing the right thing?"

"She is sitting down," says Lowell. "She is telling me that she has to come back to this question because she needs to think about it." Kristen and I spent the next hour asking questions specific to all of our lives. With each question, Lowell was able to articulate what Regina was trying to tell us in ways that felt perfectly right. "She's a feisty one," he said at one point laughing. And she was. Then, all of a sudden, Lowell stopped talking and asked for a moment to get clarity on something. It took about thirty seconds and then he said, "She is ready to talk about the girls again. She is telling me that she is torn about separating the girls from the father because he is their only surviving biological parent, but that it's the right decision to get Julia and Elizabeth away from him."

Lowell went on to tell us we would need to act swiftly but not to worry, David wouldn't resist us. He never did. She also warned that David was hiding something, something he did before she died, and that she would do everything she could to help us figure that out. We never did figure that out, but maybe it's still coming. "And tell Dad that it wasn't his fault," she said. "Tell him that I finally got one up on him," and we sat there in amazement. Lowell explained that the relationship between Regina and Dad included a lot of bantering back and forth about who was right, but it was a genuinely loving ritual and something they both enjoyed. He was right on the money. And what Regina was saying was important because Dad blamed himself for her death because he wasn't able to get her out of her marriage. And she wanted him to know that it wasn't his choice this time, it was hers, and dying, 'til death do us part,' was her way of saying, "Gottcha." It all made perfect sense. The entire reading made perfect sense.

When we were done, we thanked Lowell and he gave us a warm, meaningful hug. I knew he would hold the light for us, because that's just who he is. On our way to the car, I asked Kristen how she was feeling, "Do you feel more at peace," I said.

"I am tired but very peaceful," she said. "I mean, Regina was in the room with us! We were talking to her. And there is no way Lowell could have known any of that about Regina, her girls, David or anything we talked about because we never gave him any details."

"That's right," I said. "He has a gift and I trust him. I'm glad you do too," and then we both got in the car and silently drove home. Kristen sent a beautiful, healing email to the family explaining our experience and the gentle and loving way this total stranger was able to bring her close to her sister again. A few weeks after our visit with Lowell, Yvonne, my oldest sister and Regina's twin, needed a break, so she and I flew to Florida to hang out with Mom and Dad. Our first evening there, I played the cassette tapes Lowell recorded for us of our session. It's a wonderful thing to be able to go back and listen to the experience over and over and over. It's very healing. As I played the tapes, my mother was silent, Yvonne was somewhere far away, and tears silently streamed down my father's face.

"He got it all," my father said. "He got every bit of it. This guy is for real." From that day forward, we have never again felt uneasy about Regina's passing. Lowell was able to provide a safe, warm forum for Kristen and I to communicate with someone we loved and missed dearly, at the same time, never giving us the feeling he was any more special than we are. Even though he is.

I am delighted to say that Lowell is a household name for us now. His reading brought closure to so many of our unresolved feelings, especially my parents, and my family is transformed. We have always "known God," but now, we each understand, at our own level of comfort, that death is not division, it's just another dimension.

Kristen wrote to Lowell several months after our reading and asked if she could come more regularly because he's like a drug for those who need answers. His answer was refreshing. "Kristen, you have within you everything I do, we have just developed it differently. Trust your instincts and feelings (like Regina told her to do), and come back and see me once a year, to check on them." What is so lovely about Lowell is that he didn't encourage her to depend on *him*, rather he encouraged her to trust herself, her feelings – our greatest gift!

Sincerely,
Denise Fleissner

Rachel Wilson

My three sisters, mother, and I have had sessions with Lowell over the last few years. We usually schedule consecutive appointments and then meet up at a restaurant or someone's home later to exchange stories. Many times, Lowell's readings have given me chills, moved me to tears, and made me see things in an entirely new way. The most significant for me, however, was his reading about my third child, Elena Catherine.

I was a mother of two when I saw Lowell in the late summer of 2007. I asked many questions during our session about my life, my family, finances, work, etc. When speaking about my children, Lowell told me that I had a strong capacity for another child. He told me that I had a lot of love to give. In my mind, I was VERY MUCH done having children. I loved my son and daughter, and had just gone back to work after being a stay-at-home mom for four years.

When I found out I was pregnant, I thought of Lowell pretty quickly (and cursed him, just a bit...I thought perhaps his information made me "invite" this pregnancy). I was not at all excited or happy to be pregnant, as awful as that sounds, it was the truth. When my sisters wanted to give me a baby shower, I requested that we simply book appointments with Lowell and then gather together. They honored my request. This unborn child was the main topic on my mind at that session. Lowell immediately started explaining to me who she was. He told me that this was a second chance connection and that six years ago, she was ready to come to me, but I wasn't ready for her. Now I was farther along in my spiritual and life journey, so I was ready for her illuminating soul in my life. He had no way of knowing that six years prior, I miscarried my first pregnancy.

As soon as I processed the information, I was at peace and already in love with this "unplanned, unwanted" child. Elena was born about six weeks later. I'm so thankful that Lowell was able to make the connection for me so I would stop resisting and resenting her arrival. She is a light in our family's life and brings the deepest joy to my soul.

With gratitude,
Rachel Wilson

Janne LoFaro

Over the years I have had many readings on my journey to understanding my soul, where I've been, and where I'm going. By far, Lowell's readings are more accurate, more revealing and always timely. When my husband and I met Lowell we were trying to have a baby. His readings helped me through the emotional process. I was also encouraged to hear my guides supported me with empathy and love with my desire to be a mother. Although, in the end, I didn't conceive a child to term I knew there was a little soul waiting for us so we adopted our daughter in December 2005. We are so blessed to have found Lowell. Lowell's' readings and insight helped us find our path to our daughter.

I have suffered from severe headaches for the past eight years. I've tried all sorts of medical and alternative therapies that haven't given me much relief. The headaches started to occur once a month but throughout the years became a daily occurrence. So my quality of life was about 0% because I was always in so much pain. Through readings with Lowell I learned that in a past life I was brutally stabbed in my neck/back and had a slow painful death. The pain I feel when I begin to get a headache is in my neck. This made so much sense and gave me a better understanding on how I can "let go of the past" and "forgive" so that I could learn to live without the pain. With that information, along with Lowell's help in identifying which practitioner could help me, I have gone from 0% of quality of life to about 80% so far. I'm working on 100%!

Kindest Regards,
Janne LoFaro

Joe LoFaro

I first met Lowell at a seminar he gave on *Indigo* Children at Unity Church of Fairfax. He was personable and enthusiastic, and expressed ideas that require some degree of spiritual faith in practical terms satisfying the "engineer" in me. In fact, I found out later that we had several life experiences in common. Needless to say, he made an impression that led to my wife and I turning to him for closure in a difficult time, and then periodically to seek insights or validation of our paths individually or as a family.

Some examples of Lowell's readings having a profound impact included our resolving to adopt to add to our family, our move process from Virginia to North Carolina, and some health related issues. They have helped me though a difficult work situation, validated that I am not "lost" but on my soul's spiritual path, and to trust in my spiritual guides and The Universe. It has been amazing to experience the "ah ha" moments during Lowell's readings, and I am filled with gratitude that we have crossed paths in this life.

My Heartfelt Thanks,
Joe LoFaro

Kyla Dean

I was referred to Lowell Smith by my Chinese acupuncturist, as she thought his gifts would be able to help me to improve my health. I had nowhere else to turn as I have an incurable, non-life threatening, disease. I was up for anything so I made an appointment and my world, my universe and my mind was opened and expanded in ways I never dreamed possible from that first visit.

Not only did Lowell help me with my health, but he led me down a path of understanding of how a disease stems from several factors of physical, mental and spiritual health. He taught me to look inside myself to realize I have a very special gift of intuition. Through his teaching, I learned to hear and follow my own intuition and to trust in it. It has never let me down and I've learned it is really the most reliable ability I have. If I do not listen to it and I go against it, life will come full circle and show me a little lesson; as if to remind me to listen every time. It is an art form, in a way, that will take this lifetime to master.

As I grew and developed my intuition with the patient mentoring from Lowell, I found I had other skills that were more in-tune to the Spirit world. The most eye-opening was the day Lowell invited like-minded individuals to a historic site so that we could all explore our intuitive and sensitive abilities together. We could not research the location before the day of the trip but were instructed to just show up and see what happened. I did just that. On an early weekend morning, my adventure started as I turned down a long gravel driveway off the main road. It was a tree-lined drive with sun gleaming in through the leaves. It was a crisp autumn day and I could 'imagine' horse-drawn carts and carriages coming to and from the estate as I got closer. It seemed to me to be an estate right out of a show on television with a main house, barn and other various buildings strewn about the property. To me, it was like stepping back in time…to a time I never really thought about much before that day. Lowell instructed us to be quiet and just walk around the property for an hour then we would all get together on the porch to have a discussion.

I walked in the front door and my 'imagination' flipped on like a switch. To the left was a living room area with a big fireplace. I could envision a woman sitting there in a rocking chair with a needle-work on her lap and a calico dress on. It was the perfect spot to watch the front door and the comings and goings of the people of the house. Walking toward the back of the house, I could envision men gathering in a room looking at maps or drawings. It felt very stern and full of authority in that area. I walked up and down the hall a couple of times and kept envisioning a man in a gray military uniform with a big hat on. He was walking down the hall and out of the house with authority. I kept thinking "Colonel Custard"…but not knowing anything about history [I] had no idea what it meant.

Walking into the back yard, I envisioned picnic tables and women gathering food, kids playing among the trees and men gathering off to the side and back of the property to discuss the dynamics of war that the women and kids should not hear about. I could see several men in dirty uniforms coming through the forested area at the back of the property and setting up their tents on the property to the side and front of the house.

I walked into a small building that seemed to be a kitchen. I got so dizzy I had to sit down. I couldn't shake it for a long time. I looked around the room and something didn't seem right but I didn't know what. I could see women of different nationalities cooking over hot pots and baking bread. I finally cleared my head, stood and went upstairs. My heart felt so much compassion in the upstairs chamber. I could see a woman looking out a small window facing the long driveway. She seemed to be longing for someone to return. I felt that her love was immense but that it was a hidden love; perhaps not one people would approve of. I felt like it may have been a mixed race relationship but couldn't be specific. I felt the man she was waiting for belonged on the estate and had some authority but was a working-class man. I felt so dreamy in that little bedroom above the kitchen. I stayed for a long time and could have stayed for much longer.

We all gathered on the porch and the care taker of the property and the docent were there to verify facts with us; they had the history of the estate and surrounding area. Many people saw various things that day but I can only tell you of my own experience. Feeling a bit foolish, I raised my hand to speak of thing things that I imagined could have happened on the estate. As I described what my imagination conjured up, the owner of the house verified that one of the wives of the estate during the war, indeed, sat in a rocking chair doing needle-point and keeping warm by the fire. She verified that Colonel Custer had visited the estate at one time. She explained to everyone how there used to be an ice house in the back of the property where the men would stand behind, smoke cigars and talk of the war, out of ear-shot of the other family members. There was no evidence of the icehouse, by the way but it was in the exact location I spoke of. The docent also confirmed that troops would arrive by a river that ran behind the property, come up through the woods and set up camp in the exact locations I described. I spoke of the couple that had a secret affair and the docent told the story of the cook and the groundskeeper who had fallen in love. Due to the good nature of the owners, they let the couple live on the property in the bedroom above the kitchen. The owner explained that the kitchen area had been remodeled at one point. Lowell explained to me that intuitive people 'see' things as they were back in time. I was getting dizzy because what I was 'seeing' was not how the kitchen looked on that day. I had never heard of that but was fascinated.

Lowell and the *Indigos & Sensitives Group* over the next few weeks taught me that the *gift* I had, was seeing the "energy signatures" of the people that used to live and visit the estate. I did not know what to think about this gift and was freaked out by the whole day. It took me several days to calm down and understand what had happened that day.

That day was the beginning of my path of spiritual enlightenment and all things metaphysical. I know now that I have always had this gift and I have these visions in most historic sites. I just thought everyone had them. I know now that this is one of my sensitivities. That day, opened up so many more abilities and I have been growing and developing ever since. Thanks to Lowell, I now know the difference between an energy signature and an actual Spirit that may need help crossing over (which I have learned to do, as well). I now am no longer scared by what I *see* but use each experience to develop my knowledge of living in this physical body during this lifetime.

With Lowell being my mentor, I was able to create positive energy in my life and Aura and attract the love of my life, my husband. Not only is he a great man, but he is accepting and supportive of my developing my sensitivities. I now know that I can achieve anything and the universe will support my initiatives just as long as I set my intentions to do so.

Through past life readings with Lowell, my husband and I learned that we have been married several times in past lives. During one session, my guides explained to us that in one lifetime, our son was trying to impress my husband and fell off of a high wall and died. I never forgave my husband for letting that happen, even after many lifetimes. I carried the hurt through many lifetimes and into this one. Maybe you could have guessed that the disease that I originally came to Lowell for help was endometriosis, which is immensely painful, and infertility. Through Lowell, my guides advised that I forgive my husband so that I can mend in this lifetime and move on. I verbally told my husband that I forgave him. It made me teary-eyed to say the words. To me they seemed meaningless but to my soul were the words that tore down a dam of emotions. Through that statement and various holistic health avenues, I have been able to eliminate almost all of the pain from the endometriosis. In fact, we are currently being tested to find out if we can have a family in this lifetime together. If we are able to conceive and have a child, it will prove to us how powerful the act of forgiveness really is. Only time will tell.

I cannot thank Lowell enough for the time and caring guidance he has given me over the years. Without him, I would be shut off from the spiritual world and from knowing myself. I hope that someday, in some lifetime, I will be able to return such kindness.

Regards
Kyla

Cece Charles

It was the spring of 2004, and it had been years of suffering from what I thought was an odd "sleeping" problem. I was exhausted, burnt out, and over speaking to doctors who said everything appeared to be fine. My mom set me up with an old work acquaintance that was now practicing past life regression therapy. She thought it would be beneficial to explore other avenues, which might not be open to doctors of conventional medicine. Of course, I was nervous to meet with Maureen and talk about what I was experiencing. Half of the time it sounded crazy to me! When I first arrived at Maureen's, I was shaking with all sorts of emotions. Almost instantly she called a friend from church named Lowell Smith. She explained to me his extraordinary abilities, and said, "He will be able to tell you if there is something else going on, that maybe I cannot see." Before I knew it, he was on his way over to the house to meet with me.

I remember so clearly what the meeting did for me. He told me right away that I was very psychically sensitive. He also said in the most serious but comforting tone, "and I can see what you see." Those words lifted a huge weight off of my shoulders. He then began to explain in detail (which he could not have known unless he was me!) what I experience almost nightly, and based on my aura pattern what *gifts* I have. I didn't even have to explain anything, he already knew, as though he was just thumbing through my memories. As Lowell, spoke he said, "You get drained very easily. For example if you were to walk into a Costco, by the time you get to the meat section, you are drained of all your energy. The same thing happens to me." He continued, "As someone who is psychically sensitive, it is especially important for you to hold onto your energy and protect yourself." Lowell then introduced me to the Robe of Light Protection Prayer and explained how it protects your energy from other entities. He validated so many things for me. I couldn't help but almost cry! I was so happy to have an answer! So glad I wasn't losing my mind, and grateful I had found the puzzle piece that seemed to be missing. Lowell also told me he was being led to begin a support group for *Indigos* and physically aware teens and adults. It was May when I came home for the summer, and I went to the first meeting. I have been a member of the group ever since and it has helped me in so many ways.

After meeting Lowell and becoming apart of the group; my life has never been the same. Lowell has helped me begin to formulate a vocabulary for what I had been experiencing for years! I learned from him, I was an *Indigo*, and what it means to be termed *Indigo*. Something I had never even heard of until 2004. I learned the people I saw in my room weren't just figments of my imagination. The objects levitating, knowing things without explanation, spiritual visitations, seeing orbs, being sensitive to energies; all of it . . . wasn't just apart of some sleeping problem, it was so much more! He has guided me from being down right scared and helpless, to being in control and a work in progress. He provides loving encouragement, and opportunities to expand and nourish everyone's gifts. Lowell has really created a positive, loving, and sharing energy, for a beautiful grouping of extraordinary people.

There is never anything that can slip by him either! For example, almost always, Lowell will know things about me, before I do (or before I am willing to admit it myself). For instance, I will sense something, and hesitate to mention it in front of the group. He will look right at me and say, "I already know, go on and share, don't be afraid." I remember when we went to Harper's Ferry for a ghost tour. What an experience for a group of sensitive people! Our guide was amazed how Lowell knew stories and sensed entities, which she herself knew of, but never mentioned to anyone. From our visits to Harpers Ferry and graveyards, to our weekly meetings, I have seen a change in not only myself, but other group members as well. By being a part of the group, and listening to what others see, feel, hear, etc. has lead me to become more knowledgeable about what I experience. Lowell has taught me how to simply "be open," and living this way I can experience a much fuller and richer life. He is a wonderful teacher, who guides me on my own path, and who guides the group so we may continue to practice our purpose. It's a blessing to have a spiritual coach, like Lowell who has given me the wisdom to see the light, encouraged me to embrace my gifts, opportunities to explore a beautiful journey, and a place where I might help others.

Thanks,
Cece

Justina

I have always been highly intuitive and sensitive to energies so when I came across a flyer sponsored by the A.R.E. for a workshop to develop your psychic abilities, it grabbed my attention and I felt compelled to attend. As I was sitting in the audience I found myself leaning forward and looking at a man [Lowell] that felt very familiar to me and I noticed (to my amazement) that he was doing the same thing to me! We both recognized each other though I had never seen him or met him before in my lifetime or shall I say "this lifetime."

During a break in the workshop, I made a beeline to Reverend Lowell K. Smith and we struck up a conversation. For some reason I kept seeing in my "minds eye" Ancient Egypt and Lowell in ceremonial garments. I told him this and he stated that in fact we had a lifetime together in Egypt. He was the High Priest and I was a Priestess of the Temple – one of his students. I thought, "No wonder I kept seeing Egypt!" During our discussion he said that he had started a Teens and Adults support group for *Indigos* and psychically sensitive people and that it would be very beneficial for me to attend. I went to the next meeting and have been attending those meetings every week since then. That was about four years ago. The group has provided a loving and supportive environment where I can share, explore and expand my psychic sensitivities or abilities. As a result, my abilities have grown exponentially. I now understand the phenomena I am seeing and experiencing. I also feel that I am much more "in tune" with others and myself. I find I am able to tap into another person's thoughts or emotions more readily since coming to these weekly meetings. One time when Lowell was going to be away for a few meetings, he asked me to lead the group in his absence, which I agreed to do and discovered that my psychic abilities as well as my leadership abilities were expanded to a significant degree.

I have had several psychic readings with Lowell and have found them to be extremely accurate, helpful and relative to the experiences in my present life situations.

When my father had a series of strokes and was in failing health, Lowell made visits to the Hospice facility, Nursing Home and even to my parent's house to assist my father with healings and help him during his transitions. During the healings I was able to see the light around my father and the light of different colors that Lowell was channeling into my father's energy fields and physical body. Lowell helped me realize that I too have the ability to heal. When my father's time came to cross over I was there to help him transition and I saw the beautiful light embrace him. It really helped my father and it also helped me come to terms with my father's passing. My father and I have always been very close and have always had a special bond with each other. Even though my father passed in October 2006, I can still see his light and sense his energy, which gives me great comfort.

Through Lowell's expertise and guidance I always feel comfortable in sharing my visions, my past life recall experiences, and find clarity, further insights, and profound meanings of my dreams. Lowell and I have a strong bond or connection that spans great distances and many lifetimes and I greatly value and appreciate that connection. It is not uncommon for me to get a phone call to hear that Lowell knew that I was thinking of him and that he was sending me additional energy that I needed. I had to learn to stop taking on another person's pain when Lowell called me from Tucson to "cut it out" – stop being so empathetic. I needed to focus on my own needs. I now know the importance of recognizing a need, sending energy of Love and Light to an individual or situation without having to take on and feel the energies as my own. That has been a very valuable lesson that Lowell taught me and that I am now able to share with others.

Lowell has helped me tremendously in my spiritual, personal and professional lives. I feel that we have helped each other in many ways. I feel that I was guided to be there at the workshop in 2005 to reconnect with Lowell once again in this lifetime and I feel fortunate and blessed to know him.

Love & Light,
Justina

Comment: Justina is one of my most sensitive students, and just as in several past lives where she was also my student, she has excelled in her personal Spiritual and Psychic development. As Justina indicated in her testimonial, when I am physically not present for the *Indigos & Sensitives* meetings she facilitates those meetings and has done an outstanding job of doing so. At some future time when I either move away or pass on, I will be assured that I will leave this group in great hands.

Lowell.

Anne Marie Clotworthy

During my first of two readings with Lowell, he told me quite a number of personal details from my childhood, which he could not possibly have known. He received this information about me and it was not random, but involved specific events which have been pivotal to my development. Lowell seemed to be in a serene state while he spoke, and he seemed to be maintaining a connection to some fine, beautiful light-filled Source. Lowell delivered messages regarding events and themes in my life and he was able to explain to me how these events were related to my life's purpose. Lowell understood the meaning of the challenges I faced in my childhood within my own family, and that there was a higher purpose at work in these events. This was enormously comforting to me and gave me insights.

Lowell has a rare gift and a mission to help others. He is absolutely honest, sincere, and genuine in how he uses his psychic abilities to help and educate others.

I attended Lowell's support group for Sensitive Teens and Adults and learned things, which changed my life. Lowell taught us that it is quite normal to have these sensitivities, and that many of us learn to block or ignore these abilities and so they atrophy. Prior to joining this group, I had for the most part (except for when I was involved in healing activities), felt that the guidance I heard in my head, the strong physical sensations I received, and the vivid, highly specific dreams were a weakness and an annoyance. It turns out that these phenomena are called clairaudience and clairsentience and we all have these to some degree because it is written into our DNA. I now know how to better manage these sensitivities so that they are a help to me, rather than a puzzling hindrance. I learned techniques for how to better protect myself from negativity and negative energy.

As a result of Lowell's readings and support group, I returned to school and embarked on a new direction in my career. This is going very well, and despite many people who tried to dissuade me from taking this new direction, I used what Lowell taught me, and I followed the spiritual guidance we all can have access to. I learned how to get energized by my children versus drained, especially by my *Indigo* child whom I learned to understand in a spiritual way.

Lowell arranged a field trip to Weston House, which is reported to have Spirit activity, and my experiences there confirmed that I sense "them" through specific physical sensations. I felt a deep, penetrating, heavy coldness many places in the Weston House, which had an unusual quality, that I don't ever recall feeling before. I am a slim, middle-aged person who runs and works out regularly and I have no heart or lung ailments. I remember walking up a short flight of stairs to an upper room at Weston house. I could hardly make it up the stairs, as my heart rate became very rapid and I felt crushing weight on my chest, and I had difficulty breathing. I felt sick. I made a mental note while this was happening to me, although at the time it made no sense to me and felt alarming. I thought, "What is this, why do I suddenly feel this way, it feels like something is pushing on me?" These physical symptoms went away when I went to another area of Weston House. I later found out that this upper room had been used for very ill patients with serious heart conditions. There were more incidents in the house, and many others in our group sensed or saw things too.

I greatly appreciate all that Lowell has done for me and am grateful that he continues helping others make sense of things that seem "crazy." They are in fact real and when you understand them, it can greatly enhance your life. Thank you Lowell for being you.

Sincerely,
Anne Marie Clotworthy

Siobhan Rice

In 2005, when my spiritual life was at a point where some expert guidance to help me better understand what I was sensing and experiencing would have been very welcome, Lowell Smith appeared in my life – as if by magic. His extraordinary ability of being able to bring information from the higher realms of consciousness, and then help me do the same, has assisted me greatly in having a deeper understanding of all aspects of myself.

Over the past few years I have had several psychic readings from Lowell and the answers have always produced that 'ah ha' moment of "Now I understand, now I see the pattern more clearly." For me, having a reading is a bit like being reminded of information that I once knew but had forgotten. The guidance I have received from Lowell has always been applicable, meaningful and relevant to my daily life; for what use is a psychic reading if it doesn't change your perceptions of how to look at life? What use is past life information if the traits from those past lives cannot be understood in the context of your present life, thereby changing your behavior? All good psychic readings should assist our spiritual journey and any reading I have had from Lowell has been very beneficial and done just that.

Lowell also devotes a lot of his time and energy to helping people realize their potential and to understand their own sensitivities. To assist in this work he started two groups several years ago called *The Indigos & Sensitives Group* and a *Search for God Group*. I personally attended both of these groups for a long time and I was very grateful for the friendships and the sharing I encountered there.

In particular, as a parent of both *Indigo* and *Crystal* children, Lowell's interpretations of their traits and characteristics were unfailingly accurate. I watched with awe and interest as he assisted many parents and children who attended the *Indigos & Sensitives* meetings to better understand their own particular sensitivities.

Nowadays you can find psychics just about anywhere but finding a good one is a real blessing. Lowell's appearance in my life has been a Godsend and I greatly appreciate his friendship and support in helping me join the proverbial dots in my life.

Thank you Lowell,
Mary Siobhan McGibbon [Rice]
The Paul Solomon Foundation

Connie (Walker) Hartz

Lowell gave a reading for my granddaughter, Jackie, from a photograph. He said she was a *Crystal* child, had three Spirit Guides, had the ability to discern what plants needed, had the ability to heal, etc. Jackie was about eight years old at the time. I did not know how to talk to her about what Lowell had told me. I wanted to be sure to nurture or have nurtured the *gifts* she had. These little ones are so important. But what to do!

Confirmation of what Lowell told me about Jackie.

I was visiting Jackie – she was now nine years old. I told her I had something on my hand and could she look at it. She looked at me and calmly said, *"Sounds like you want me to heal you."* I was hemming and hawing not knowing what to say. Her words – and the way she said it – blew me away and my mistake was not to go further with it.

On her tenth birthday I called to wish her Happy Birthday. She mentioned she had a bad dream and that she was keeping a journal of her dreams. I told her she had nothing to fear, the angels were around her. She said, "Oh, yeah, I know" in a tone that said, "So what else is new." I thought now is my chance to broach the subject of Spirit Guides. I said "and you have your guides." Her response: "Yes. I know Charles, he is teaching me to look at the future and the past but I can't always tell the difference but I don't know the names of the two girls," confirming what Lowell said – she has three guides. And she was familiar with them.

Jackie is now fifteen and a typical teenager. God help her parents! When she was visiting me in Virginia Beach at Thanksgiving last year, she wanted a massage so I arranged for one at A.R.E. On our way there, she said, "I know I can heal but I'm not sure how to go about it." After the massage we went to the bookstore and picked out a few books on the subject.

Thanks, Lowell, for giving me insight into Jackie. Continue your work with these precious *Indigo* and *Crystal* children.

Much Love,
Connie

C. Cohen

I met Lowell in August of 2008 when he did a brief Aura and Past Life Regression reading involving my late husband. The information was startling and valuable, leading me to recommend him to a family member and an acupuncturist who both found his work to be superior.

Since then, I have consulted Lowell about various business and family problems and have been struck by the accuracy of his readings on individual's strengths, weaknesses and motivations. He is an amazingly perspicacious person who I continue to value as an adviser.

Very truly yours,
C. Cohen

James E Shotts, MD

I first met Lowell at a meeting in upstate New York held at Omega Institute conducted by the best selling author on Past Life Regression, Brian Weiss, MD. I knew immediately that Lowell was someone very special and one who indeed possessed extraordinary gifts. During subsequent conversations, I came to realize he was a gifted psychic, and one who was grounded with integrity, wisdom, and compassion. His mastery was clearly apparent.

I look forward to the opportunity of future consultation with him, and the benefit that can be derived from his insight and guidance.

Thank you,
James E Shotts MD

The Abarcas

My husband and I met Lowell at a past life regression workshop at Omega Institute in the summer of 2008. After the week-long workshop was over, I asked Lowell if he had time to do a brief reading for us. Since the five-day workshop was very intense, I was not sure that Lowell would have the energy; however, he graciously agreed stating that he never felt too drained to do a reading.

Lowell first did a brief, past life reading for me. During this reading, he pulled information from the Akashic Records to help me better understand my life's purpose. The lifetime that he accessed had a powerful parallel to my current lifetime. Since I had just met Lowell and had not talked about my current life, there is no way he could have known about my current job situation. Learning about this parallel and contemplating Lowell's reading, helped me to see my life's purpose in a different way. I had just begun to examine my own religious beliefs and spirituality and Lowell's reading supported this journey.

Lowell next did a reading for my husband, Alberto. My husband's reading was even more life changing than my own. It explained so many unanswered questions in his current life. For example, his stomach has always slightly bothered him and no doctor has been able to determine the cause. It all made so much sense when he was reminded of a lifetime as a Roman soldier in which he died by the blade of a sword to his intestines.

The reading stated that as a soldier in that lifetime, he visited villages before and/or after Jesus visited the same villages, without having actually met him in person. Although he was a follower of a pagan religion at the time, he always felt a connection with Christ. However, it was not until Alberto died that he saw Jesus' face and felt his wonderful spiritual essence as he (Alberto) passed to the Other Side. In his current life, Alberto has felt a vague recollection of having known Jesus and was confused by this when he was a small boy. This reading helped him understand the connection.

In addition, Alberto has always had an irrational fear of our son dying. If our son gets a fever, Alberto immediately worries that we might need to take him to the doctor or hospital. When Lowell told Alberto that in a past life our son was Alberto's little brother whom he lost in a tragic accident, his irrational fear made so much sense.

The reading indicated that in that past life in ancient Greece, Alberto had a very strong relationship with his little brother. His brother followed him everywhere. Alberto delighted in daredevil feats and his little brother joined him in a few of these antics. One day Alberto decided to dive off a cliff about forty feet above the water below. He never dreamed that his brother would follow him. Unbeknownst to Alberto while he was in the water, his little brother followed him up the cliff. When he got to the top, he slipped and fell to his death. Alberto was crushed with anguish. He carried his brother back to his parents' village all the while wailing his grief. The intensity of this grief was so strong that Alberto lapsed into a deep depression lasting ten years. On the eve of the day that he contemplated suicide, his brother came to him in a vision. Frightened beyond imagination, Alberto listened as his brother gave his forgiveness and encouraged Alberto to forgive himself thus saving Alberto from death. Alberto clung to the message of forgiveness from his brother for the rest of that lifetime.

Lowell assured my husband that his current fear of losing our son in this life is his sense of losing him in the past life in ancient Greece. He encouraged Alberto to focus on the joy of his interactions with our son as opposed to dredging up past grief. This past life also highlighted our son's extreme cautiousness in this life of doing physical things in which he feels he could become injured. The intensity of the reading was extremely powerful and emotional. We are deeply indebted to Lowell for helping to heal my husband's fear of losing our son.

Lowell also confirmed that our son has crystalline energy. We have known about our son's strong spiritual presence and Lowell's confirmation and suggestions to foster this energy have been very helpful. I have never met someone as strongly intuitive as Lowell. Even before I asked a question, he was there with an answer.

With grateful hearts,
Beth and Luis

Jim (Bart) Bartelloni

Lowell did a reading for me in March 2008 which helped me discover my spiritual essence and helped answer many of the dreams and inner dialogue questions that I had been having. By listening to Lowell and meditating on the information that he gave me, I was able to harness a connection to Spirit, which I never would have known existed. It was very helpful that we were able to discuss my deceased father and his spiritual being and how easy I could connect to him. I was so impressed with his genuine and passionate personality that I had my daughter's reading conducted by Lowell. This has helped her understand potential college choices and her life direction.

Many Thanks,
Bart

Margaret Miller

I met Lowell at a friend' home in October of 2008. It was a very nice get together. However at the time, I did not realize how much I would benefit from that visit. My son had passed away ten years previously. I had always been troubled regarding his demise because on the death certificate it was determined that he had died by suicide. I had attended several SOS meetings after my son's death, but I never felt that I belonged. After meeting with Rev. Smith, I understood why. Rev. Smith told me that my son's death was not self inflicted – that there were others involved. Lowell also brought out some others factors that no one knew but myself.

Lowell also talked about my late husband. My late husband developed tonsil cancer and had surgery five years previously. He passed away from complications from pneumonia on March 27, 2003 and on that same day, my mother was hit by a car and killed twelve years earlier. Lowell remarked that there was something wrong with Rod's voice as he couldn't speak very clearly, and in fact Lowell was having difficulty speaking [he was coughing] when he told us this. To my surprise Lowell commented that Rod would rather be where he is [in Spirit] because his [Rod's] voice was very important to him, as he was a pilot for many years. This was so true about my husband, and Lowell could not have know that.

I am looking forward to visiting with Lowell in the future, as he is very much an inspiration. His bringing forth the information that he did in such a caring and gentle manner was truly a blessing.

Sincerely
Margaret R. Miller

Nancy Robinson

I met Lowell several years ago and at that time he encouraged me to follow my instincts and do what I knew was best for me. He warned me that my son needed support and help with a personal issue. I said unfortunately my son insisted on being out of communication with me and would not accept my calls. Lowell suggested that I have my son call him, but my son would not.

Lowell's reading about my health issues gave me confidence in my own intuition. I could feel his strength when he communicated messages from beyond the visual. He assured me that my main issue, my stomach, was being caused, as I had suspected, by an osteoporosis medicine I was taking at the time. I dropped the medicine and its sister variations. I increased my exercise, walking, weight training, and Hatha yoga. Two years later, my doctor was amazed that I was definitely improved. A colonoscopy confirmed that my stomach was probably being damaged by those osteoporosis medicines.

Another issue at that time had to do with a new friendship I had just begun. Lowell teased me a bit and asked, "Why are you both being so formal and stand offish?" I laughed and said it felt correct to do so. He said, "Just trust that your friendship is just what you think it is." I smiled. Three years later I have to admit that this is the most nurturing friendship of my life. I am amazed that I am so content.

Recently, my life has been going well but my son, who still refuses communication, was in serious trouble. Lowell envisioned that this son was on the cusp for either positive change or destruction. I shuddered for I realized how volatile his life had become. He was an early member of the group facing foreclosure, more than that, he was recently divorced, had lost his job and company, had wrecked his truck, and was facing bankruptcy. By now he had refused to speak to me for the past four years. After the session with Lowell I prayed for this son regularly as Rev. Smith had encouraged me to do, and when I was notified that he was suicidal, from behind the scenes I supported the family's efforts to show him alternatives to his self destruction. I held off personal communications until he approached me. Recently, in our own communications, I mentioned that he seemed to be grieving his recent losses. That comment released a flood of heartfelt comments. Now he and I are again in communication. I pray he is gaining the strength and wisdom to face and solve his problems. He seems to have come through the fire of self-doubt and gained the courage and strength to move forward in his life.

I thank Lowell for giving me the courage to trust my own instincts in difficult times and act or not act from my own power. Lowell is a soul felt presence in times of need for me.

With grateful respect,
Nancy Robinson

Craig B.

My family and I have had several readings with Lowell and we have found the information in the readings to be accurate and helpful in understanding ourselves. He has provided past life links that help explain current situations and directions. This has helped me awaken more to my spiritual side and help me grow as a soul. An example is that I have always enjoyed the outdoors and being in a forest and places where there is a chill in the air. I feel a certain peace and renewal there. I also love maps and learning about new cultures. I had not mentioned this to Lowell before. In my first reading, Lowell told me how in a past life I was an explorer of the Ohio and Wisconsin areas and that I was attuned to nature and enjoyed that lifetime so much I could even do some similar work today. I felt inside he was spot on and even now I can see the lure of that type of experience.

When I lost my job of 23 years, I was worried and went for a reading with Lowell. He told me that the Universe was creating an opportunity for me to move in a different direction, that this was not a punishment but an opportunity. This allowed me to move past the shock and fear of the situation and move into the light. I used this to help propel me to find a new job. I wrote up eleven qualities of my new job and I found a job that matched all of the qualities.

Lowell has helped my family come to a better understanding of our dynamics and how we can get through some challenging situations. We have come upon information through Lowell that has helped us understand certain feelings, which allowed us to close the loop on some experiences and to move forward. Every time we saw Lowell we have always left feeling better and more enlightened than when we arrived.

Lowell has a good understanding of how to relate psychic information he receives into helpful information for the healing and growth of the soul seeking advice.

With much appreciation,
Craig

Leo Sveikauskas

I have been on a spiritual path for many years, studying the Search for God books of Edgar Cayce and meditating and praying for people. It is lonely work, since many people are not aware of spiritual currents or the spiritual dimensions of everyday life.

I have had eight readings from Lowell. It is remarkable that he is able to read a person's spiritual development accurately, with a clear understanding of how Spirit is developing within a person, and how it will express itself and develop in the future. Lowell can also see the motivations and spiritual level or potential of other people in one's life, which is often very helpful. Lowell's readings have helped me greatly in focusing on the central issues of my spiritual growth and allowed me to advance on this path more rapidly. Many of my friends, from Search for God Groups or others, have also received readings from Lowell and similarly consider the insights they have obtained on their own lives to be remarkable.

That sums it up, but perhaps some specific examples will give a flavor of how all this works. In my first reading, Lowell was able to note that my father had been interested in spiritual issues, but had not been able to carry out these interests very much. Lowell also remarked that my twin brother had once been much poorer than I but was now much richer. I came to another reading with much spiritual energy after listening to the Dalai Lama and some Tibetan monks. Lowell began that reading by noting the spiritual presence of a Tibetan monk.

My wife Cathy has also had several readings from Lowell. Lowell generally starts out by discussing exactly the issues she had been thinking about in her drive over to Fairfax County. When my wife asked Lowell about her health, he mentioned she was about to have a hip condition. About eight months later, a pain in the hip arrived due to sciatica.

Though specific examples such as these can provide some impression of the type of information that comes through, the real heart of the readings is the clear vision of each person's individual development. To know that Lowell is capable of such a detailed knowledge of each individual human life has changed my understanding of how the universe works, and the depths of helpfulness to which each person may aspire.

I believe that when this book is published, and Lowell appears on the Oprah Winfrey show (my guess), people around the world will learn about the insights and guidance that Lowell can provide. I just hope that my wife and I will still be able to schedule an occasional reading. (I would hopefully suggest that Lowell reserve 9:00 am to 11:00 am readings every morning for pre-Oprah clients.) Whether we are ever able to see Lowell again or not, we will remain grateful for the readings and appreciate the insights we have learned from them.

Leo Sveikauskas
Bethesda, Maryland

Steve Bracewell

I have been on a spiritual quest for many years before meeting Lowell at a spiritual gathering at a community center about six years ago. I saw an ad for a psychic fair at the Unity Church in Frederick, Maryland and felt drawn to go. When I arrived, there were a number of booths and tables and as I walked around, I was drawn to Lowell's table. He was in a session with another person and there was a waiting list but I was drawn to sign up and bided my time at other tables until the appointed time. The other sessions ran longer than expected and when it was my turn, the place was closing. Because of the chaotic and disruptive nature at the end of the day, we decided to schedule another time and we met about a week later (everything happens for a reason).

Here I must digress – I have had a number of readings over the years and learned there are readers out there that are just not for you. However, Lowell's reading was to the point and did not have a lot of BS included. He uses an avenue that is not used by many psychics. That is the tapping into what is known as the Akashic records. I had experienced other readers that used that method and always have been impressed with the accuracy. Lowell's accuracy was very impressive. When I left, I had a very good feeling about the reading and Lowell's ability to get his own stuff out of the way. This became much more impressive when years later, I found out there was a lot of experiences that Lowell had come through that could have gotten in the way. Almost all of the information that has come through has had a meaning to me.

Some of Lowell's readings have been so accurate to include possible future choices I had to make that at the time. The information made no sense to either of us at the time. And the readings have always included information that there is no way Lowell could have known. I have always interpreted this to be a possible direct communication with my higher self.

I have referred several of my friends to Lowell and everyone has been helped with his readings. Each one that I referred has later called me to thank me for my suggestion.

Sincerely,
Steve Bracewell

Terasama Masaji

I tried several times in many different ways to get information about my past lives. For example, I went to The Monroe Institute and took several classes, and a few times I had private readings by phone, but none of these worked for me. I met Lowell at The Monroe Institute several years ago [Jan 2005] and kept communicating with him because I noticed that there was something different about Lowell from other psychics I had met. One day I asked Lowell for a past life reading which he agreed to do.

During the reading, I found out that I had a life in China as an art performer, which I am in my current life. I also learned that my father was killed in that lifetime and I told Lowell that I had bad dreams about that experience every once in awhile throughout my life. Since that reading I have had no more bad dreams. I also learned that in another lifetime in Japan, I was killed by being shot in my neck by an arrow. Although Lowell could not have known this, I had been having trouble with my neck for a very long time. However, after that reading, my neck pain is almost gone. I was very surprised that I had such kinds of past life experiences. To be able to review my past lives has been very powerful and interesting, and these reviews have also cleared up several physical troubles I have experienced as well. Lowell is truly amazing.

Sincerely,
Terasama "Candyman" Masaji
masajiterasawacandyman@hotmail.com

Comment: Masaji performs at Disney World in Orlando and throughout the United States, Europe and, of course, Japan. He is an amazing artisan creating these amazing 'origami' like figures out of 'candy.' He has a great gift that he brought from a past lifetime and I am honored being called a friend. Check out the following video link for his work:

http://www.masajicandyman.net/

Art Mitchell, Ph.D.

To me, Lowell represents a connection with reality, a link to what I "think" I cannot access myself. Too much identification with the physical world and my thoughts, and dare I say those of others, get in the way. I consider someone with Lowell's abilities "a miracle." I trust him explicitly, and the readings he did for me as well as for my *Indigo* children had a great impact; always uplifting, encouraging and never boring! He has advised me on past lives and recurrent themes of embracing challenges and exploration. He has enabled me to understand that certain insecurities such as low self-esteem, which were prevalent when I was younger, have a basis in unresolved actions in the distant past. Knowledge is power and can break old patterns. He has advised me also on strategies to deal with whatever comes my way with the understanding that not just "this too shall pass" but rather I do not have to react from a place of past events. I am learning that "wherever I go, there I am," an obvious statement but actually quite profound as it points to the joy of living in the Present. More and more each day I am able to do this, focusing not on the goal but rather the steps, and it brings great joy to the moment. So, thank you Lowell, my friend, for being who you are and doing what you do so well.

Namaste,
Art Mitchell

Ingrid

I had a session with Lowell when I was under a great deal of stress from multiple sources. Without explaining my current situation to him, Lowell said that he had an image of hot lava churning underneath the surface, and that I was bouncing along above it. That was exactly me at that time. It was so comforting and validating for me to know that someone truly understood how greatly distressed I was. His spiritual counsel helped me put things in perspective.

I was very close to my mother and when she died I missed her very much. Through Lowell's contact with my mother, he gave me insight into her life on the other side. I was very comforted to know about her learning and good works.

Take care and good luck finishing the book,
Ingrid

Conclusion and Going Forward

As a person born psychically sensitive, I have had the responsibility and privilege of *sensing, seeing, hearing,* and *knowing* things psychically most of my life. It has been my life's work to understand, develop and expand my sensitivities, and learn how to use them to help others. I have had to learn that it is not about being right (which is ego driven) but about conveying the information I am *shown, sense, hear,* etc. in such a way that the person I am reading for, or simply communicating with, recognizes the truth of what I am saying within themselves. It is never mine to judge, but it is my responsibility to hold to the light, those truths that my clients, my friends, or simply others that God sends my way, need to hear or be made aware of, even if they don't want to hear it or know it. To the extent that I stay in tune with my higher self's purpose and remain out of the way of the information, the people that God or the Source sends my way, will "get" the messages they need to hear or become aware of at that particular moment. Hopefully I have been able to do that in this book, and each of you will get out of this book that which you need to hear or become aware of, to help you be (or become) a better parent, a better sibling, a better coworker, a better lover, a better spouse, a better friend, a better whatever, and most of all a better person – one who is more fully connected to the Source of your being; your God.

Having read my "story," hopefully the reader has a better appreciation for what it's like to grow up psychic, and gained an understanding that "things" that are perceived via one's psychic sensitivities are just as real as anything one experiences with their five physical senses. As an Engineer and Scientist well educated in the Physical Sciences *AND* a Psychic who experiences many paranormal phenomena, I have come to understand that the old scientific paradigm that dictates, "If you can't experience it with your five physical senses, or can't measure it, it doesn't exist," is invalid. I have come to understand and accept that what I *sense, see, hear* and *know* with my psychic sensitivities is just as real and valid as any scientifically measurable phenomena. That is what Metaphysics is all about. Understanding and using Universal Laws and principles that are outside the purview of our five physical senses. I have been allowed to "walk" in both the world of science and the world of the paranormal, and that has significantly enhanced my life. It has also permitted me to be of much greater service to those who are open to understanding and exploring "things" that are beyond their five physical senses.

Hopefully I have convinced each of you that *ALL* children are born psychically sensitive! And that it is only after they have repeatedly been told that the things they *see, hear, sense, feel* or *know* is "just their imagination" do they reluctantly turn their sensitivities off. The reader needs to understand that just because you as a parent, caretaker, teacher, counselor, etc. cannot *see, sense, hear* or *know* those same things does not mean that your child doesn't experience them. We all need to be sensitive to that, and rather than tell them "it is just your imagination," begin asking questions and try to learn exactly what their experience is. If you work to validate their experience rather than trying to convince them that it is their imagination, you might just be surprised and learn that you can become aware of those sensitivities again yourself. Some children never completely lose their sensitivities, while others just ignore their sensitivities in favor of "fitting in" with their peer group and society's limited awareness expectations.

Over the years, I have learned that along with the *gift* of being psychic comes a great responsibility. Psychic sensitivities must never be used against someone, or to harm someone, but can be used to protect yourself or protect others. Psychic sensitivities must be exercised just like any muscle, and from my experience, this is best accomplished by sharing your psychic sensitivities with others. As a professional psychic, I believe that the *gift* of being psychic is priceless and needs to be openly shared in a loving and caring manner. However, there is nothing wrong with being paid for your time as you perform a reading.

The best way to enhance ones psychic sensitivities, in addition to doing readings, is Meditation, Dream Journaling, Spiritual or Metaphysical studies, as well as Yoga, Tai Chi or Chi Gong, where the Spiritual component of these disciplines is included in the training.

Children of The New Consciousness

As I have indicated previously, the *Indigos, Crystals,* and *Star* Children – who I sometimes call *New Age Kids* – come into this earth plane with a New or Higher Consciousness, which reflects their special Spiritual purpose:

> *To break up the paradigm of Competition, greed and self centeredness, and begin instituting a paradigm of Cooperation, sharing, and economic and social equality.*

That means being responsible for both what one is contributing and what one is taking. Many of these kids and young adults need to be reminded of this, while many others already know it and are doing their part in trying to implement this, even if they have not heard it stated this way.

They, not me or my generation are the ones who will shape the future of humankind. My role is simply to help awaken them to their true purpose and help them realize that they need to embrace the Cooperation paradigm and consciously and deliberately work to destroy the Competitive greed paradigm by showing that it creates separation. These *New Age Kids* have the opportunity to grasp and use their natural psychic sensitivities to assist them in the process of creating a world that benefits all mankind. It is my generation's responsibility to help them not get caught up in the individual wealth and ego glorification energy that so dominates our Competition-driven Capitalist society.

My desire is to work toward creating Spiritual and Psychic Support and Discussion Groups worldwide for these *New Consciousness Beings* that will be facilitated by Spiritually aware and responsible adults. Adults who can "leave their ego's at the door" as they take on the opportunity to guide and be open to these kids and young adults. Indeed, the best teacher is one who can humble themselves enough to learn from their students.

I strongly encourage all of my *Indigos & Sensitives Support Group* students, my SFG Study Group students, as well as anyone else God directs my way, to develop and expand whatever innate psychic sensitivities they might have, because those sensitivities will allow them to be of greater service to their fellow man and woman, and create a closer connection with the source of their being – God.

Going Forward

I believe that the world is becoming much more open to the possibility that there is more to life than can be experienced by our five physical senses. With such primetime TV shows as *The Medium*,[89] *Ghost Whisperer*,[90] *The Mentalist*,[91]", and off hours shows like *Psychic Children*,[92] and *Ghost Hunters*,[93] the public is being introduced to psychic and mediumistic shows that although exaggerated or misrepresented at times, are indicative of an opening up of consciousness of the mainstream media, and from my perspective that is very encouraging.

---

[89] *Medium* is a CBS TV series
[90] *Ghost Whisperer* is a CBS TV series
[91] *The Mentalist* is a CBS TV series
[92] *Psychic Children* is an A&E TV program
[93] *Ghost Hunter* is a SciFi.Com TV program

Hopefully my "stories" have helped you the reader to understand that you have the potential to become aware of an entire new world, or as I would say, reconnect to a world you may have forgotten.

I am looking forward to dying someday, not because I have a morbid death wish because I don't. In fact I would like to stick around and see how these *New Age Kids* or *New Consciousness Beings* implement their soul's purpose, but I will probably have to see that from the "other side." However, I am looking forward to validating what I have *seen, heard,* and *sensed* via my psychic sensitivities and awarenesses. I have to say that I have occasionally thought, "What if all of my awarenesses and sensitivities are simply my creative imagination and the whole story about God is not what I have thought it was? How would I feel about that?" An interesting question to ponder but as I write this, I don't know that anyone knows "definitively" what really is on the other side of death. I only know that from what I have been *shown* and understand, death is not to be feared nor sought, but honored as simply a process, just as birth in this life is a death from "the other side."

With great love & hope for all mankind
Rev. Lowell K. Smith

2150 AD Holographic Macro Images

As I indicated in Chapter 5, while preparing for the 1989 Northern Virginia A.R.E. Mid-Atlantic Retreat – *Creating Your Own Future Now*, with Thea Alexander, I began *seeing* 3D holographic images associated with each of the ten Macro Society levels (Alpha-1 through Macro-10) detailed in her book, *2150 AD* along with an explanation of what each symbol means. I am including a copy of these images and their meaning on the following pages.

Alpha - 1 	Alpha - 1 The STAR of one's Macro awareness being connected in harmony to the STAR of the conscious individual being. Various changing colors for different individuals, and wave seems to flow, but is always one complete cycle. Phasing of the wave appears different for different individuals and changes as individual's awareness changes.
Beta - 2 The connection between one's Macro/higher self (top curl) and the conscious mind (lower curl) showing the beginning awareness that the path between the two awarenesses loop back on itself at both ends. The line between the two curls is constantly undulating and is different for each individual.	Beta - 2 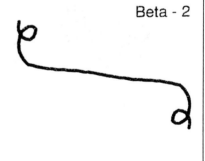

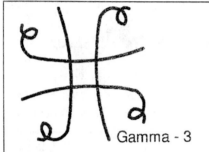

Gamma - 3

Gamma - 3

The four aspects of one's being; Physical, Etheric, Astral and I AM intertwined to make up one's present life pattern.

Figure is twisted differently for each individual and is constantly rotating in space.

Delta - 4

The infinity that you are in the conscious world and the Macro world, within the infinity of the Universe.

Figure eight pulsates and shrinks and grows and is not balanced for all individuals. There are more figure eights in different dimensions both within and with-out (representing different aspects) but I don't know how to represent that here.

Delta - 4

Aton - 5

Aton - 5

The path of Macro mind or Higher consciousness evolution is an ever-expanding spiral of awarenesses, all tied to your present state (bottom curl), which is a figure over the crown Chakra of all individuals.

Figure spirals without bottom curl moving and is tighter for some individuals than for others but appears to always be seven rotations.

Zton - 6

The whole awareness of the Yin and Yang but with individual awarenesses on conscious and unconscious planes beginning to evolve (spiral) within their own plane.

Star in each orb represents the Astral connection between the two. You cannot evolve unconsciously without affecting your conscious world and vise versa. Spirals move at a different rate for different individuals. When one is in tune with their "other" selves, spirals move in synchrony

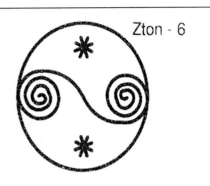

Zton - 6

Kton - 7

Kton - 7

The complete spiraling universe of one's Macro mind or Higher consciousness connected to a Soul Mates Macro mind or Higher consciousness. Thread can be broken if harmonious connection (crossing lines) becomes out of phase.

Figures pulsate slowly and move toward and away from each other and the observer, in a slow undulating manner. At the same time, crossing lines are moving.

Muton - 8

The complete oneness of who you are, on all levels, connected to the complete oneness of who you are on (or in) a different dimension, world, or awareness.

Focal point changes from a human figure to a pulsating bright light, to a multi-dimensional rainbow burst, back to a different figure and is constantly changing. Wave between focal points is intensely bright and changes color but is incredibly soothing and represents the GOD consciousness connection between two completely different worlds existing simultaneously in space / time / consciousness.

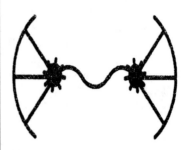

Maxon - 9

The increasing awareness of souls all aimed or focused at some Universal entity or awareness. Double lined ALPHA represents the Macro awareness *"being"* of groups connected in harmony to the conscious awareness of the same groups. The feeling is of an upward movement in consciousness of a massive number of entities. Varying colors and hues moving from a brownish gray and brownish yellow/ orange/red below the ALPHA line, to the brighter and purer greens, blues and violets with touches of beautiful reds and eventually white at peak of arrow.

Macro - 10

The completion of all that is. The Physical and Astral have connected at the bottom via the subconscious (Moon), the Spiritual (Water). The Etheric (Cloud), and the I AM (Star) are connected at the top, and enclose the full potential "being" that you are, which is the Sun/Son at the center. Curls represent connections to other souls, dimensions and/or awareness.

Moon, Water, Cloud, and Star appear to be different sizes and have different colors and "feel" for different individuals, and the Sun at center is brighter for some people.

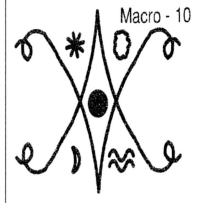

Macro - 10

List of Books and Web Sites

The following is a list of books that I have come across on *Indigos, Crystals,* and other *"New Age Kids."* This list is expanding almost weekly as additional authors write about this new "phenomena."

- *The Indigo Children – The New Kids Have Arrived* (1999); Lee Carroll and Jan Tober
- *An Indigo Celebration - More Messages, Stories, and Insights from the Indigo Children* (2001); Lee Carroll and Jan Tober.
- *The Care and Feeding of Indigo Children* (2001); Doreen Virtue, Ph.D.
- *How To Raise An Indigo Child – 10 Keys for Cultivating a Child's Natural Brilliance* (2002); Barbara Condron, D.M., D.D., B.J.
- *Anger and the Indigo Child* (2002); Dianne Lancaster.
- *The Crystal Children: A Guide to the Newest Generation of Psychic and Sensitive Children* (2003); Doreen Virtue, Ph.D.
- *Indigo, Crystal, and Rainbow Children: A Guide to the New Generations of Highly Sensitive Young People* (a 2-CD set); Doreen Virtue, Ph.D.
- *Edgar Cayce on The Indigo Children* (2004) re-titled *Psychic Children: A Sign of Our Expanding Awareness* (2004), Peggy Day and Susan Gale.
- *Beyond the Indigo Children – The New Children and the Coming of the Fifth World* (2005); P.M.H. Atwater, LHD.
- *The New Generation: The Spiritist View on Indigo and Crystal Children* (2006); Divaldo Franco and Vanessa Anseloni.
- *Spiritually Healing the Indigo Children (And Adult Indigos, Too!);* Wayne Dosick, Ph.D. and Ellen Kaufman Dosick, MSW.
- *The Children of Now*; (2007), Meg Blackburn Losey, Msc.D., Ph.D.
- *Conversations with The Children of Now* (2008), Meg Blackburn Losey, Msc.D, PhD.

Web Site Links

The following is a list of web sites dedicated to or about **Indigo Children, Crystal Children** and **Star Children** that I believe contain important or useful information. This list is constantly changing and will, I am sure, be out of date by the time this book is published.

http://www.childspirit.org – This web site provides a network for families, researchers, teachers, health care providers, community and religious leaders, and scholars interested in the spirituality of children. ChildSpirit is a non-profit organization dedicated to understanding and nurturing the spirituality of children and adults (Dr. Tobin and Mary Hart).

http://www.childrenofthenewearth.com – This web site was created to give inspiration, information and a voice to the growing international community of teachers, psychologists, doctors, healers, caregivers and conscious parents who foresee the necessity for a paradigm shift in the way we feed, nurture, educate and relate to our children. They publish a monthly *Children of The New Earth* magazine. Advisory panel Lee Carol and Jan Tober, Dr. Doreen Virtue, and many others.

http://www.indigothemovie.com – The *Indigo Children* Movie web site link (James Twyman, Neale Donald Walsch, and Stephen Simon).

http://www.indigochild.com – This Internet site is meant to complement the books *The Indigo Children* and *An Indigo Celebration*, published by Hay House (Lee Carol and Jan Tober). Includes a list of recommended schools for "gifted" children.

http://www.metagifted.org/topics/metagifted/indigo – A site created by Wendy Chapman, a self proclaimed *Indigo Adult*, with an emphasis on *Indigo Children*, *Indigo Adults* and *Crystal Children*.

http://www.indigochild.net/a_homeframe.htm – This is a multi-lingual site dedicated to *Indigo Children*. It has a list of books and articles, an *Indigo* Questionnaire, information on Health and Behavior, information about an "Indigo Lightring" which (I believe) she explains in her book (currently only in German).

http://www.starchildglobal.com/starchild – A multi-lingual and global site devoted to the empowerment of all who live on Planet Earth, through an understanding of Who You Really Are and how you can live a Creative and enjoyable life. Includes information on "A Global Network for Lightworkers," as well as links for information about *Indigo* and *Crystal Children and Adults*, as well as *Starseeds*, the *Starchild* and *Earthchild* (Celia Fenn, Capetown, South Africa).

http://www.davincimethod.com/indigo.html – A site dedicated to the book *The Davinci Method* by Garret LoPorto, which the web site says is about "How to Celebrate and Nurture the Indigo Temperament". Site by Media for Your Mind, Inc., a creator, publisher, and distributor of life enhancing and educational media, such as K-12 textbooks, self-help books, ebooks, audio-programs and websites.

http://www.indigochildren.meetup.com – A site dedicated to allowing *Indigos*, their families and/or others interested in the *Indigo* consciousness to connect. Lists many Indigo and Parent groups throughout the world. (Co-founders Peter Kamali and Matt Meeker).

http://www.thestarchildren.com/star_children-fl.html – A site with products such as "The Star Children," a 2-part CD presentation, articles, and links dedicated to Star Children, their parents and others interested in this topic. Has a link to a "Star Kid/Star Seed Identification Questionnaire" (site by Daniel Jacobs).

http://www.theindigoevolution.com – This site features the Artist, Poet Alaine – a brilliant and talented Crystal Child (she has her own web site) as well as information and articles on Indigo products and The *Indigo* Movie. Site is by James Twyman, Stephen Simon, and Doreen Virtue, Ph.D. It has a 12 question Quiz, "Is Your Child an Indigo?"

http://www.emissaryoflight.com – James Twyman and The Beloved Community web site.

http://www.spiritualcinemanetwork.com – Spiritual Cinema Network – The Official Hosts for Spiritual Cinema Premiers Worldwide. Site has a QuickTime player version of the trailer to the upcoming movie *"Illusion."* w/ Michael Goorjian and Kirk Douglas.

http://www.spiritualcinemacircle.com – Spiritual Cinema Circle site dedicated to the distribution of Spiritual Cinemas. Neale Donald Walsch's movie *Conversations With God* was released in Feb 2007.

http://www.angeltherapy.com – Site about Angel Therapy, *Indigo and Crystal Children*, etc. Site by Doreen Virtue, Ph.D.

http://www.cosmikids.org – A site dedicated to providing a unique play space that provides fun and challenge with games, crafts, events, and interactive play, all designed to encourage children to appreciate their talents and to discover their inner strength.

About The Author

Rev. Lowell K. Smith was educated as an Electrical Engineer at the University of Delaware (BEE '69, MEE '71) and as a Computer Scientist at Pace University (MSCS '94). He worked in that capacity for over 30 years.

As a highly intuitive, A.R.E. Field Tested Psychic, Lowell has been sensitive to Auras and other psychic information since he was a small child. He learned that he had the ability to read the *Akashic Record*, the holographic record of everything a soul has done in a past or present life, as well as potential paths a person has the possibility of creating for their future. From this record, Lowell is able to obtain information that helps his clients understand challenges and strengths concerning their life purpose, talents, relationships, career options, health, finances, personal issues and belief systems.

Lowell has been doing conscious psychic readings and channeled readings as well as teaching Metaphysical and Religious classes for the past 30 years. In addition to reading Past Life Information from the Akashic Record, Lowell has been trained in Past Life Regression Therapy by Dr. Brian Weiss and uses this Hypnotherapeutic approach with some of his clients as well.

As a Medical Intuitive, Lowell can "scan" a person's body and *see* and *sense* physical difficulties and provide information that clients can take to their doctor. In 1996, Lowell's medical intuitive abilities were demonstrated through his personal experience of accurately diagramming the location of his own brain tumor. Your can learn more about Lowell on his web site.

http://www.ReflectionsInLight.org

CPSIA information can be obtained
at www.ICGtesting.com
Printed in the USA
FFOW01n1830220316
22504FF